Leaders on Leadership

Interviews with Top Executives

With a Preface by Warren Bennis

Library of Congress Cataloging-in-Publication Data

Leaders on leadership : interviews with top executives / with a
    preface by Warren Bennis.
        p.   cm. — (The Harvard business review book series)
        Includes index.
        ISBN 0-87584-307-7 (acid-free paper)
        1. Chief executive officers—United States—Interviews.
    2. Executives—United States—Interviews.   3. Leadership.
    I. Harvard business review.   II. Series.
    HD38.5.U6L4   1992
    658.4′092—dc20   91-40754
                                                              CIP

The *Harvard Business Review* articles in this collection are available individually. Discounts apply to quantity purchases. For information and order-
ing contact Operations Department, Harvard Business School Publishing,
Boston, MA 02163. Telephone: (617) 495-6192. FAX: (617) 495-6985.

Printed in the United States of America.

96   95 94 93 92   5 4 3 2 1

Contents

Part IV Perspectives on Change

Part V The Politics of Leadership

Preface

As I write this preface in the vertiginous fall of 1991, I wonder what's in store for the world this time next year. Last year this time, the events of the previous year would have surprised us as much, perhaps even more. The collapse of Communism in Eastern Europe, the crumbling of the Berlin Wall, the Persian Gulf war were hardly imaginable until they began to unfold on CNN. As I remind my students, only half-joking, the four shining icons of the 1980s collapsed within 36 hours in February 1989: junk bonds, Perrier, the Trumps' marriage, and Michael Tyson.

The sudden emergence of America as the world's largest debtor, Japan as the globe's richest creditor, and the Soviet Union as its most ardent preacher of pacifism seem, to many Americans, to have turned the world upside down, raising doubts about whether America can, or should, continue to lead. *The Washington Post* cautions its readers, "Kiss Number One Goodbye, Folks." A headline in the *International Herald Tribune* warns, "America, Europe Is Coming."

Inevitably, global change has had corporate repercussions. If there is reason to despair and join the doomsayers in handwringing and headshaking, it is because traditional American managers were brought up in a simpler time, when all they had to do was build the best mousetraps and the world beat a path to their doors. "Leadership in a traditional U.S. company," says R.B. Horton, CEO of British Petroleum America, "consisted of creating a management able to cope with competitors who all played with basically the same deck of economic cards." And it was an American game. The competition may have been fierce, but it was knowable. If you played your cards right, you could win.

But that game has changed—dramatically, as the 16 leaders in the following pages tell us—and strange new rules have appeared. The deck has been shuffled and jokers added. Never before has

American business faced so many challenges. Uncertainties and complexities abound. There are too many ironies, polarities, confusions, contradictions, and ambivalences for any organization to understand fully. The only truly predictable thing right now is unpredictability. The new chic is chaos chic. Yogi Berra had it right: "The future ain't what it used to be."

Constant change disturbs managers. It always has, and it always will. Machiavelli's observation that "change has no constituency" still rings true. In his recent book *Adhocracy: The Power to Change,* Bob Waterman tells us that most of us are like the characters in Ibsen's play *Ghosts.* "We're controlled by ideas and norms that have outlived their usefulness, that are only ghosts but have as much influence on our behavior as they would if they were alive. The ideas of men like Henry Ford, Frederick Taylor, and Max Weber—these are the ghosts that haunt our halls of management."

Most of us grew up in organizations that were dominated by these men, the fathers of the classic bureaucratic system. Bureaucracy was a splendid social invention in its time—the nineteenth century. In his deathless (and deadly) prose Weber first brought to the world's attention that the bureaucratic, machine model was ideal for harnessing the manpower and resources of the Industrial Revolution. To this day, most organizations retain the macho, control-and-command mentality intrinsic to that increasingly threadbare model. Indeed, it is possible to capture the mind-set created by that obsolete paradigm in three simple worlds—Control, Order, and Predict (COP).

Reading these remarkable, sometimes profound interviews collected here, I am reminded of Tolstoy's remark that all happy families are alike. Several themes appear again and again.

However much the CEOs represented in this volume differ in experience and personal style, they constitute a prism through which the fortunes of the modern world are refracted. These leaders are emblematic of their time, forced to deal not only with the exigencies of their own organizations, but also with a new social reality. Among the broader factors that inform all their decisions: the accelerating rate and complexity of change, the emergence of new technologies, dramatic demographic shifts, and globalization. For me, all of them are reflected in a single incident. Several years ago I invited the Dalai Lama to participate in a gathering of leaders at the University of Southern California. The living embodiment of thousands of years of Tibetan spiritual wisdom graciously declined—by fax.

Each of these leaders has discovered that the very culture of his organization must change because, as constituted, that culture is devoted more to perpetuating itself than to meeting new challenges.

Each of these individuals is a leader, not a manager. Jack Welch, chairman and CEO of General Electric, has predicted (correctly, I believe) that "The world of the '90s and beyond will not belong to 'managers' or those who make the numbers dance, as we used to say, or those who are conversant with all the businessese and jargon we use to sound smart. The world will belong to passionate, driven 'leaders'—people who not only have an enormous amount of energy, but who can energize those whom they lead."

Each of these individuals understands that management is getting people to do what needs to be done. Leadership is getting people to *want* to do what needs to be done. Managers push. Leaders pull. Managers command. Leaders communicate.

Without exception every CEO interviewed has become the chief transformation officer of his organization. As Robert Haas, chairman and CEO of Levi Strauss, observes, change isn't easy, even for those committed to it. "It's difficult to unlearn behaviors that made us successful in the past. Speaking rather than listening. Valuing people like yourself over people of a different gender or from different cultures. Doing things on your own rather than collaborating. Making the decision yourself instead of asking different people for their perspectives. There's a whole range of behaviors that were highly functional in the old hierarchical organization that are dead wrong in the flatter, more responsive empowered organization that we're seeking to become."

One CEO who shares the vision reflected in these pages is John Sculley, CEO of Apple. As he told me recently: "The new model is global in scale, an interdependent network. So the new leaders face new tests such as how to lead people who don't report to them—people in other companies, in Japan or Europe, even competitors. How do you lead in this idea-intensive, interdependent-network environment? It requires a wholly different set of skills, based on ideas, people skills, and values." Sculley also predicted that the World War II fighter pilot (the formative experience of several corporate heads as well as President Bush) would no longer be our principal paradigm for leaders.

As described by the leaders in this volume, the organizations of the future will be networks, clusters, cross-functional teams, temporary systems, ad hoc task forces, lattices, modules, matrices— almost anything but pyramids. We don't even know yet what to call these new configurations, but we do know that the ones that succeed will be less hierarchical and have more linkages based on common goals rather than traditional reporting relationships. It is also likely that these successful organizations will be described by Rosabeth Moss Kanter's "5 F's: fast, focused, flexible, friendly, and fun."

A few weeks ago I was talking with Alvin Toffler, the all-time change maven whose paradigm-shifting book, *Future Shock,* was published in 1970. We were trying to name an organization that exists in today's environment that was immune to change and had been stable and prosperous. We couldn't think of one.

If the world were a stable, placid, predictable place, where the rules of five or ten years ago would still work, I suspect all our CEOs would say, "Terrific. Let's stick with the COP model." But the message that comes through loud and clear in these pages is that a new model of leadership is required.

All these CEOs understand that contemporary organizations face increasing and unfamiliar sources of competition as a result of the globalization of markets, capital, labor, and information technology. To be successful, these organizations must have flexible structures that enable them to be highly responsive to customer requirements and adaptive to changes in the competitive environment. These new organizations must be leaner and be able to engage in transnational and nontraditional alliances and mergers. And they must understand a global array of business practices, customs, and cultures.

The question all these leaders are addressing, with apparent success, is: How do you change relatively successful organizations, which, if they continue to act today the way they acted even a few years ago, will undo themselves in the future? (Remember that 47% of the companies that made up the *Fortune* 500 in 1979 were not on the list in 1989.) It seems to me that the CEOs are telling us that the new paradigm for success has three elements: Align, Create, and Empower, or ACE. This trilogy is what effective leadership is all about.

Today's leader needs to *align* the resources of the organization, particularly the human ones, creating a sense of shared objectives worthy of people's support and even dedication.

Vision animates, inspirits, transforms purpose into action. But people cannot be expected to enroll in just any exciting vision. Some visions and concepts have more staying power and are rooted more deeply in our human needs than others. One of these is the concept of quality. Often quality is not measured at all but is appreciated intuitively. Our response to quality is a feeling. And clearly linked to the concept of quality is that of dedication to, even love of, our work. This dedication is evoked by quality and is the force that energizes high-performing systems. What all of the leaders convey in the interviews is the understanding that when we love our work, we need not be managed by hopes of reward or fears of punishment.

Ultimately, in great leaders and the organizations surrounding them, there is a fusion of work and play to the point where, as Robert Frost says, "Love and need are one." These leaders, under review here, have this capacity to create a compelling vision, one that takes people to a new place, and to translate that vision into reality.

Today's leader must *create* an organizational culture where ideas come through unhampered by people who are fearful. Such leaders are committed to problem-finding, not just problem-solving. They embrace error, even failure, because they know it will teach them more than success. As Norman Lear once said to me, "Wherever I trip is where the treasure lies."

Effective leaders create adaptive, creative, learning organizations. Such organizations have the ability to identify problems, however troublesome, before they become crises. These organizations are able to rally the ideas and information necessary to solve their problems. They are not afraid to test possible solutions, perhaps by means of a pilot program somewhere in the organization. And, finally, learning organizations provide opportunities to reflect on and to evaluate past actions and decisions. This becomes a "learning wheel."[1]

Empowerment, that overused word from the 1960s, involves the sense people have that they are at the center of things, rather than on the periphery. In an effectively led organization, everyone feels he or she contributes to its success. Empowered individuals believe that what they do has significance and meaning. Empowered people have both discretion and obligations. They live in a culture of respect where they can actually do things without first getting permission from some organizational parent figure. Empowered

---

[1] I am indebted to Charles Handy and his book, *The Age of Unreason,* for these insights about learning.

organizations are characterized by trust and systemwide communication.

The ability to align, create, and empower will characterize successful leaders well into the twenty-first century. But there is another theme that surfaces provocatively in some of the interviews in this book, most notably in the remarks of Percy Barnevik, president and CEO of Asea Brown Boveri. That is the emergence of federation as the structure uniquely suited to balancing the seemingly incompatible drives toward global cooperation and the putting down of deep local roots. This paradox is evident in world politics, where intense ethnic and national identities coexist with the widespread recognition that new economic and political alliances must be forged outside one's borders. I'm convinced that federation will be the watchword of the 1990s. And I can imagine a time when corporations such as ABB that are simultaneously global and deeply rooted in local cultures serve as models for nations that aspire both to survival in an international economy and to national self-expression.

Whatever shapes the future ultimately takes, the organizations that will succeed in the white-knuckle decade of the 1990s are those that take seriously—and sustain through action—the belief that their competitive advantage is based on the development and growth of the people in them. And the men and women who guide those organizations will be a different kind of leader than we've been used to. They will be maestros, not masters. They will be coaches, not commanders.

In the postbureaucratic world, the laurel will go to the leader who encourages healthy dissent and values those followers brave enough to say no. The successful leader will have, not the loudest voice, but the readiest ear. And his or her real genius may well lie, not in personal achievement, but in unleashing other people's talent.

November 1991   Warren Bennis
Santa Monica, California

PART

I

An Overview

1
The State of American Management

Walter B. Wriston

Walter Wriston, the former president and chairman of Citicorp, reflects on the state of American management—its past, present, and future. Entrepreneurship and leadership describe the spirit of today's management. Today's manager must find the best people, motivate them, and give them the freedom to perform their jobs in their own way. Managers must also be articulate, focused on company goals, and know how that goal will be achieved.

The changes occurring in the practice of management are also having effects on the organization and its structure, which is becoming hierarchically flatter as well as streamlined.

The author discusses other factors influencing management and its new directions such as the accelerating pace of knowledge, globalization, and the new thinking—using accounting practices as an example—that characterize the Information Age rather than the Industrial Age.

According to the author, during this time of transition for both management and the work force, workers must receive better education that includes computer literacy, because the trend is away from the manual worker to the knowledge worker. It's a challenge that America can meet because it's a challenge America has met in the past.

The state of American management today is good. I am not one of those people who believes that America is not "competitive." In fact, to me "competitive" is really just a code word for protection. I believe that American managers are part and parcel of the most dynamic economy in the world—and that American managers deserve a great deal of the credit for keeping that economy healthy and growing. Today we are in the seventh year of an unprecedented

economic expansion—an expansion for which the classical economists have been lighting candles every quarter since I can
remember.

But what they don't know or keep forgetting is the fundamental
truth about the United States and its economy: this is the only
country in the world that renews itself every day. All of the economists, all of the academics, all of the people who wring their
hands over America's decline forget that coming off the boat down
at the docks this morning were 25 Koreans, 150 Mexicans, 3 Hun-
garians, and many more. Go look at U.S. colleges today. The leading students, the brightest scholars are from China or Taiwan or
practically anywhere on earth. All of us, except American Indians,
originally came from somewhere else. The world is America's talent
pool. The great genius of America is that it takes all these people
from different places and somehow turns us all into Americans.
There is nowhere else like this—there has never been anything like
it in the history of the world.

There is a second great advantage that America has over any
other country in the world: this is the Age of Pluralism, and U.S.
society is based on pluralism. There are thousands of different
power centers in the United States; thousands of little companies
on Route 128, in Silicon Valley, and spread across the country. And
of course, there are the huge companies that have grown up over
the last half-century. Between these two ends of the economy, there
is enormous pressure—competing for the talent and intellectual
horsepower that each end can attract and hold, for the products
that each will produce, for political balance as each jockeys for
recognition and advantage. These competing power centers are the
expression of the uniquely American system; they are the vehicle
through which U.S. managers contribute to their economy. And
they shape the important changes that are going on in the practice
of management—changes that will help keep managers and companies strong and competitive in the future.

Today the spirit of the entrepreneur has entered the mainstream
of U.S. management. Entrepreneurship is transforming the corporate bureaucracy. And today we hear the word "management" less
and the word "leadership" more. In the past, top managers were
fascinated with finance and control: they dealt with secondary
funding, adjustable preferreds, or they crunched the numbers sitting in the controller's bottom drawer.

Today a lot of the battles are won on the factory floor. And today more and more of U.S. industry consists of knowledge workers—people whose loyalty, whose affinity, is not to the old company logo but to doing the job right and contributing to how the work gets done. That means managers have to figure out how to motivate, coordinate, and conduct these collections of individuals, whether on the factory floor or in the office pools. It starts with articulating clear, limited goals about where the division or the company should go.

But even that has many different levels. Is the goal to continue on the trajectory that is on the best-fit curve right now? Or do you want to throw away 20% of your product line and use that money to concentrate on the other 80% of your products—products that represent the future? Do you want to make things the way you used to make them? Or are you convinced that you have to adopt a totally new approach in order to compete in the future?

Managers have always had to ask these questions. But today to be a leader, top executives need to be more like politicians than like the number-crunchers of yesterday. If there is a meter that measures the work of the manager, and at one end of the gauge are traditional management skills—all the technical information of finance, marketing, and the rest of the curriculum—and at the other end are leadership, goal setting, motivation, and articulation, then today the needle has swung from conducting monthly budget reviews to articulating where the company is going, for what purpose, and how it's going to get there.

With this change in the work of the manager is coming a change in the shape of the organization. In well-run corporations, in the corporations that will survive and create the future, layers of management are disappearing. They are disappearing for two reasons: first, because micromanagement from the top is less important than inspiration, and second, because information flows to all levels of management, dispensing the same data at the same time to all. These changes make obsolete the extra layers of management—layers that once had to control and relay information. These managers would ask the people working under them what they were doing; then they would tell the people working above them what they said. They were transmission lines. But they spun not, neither did they weave; nor did they produce anything of added value. These are the layers that are coming out—and that need to come out.

They are coming out for still another reason, one that U.S. managers should have known all along but are learning now in company after company: the people who actually do a job, who are the closest to the work, know more about it than the manager. Today workers at all levels of the company are by definition knowledge workers. They have access to vital information, they take pride in their craft, and they understand things that no one else in the organization can.

I saw this firsthand 15 years ago, when New York City was close to bankruptcy and lacking funds to maintain roads and subway lines. The man who ran one of the public employees' unions was a friend of mine, and I remember when he told me, "The next subway wreck will be on the Coney Island line." I was astonished. "How do you know that?" I asked. "It's easy," he said. "My guys maintain the tracks, and those tracks are in the worst shape of any in the system." Naturally I asked him, "Why don't you tell the manager?" His answer was a lesson for all of business. "Because," he told me, "management's priority is the big PERT chart, with its red, blue, and green dots. And on that chart, top management has decided to repair the E line going into Queens—and by the way, my guys tell me that line's in pretty good shape."

Not long ago, I saw how GE learned this lesson. One of its plants, which makes very complex machines, went on strike. To keep the plant running, the company brought in the supervisors who had designed the machines. They ran the factory beautifully, but after the strike was settled, they all said the same thing: "If I had actually worked the design out on this drill press instead of in my head, I could have made it better." The lesson is the same. Top managers have got to go back to basics and ask the people who have the problem, who have the skills, who have the hands-on knowledge, "How do you do it?"

There's another reason why this change is essential for U.S. managers—the accelerating pace of knowledge. It is a simple fact that roughly 85% of all the scientists who ever lived on this planet are alive today. Knowledge is doubling every 10 to 12 years. And as a result, the time between the realization of a brilliant idea and the delivery to the marketplace of a product based on that idea is the shortest it has ever been in history. It took almost 200 years for gunpowder to move from the laboratory to artillery. Today products can come out of the laboratory and be in the marketplace in a few months. But for that to happen requires a different kind of management and organization than we have prided ourselves on in the past.

More than ever, it means talent. It means that every organization is more reliant on the talents of its people than ever before. Talent is the number one commodity in short supply. You can't have enough good people in your organization. Because the terrible truth is that good people can make bad systems work. And bad people can ruin even the best system. So the job of the manager today is very simple and very difficult: to find the best people you can, motivate them to do the job, and allow them to do it their own way. Interestingly, it's this description of the manager's job that is at the heart of the age we are entering, the Age of Restructuring. Whether it's the threat of global competition, the threat of the takeover, the threat of 1992, or just the fact that every so many years, industry, to survive, must restructure itself—U.S. managers no longer accept a business that is a loser, even if the balance sheet can hide the loss by rounding out the numbers. Managers are both listening more carefully to their people and asking them tougher questions. They are looking at their businesses and asking, "How can we create more value?" Answering that question will make companies lean and mean, run faster and be more agile, achieve world-class success—all the words that describe the new world of the business leader.

Unquestionably, globalization is a large part of this new age, not only in terms of products but also in the range of decisions that managers must make. Today a lot of people talk about the global market—but only a very small group understand what it really is. It's not a transnational corporation. It's a horizontal integration of production across many different countries. If you have value added in ten countries, in the end you don't export a product; you export value added. How you integrate that entire operation requires a different set of skills than if you simply set out to build a greenfield plant in Spain to make widgets.

Years ago, the economist Milton Friedman called a lot of attention to Leonard Read's story of the simple, old-fashioned lead pencil by using it to illustrate the role of prices in communicating in the marketplace. Today you could use that same lead pencil to illustrate the impact of the globalization of business. In the first place, that old-fashioned lead pencil isn't made out of wood anymore. It's made out of plastic—plastic that looks like wood, has a wood feel, and even sharpens like wood. But it's plastic nonetheless. And the plastic could have been made in a distant foreign country or it could have been made in Detroit or it could have been made in a small town in the South. The carbon for the lead pencil came from still another source and the eraser from a third source. And after it's all been assembled and delivered to the store and it comes time for you to buy that pencil, you don't really care where all the components came from.

That's the globalization of business from the customer's point of view. From the manager's viewpoint, you're in a marketplace where you're suddenly waking up with a guy you've never heard of from a country you're not too sure where it is, who's eating your lunch in your hometown. That's new. And it requires new skills in managers—it means that leaders must have a wide enough span, a broad enough vision to understand that world and operate in it. It means that they must understand the law of comparative advantage. They need to know that for some production phases, they will not necessarily find comparative advantage in Des Moines, Iowa. It may be in Taiwan or Mexico or some equally good place. They have to be able to decide that, if that's where the value added should be, that's where they'll put it.

Make no mistake—this isn't just a managerial issue for large corporations. In fact, what fascinates me are the little companies that are far ahead in making global decisions. Take, for example, one little $300 million New England-based company that makes connectors. It makes the pins in Switzerland, assembles them in Germany, and sells them here. That would not have been possible 20 years ago.

Of course, it's just as true for the largest corporations. Again, take GE as an example. It makes the high end of its CAT scanners in Milwaukee, Wisconsin—and that equipment is the best in the world. For the low end of the market—a $1 million piece of equipment—it turns to Japan for manufacture. And the middle market in other equipment is covered by General Electric CGR S.A. in Europe. This is a completely global market. Engineering skills pass horizontally from the United States to Japan to France and back again. Each subsidiary company supplies the marketing skills to its own home market.

But the best example is IBM's superconductivity project. It's a global R&D exercise pioneered in Switzerland by the U.S. company working with the talents of a German scientist and a Swiss scientist. Talent doesn't carry a passport in this new age. In fact, to be successful, managers must be able to work with people who don't speak their language, who may not share their value systems, but who have the talent the business needs.

It's true of individuals. But it's also true of other companies from other countries. The name of the game today is "Alliances." It's named marketing agreements, partnerships, and joint ventures. That's how managers are learning to compete against world-class competitors in a global market. All of this horizontal integration, global production, transborder capital flows, all linked together by an electronic global marketplace—all of this has so locked the world together that politicians worldwide have no choice but to accept it or watch their nation fall behind. The drive toward the European Community 1992 in the Common Market isn't being led by the bureaucrats, the customs clerks, and passport stampers who will all be out of a job. Business is driving it. The Italians were first, largely because many of their businesses had to operate almost in spite of their government. Then came the French, followed now by the Germans, who were slow off the mark. Now it's going on around the world. The New Zealanders are on the hunt—they're looking at alliances and markets. The whole world is restructuring, driven by the realization that it's a global marketplace. Borders and control of land are less and less important. The traditional notion of sovereignty is becoming obsolete. All of this will create immense management problems in the future that will have to be handled with skill—and some alliances will fail.

Globalization is one big change that U.S. managers are now confronting around the world; there are also several important issues here at home that command our attention. We must reconsider many of the systems and assumptions that underlie how we do business and how we manage. Too often we try to apply tools from the Industrial Age to the Information Age. We might as well attempt to power our modern ships with men at oars, all lined up and facing backward, rather than using the latest technology and a forward-looking crew.

Here is just one example: our accounting system. It was designed for a rapidly fading Industrial Age—and it ignores the new realities of the information society. Today FASB is looking at the question of what constitutes an asset. Now, in my book, an asset is something that creates a stream of income. But take that definition and apply it to the modern factory. Today the biggest asset in the business is intellectual capital, the software that actually runs the factory, that controls the operation and makes it productive. But how do we treat software? Because software came after the Industrial Revolution, because it isn't tangible, we expense most of it. And how do we treat the plant—the shell that stands idle until the software brings it to life? We capitalize it. When you know for a fact that if all the software disappeared, all the planes would stop flying, all the streetlights would go off, all the plants would stop producing—and you still can say with a straight face that software isn't an asset—then you must acknowledge an enormous gap between reality and practice.

The same is true in the way we now treat company names. Accounting says that the name Citibank or Coca-Cola or IBM or Apple is valueless; it is "good will." It should be written off—as if 100 years of marketing had no value. But common sense tells you that a trademark is worth something. Otherwise it wouldn't be patentable. And if you look at how some of America's oldest, established companies have tried to put their names back to work for them in the marketplace as a store of value, then it's clear that a company's name can be worth more than its prestigious headquarters building. Especially since some of these companies are fighting to keep their good names and simultaneously selling off their fancy buildings.

The fact is that this system is backward, obsolete. But if you say that out loud, if you try to operate in a way that actually conforms to the way the world now works, then the keepers of the accounting flame accuse you of cooking the books and watering the balance sheet.

There's another accounting problem that's even worse, and that's our national accounts. These numbers are so bad that even the daily newspapers are starting to notice it—but smart managers have known it for years. The problem is this: Washington comes out with GNP numbers that are revised several times and aren't final for three years. And when they're finally adjusted, it often turns out that they're double or half what the government had first announced. It poses a very difficult question for U.S. managers: How do you make decisions in a society where the numbers aren't any good? It is more than ironic that we live in an information-driven economy where much of the critical information the government puts out is simply inaccurate. And as a consequence, managers must think longer term in all their decisions—but not necessarily for a good reason. Rather, your thinking becomes longer term when you know that all your decisions in the present are based on information that is totally untrustworthy. In that situation, the manager has to rely on his or her instinct and on the passage of time to illuminate what is missing from unreliable statistics.

Another important element of the information society is the change it is bringing in the work force. We are going to continue to see growth in the importance of the knowledge worker compared with the manual worker. It is simply a matter of power and leverage. I remember a presentation on handheld calculators that I attended years ago when they were first appearing. In front of a group of doubting CEOs was a visionary, defending the notion of the calculator, trying to convince these tough-minded managers of its value. Of course, they knew better. "I don't need one of those things," was their attitude. "I know how to add and subtract." And what he told them back then about the simple handheld calculator was this: "You can dig a hole with a shovel too, but it's better to have a bulldozer. What I'm giving you is the hydraulics of the mind." That stopped some of those stiff-collared types. Because the hydraulics of the mind is what is transforming the entire world. Intellectual capital is becoming relatively more important than physical capital.

We have one more important piece of work to attend to in the United States—and that is education. Our education system and our approach to its problems are perfect reflections of the pluralism of America. And one of our redeeming features is that, if something gets bad enough in this country and if people come to understand it, then we work on that problem. That's the case with education today.

In New York, the most pluralistic of all cities, we probably have the five best schools in the world—and the five worst. The Bronx High School of Science will likely produce more Nobel laureates than any school in the world. And it sits in a neighborhood that is a disaster. We have the Manhattan Center for Science and Mathematics, which graduated 100% of its entering class. We have School District 4, which is a model for the world. This district in East Harlem serves over 14,000 students, 60% Hispanic, 35% black, 4% white, 1% Asian. About 80% are eligible for free or reduced-price lunch programs. Its students show dramatic progress compared with students in other districts. And we also know that we have many kids who can't read and write and a huge bureaucracy that shows little interest in change because it's job threatening.

But we know one solution: free choice—creating a marketplace in education. And what's more, we know this isn't the first time we've had to deal with this problem. Years ago, we had people coming right off the boat and into the factory. They couldn't read; they couldn't write. At least not when they started. But we taught them; we taught remedial reading and writing then—today we're teaching remedial computer literacy. It's the same problem.

Is it easy? Of course not. But I believe that we can handle it, that pluralism is our greatest protection. I believe that just as the best land-grant colleges have traditionally challenged the private universities, just as the best public hospitals have challenged private ones—so today in our efforts to improve primary and secondary public education, our greatest strength is choice and pluralism.

Because the most basic fact about the world we live and work in is this: information is a virus that carries freedom. What's happening today in America and around the world is irreversible. While events never move in a straight line without setbacks, what's happening in the Soviet Union, in China, in Eastern Europe is going to change the world. And change it permanently. The Information Age means that there simply isn't anyplace to hide anymore. Whether it's an oil spill in Alaska, a nuclear disaster in Chernobyl, or a massacre in Tiananmen Square, today television shoves that event into more than 100 million homes simultaneously. Information creates freedom because revolutions occur when people become aware of alternatives. And for America and American managers, that's the promise of the best kind of future there is.

PART
II
The Importance of Values

1
Speed, Simplicity, Self-Confidence: An Interview with Jack Welch

Noel Tichy and Ram Charan

John F. Welch, Jr., chairman and CEO of General Electric, leads one of the world's largest corporations. It is a very different corporation from the one he inherited in 1981. GE is now built around 14 distinct businesses—including aircraft engines, medical systems, engineering plastics, major appliances, NBC television, and financial services. They reflect the aggressive strategic redirection Welch unveiled soon after he became CEO.

By now the story of GE's business transformation is familiar. In 1981, Welch declared that the company would focus its operations on three "strategic circles"—core manufacturing units such as lighting and locomotives, technology-intensive businesses, and services—and that each of its businesses would rank first or second in its global market. GE has achieved world market-share leadership in nearly all of its 14 businesses. In 1988, its 300,000 employees generated revenues of more than $50 billion and net income of $3.4 billion.

GE's strategic redirection had essentially taken shape by the end of 1986. Since then, Welch has embarked on a more imposing challenge: building a revitalized "human engine" to animate GE's formidable "business engine."

His program has two central objectives. First, he is championing a companywide drive to identify and eliminate unproductive work in order to energize GE's employees. It is neither realistic nor useful, Welch argues, to expect employees of a decidedly leaner corporation to complete all the reports, reviews, forecasts, and budgets that were standard operating procedure in more forgiving times. He is developing procedures to speed decision cycles, move information through the organization, provide quick and effective feedback, and evaluate and reward managers on qualities such as openness, candor, and self-confidence.

Second, and perhaps of even greater significance, Welch is leading a transformation of attitudes at GE—struggling, in his words, to release "emotional energy" at all levels of the organization and encourage creativity and feelings of ownership and self-worth. His ultimate goal is to create an enterprise that can tap the benefits of global scale and diversity without the stifling costs of bureaucratic controls and hierarchical authority and without a managerial focus on personal power and self-perpetuation. This requires a transformation not only of systems and procedures, he argues, but also of people themselves.

Noel Tichy was manager of GE's Management Education Operation from 1985 through 1987. He is a professor at the University of Michigan's School of Business Administration, director of its Global Leadership Program, and coauthor of *The Transformational Leader* (John Wiley & Sons, 1986). Ram Charan is a Dallas-based consultant who advises companies in the United States, Europe, and Asia on implementing global strategies.

HBR: What makes a good manager?

Jack Welch: I prefer the term business leader. Good business leaders create a vision, articulate the vision, passionately own the vision, and relentlessly drive it to completion. Above all else, though, good leaders are open. They go up, down, and around their organization to reach people. They don't stick to the established channels. They're informal. They're straight with people. They make a religion out of being accessible. They never get bored telling their story.

Real communication takes countless hours of eyeball to eyeball, back and forth. It means more listening than talking. It's not pronouncements on a videotape, it's not announcements in a newspaper. It is human beings coming to see and accept things through a constant interactive process aimed at consensus. And it must be absolutely relentless. That's a real challenge for us. There's still not enough candor in this company.

What do you mean by "candor"?

I mean facing reality, seeing the world as it is rather than as you wish it were. We've seen over and over again that businesses facing market downturns, tougher competition, and more demanding customers inevitably make forecasts that are much too optimistic. This means they don't take advantage of the opportunities change usually offers. Change in the marketplace isn't something to fear; it's an enormous opportunity to shuffle the deck, to replay the game. Candid managers—leaders—don't get paralyzed about the "fragility" of the organization. They tell people the truth. That doesn't scare them because they realize their people know the truth anyway.

We've had managers at GE who couldn't change, who kept telling us to leave them alone. They wanted to sit back, to keep things the way they were. And that's just what they did—until they and most of their staffs had to go. That's the lousy part of this job. What's worse is that we still don't understand why so many people are incapable of facing reality, of being candid with themselves and others.

But we are clearly making progress in facing reality, even if the progress is painfully slow. Take our locomotive business. That team was the only one we've ever had that took a business whose forecasts and plans were headed straight up, and whose market began to head straight down, a virtual collapse, and managed to change the tires while the car was moving. It's the team that forecast the great locomotive boom, convinced us to invest $300 million to renovate its plant in Erie, and then the market went boom all right—right into a crater. But when it did, that team turned on a dime. It reoriented the business.

Several of our other businesses in the same situation said, "Give it time, the market will come back." Locomotive didn't wait. And today, now that the market is coming back, the business looks great. The point is, what determines your destiny is not the hand you're dealt; it's how you play the hand. And the best way to play your hand is to face reality—see the world the way it is—and act accordingly.

What makes an effective organization?

For a large organization to be effective, it must be simple. For a large organization to be simple, its people must have self-confidence and intellectual self-assurance. Insecure managers create complexity. Frightened, nervous managers use thick, convoluted planning books and busy slides filled with everything they've known since childhood. Real leaders don't need clutter. People must have the self-confidence to be clear, precise, to be sure that every person in their organization—highest to lowest—understands what the business is trying to achieve. But it's not easy. You can't believe how hard it is for people to be simple, how much they fear being simple. They worry that if they're simple, people will think they're simpleminded. In reality, of course, it's just the reverse. Clear, tough-minded people are the most simple.

Soon after you became CEO, you articulated GE's now-famous strategy of "number one or number two globally." Was that an exercise in the power of simplicity?

Yes. In 1981, when we first defined our business strategy, the real focus was Japan. The entire organization had to understand that GE was in a tougher, more competitive world, with Japan as the cutting edge of the new competition. Nine years later, that competitive toughness has increased by a factor of five or ten. We face a revitalized Japan that's migrated around the world—to Thailand, Malaysia, Mexico, the United States—and responded successfully to a massive yen change. Europe is a different game today. There are great European businesspeople, dynamic leaders, people who are changing things. Plus you've got all the other Asian successes.

So being number one or number two globally is more important than ever. But scale alone is not enough. You have to combine financial strength, market position, and technology leadership with an organizational focus on speed, agility, and simplicity. The world moves so much faster today. You can be driving through Seoul, talking to France on the phone and making a deal, and have a fax waiting for you when you get back to the United States with the deal in good technical shape. Paolo Fresco, senior vice president of GE International, has been negotiating around-the-clock for the past two days on a deal in England. Last night I was talking with Larry Bossidy, one of our vice chairmen, who was in West Germany doing another deal. We never used to do business this way. So you can be the biggest, but if you're not flexible enough to handle rapid change and make quick decisions, you won't win.

How have you implemented your commitment to simplicity at the highest levels of GE, where you can have the most direct impact on what happens?

First, we took out management layers. Layers hide weaknesses. Layers mask mediocrity. I firmly believe that an overburdened, overstretched executive is the best executive because he or she doesn't have the time to meddle, to deal in trivia, to bother people. Remember the theory that a manager should have no more than 6 or 7 direct reports? I say the right number is closer to 10 or 15. This way you have no choice but to let people flex their muscles, let them grow and mature. With 10 or 15 reports, a leader can focus only on the big important issues, not on minutiae.

We also reduced the corporate staff. Headquarters can be the bane of corporate America. It can strangle, choke, delay, and create insecurity. If you're going to have simplicity in the field, you can't have a big staff at home. We don't need the questioners and the checkers, the nitpickers who bog down the process, people whose only role is to second-guess and kibitz, the people who clog communication inside the company. Today people at headquarters are experts in taxes, finance, or some other key area that can help people in the field. Our corporate staff no longer just challenges and questions; it assists. This is a mind-set change: staff essentially reports to the field rather than the other way around.

So many CEOs disparage staff and middle management—you know, "If only those bureaucrats would buy into my vision." When you talk about "nitpickers" and "kibitzers," are you talking about lousy people or about good people forced into lousy jobs?

People are not lousy, period. Leaders have to find a better fit between their organization's needs and their people's capabilities. Staff people, whom I prefer to call individual contributors, can be tremendous sources of added value in an organization. But each staff person has to ask, "How do I add value? How do I help make people on the line more effective and more competitive?" In the past, many staff functions were driven by control rather than adding value. Staffs with that focus have to be eliminated. They sap emotional energy in the organization. As for middle managers, they can be the stronghold of the organization. But their jobs have to be redefined. They have to see their roles as a combination of teacher, cheerleader, and liberator, not controller.

You've dismantled GE's groups and sectors, the top levels of the corporate organization to which individual strategic business units once reported. That certainly makes the organization chart more simple—you now have 14 separate businesses reporting directly to you or your two vice chairmen. How does the new structure simplify how GE operates on a day-to-day basis?

Cutting the groups and sectors eliminated communications filters. Today there is direct communication between the CEO and the leaders of the 14 businesses. We have very short cycle times for decisions and little interference by corporate staff. A major investment decision that used to take a year can now be made in a matter of days.

We also run a Corporate Executive Council, the CEC. For two days every quarter, we meet with the leaders of the 14 businesses and our top staff people. These aren't stuffy, formal strategic reviews. We share ideas and information candidly and openly, including programs that have failed. The important thing is that at the end of those two days everyone in the CEC has seen and discussed the same information. The CEC creates a sense of trust, a sense of personal familiarity and mutual obligation at the top of the company. We consider the CEC a piece of organizational technology that is very important for our future success.

Still, how can it be "simple" to run a $50 billion enterprise? Doesn't a corporation as vast as GE need management layers, extensive review systems, and formal procedures—if for no other reason than to keep the business under control?

People always overestimate how complex business is. This isn't rocket science; we've chosen one of the world's more simple professions. Most global businesses have three or four critical competitors, and you know who they are. And there aren't that many things you can do with a business. It's not as if you're choosing among 2,000 options.

You mentioned review systems. At our 1986 officers' meeting, which involves the top 100 or so executives at GE, we asked the 14 business leaders to present reports on the competitive dynamics in their businesses. How'd we do it? We had them each prepare one-page answers to five questions: What are your market dynamics globally today, and where are they going over the next several years? What actions have your competitors taken in the last three years to upset those global dynamics? What have you done in the last three years to affect those dynamics? What are the most dangerous things your competitor could do in the next three years to upset those dynamics? What are the most effective things you could do to bring your desired impact on those dynamics?

Five simple charts. After those initial reviews, which we update regularly, we could assume that everyone at the top knew the plays and had the same playbook. It doesn't take a genius. Fourteen businesses each with a playbook of five charts. So when Larry Bossidy is with a potential partner in Europe, or I'm with a company in the Far East, we're always there with a competitive understanding based on our playbooks. We know exactly what makes sense; we don't need a big staff to do endless analysis. That means we should be able to act with speed.

Probably the most important thing we promise our business leaders is fast action. Their job is to create and grow new global businesses. Our job in the executive office is to facilitate, to go out and negotiate a deal, to make the acquisition, or get our businesses the partners they need. When our business leaders call, they don't expect studies—they expect answers.

Take the deal with Thomson, where we swapped our consumer electronics business for their medical equipment business. We were presented with an opportunity, a great solution to a serious strategic problem, and we were able to act quickly. We didn't need to go back to headquarters for a strategic analysis and a bunch of reports. Conceptually, it took us about 30 minutes to decide that the deal made sense and then a meeting of maybe two hours with the Thomson people to work out the basic terms. We signed a letter of intent in five days. We had to close it with the usual legal details, of course, so from beginning to end it took five months. Thomson had the same clear view of where it wanted to go—so it worked perfectly for both sides.

Another of our jobs is to transfer best practices across all the businesses, with lightning speed. Staff often put people all over the place to do this. But they aren't effective lightning rods to transfer best practice; they don't have the stature in the organization. Business leaders do. That's why every CEC meeting deals in part with a generic business issue—a new pay plan, a drug-testing program, stock options. Every business is free to propose its own plan or program and present it at the CEC, and we put it through a central screen at corporate, strictly to make sure it's within the bounds of good sense. We don't approve the details. But we want to know what the details are so we can see which programs are working and immediately alert the other businesses to the successful ones.

You make it sound so easy.

Simple *doesn't* mean easy, especially as you try to move this approach down through the organization. When you take out layers, you change the exposure of the managers who remain. They sit right in the sun. Some of them blotch immediately; they can't stand the exposure of leadership.

We now have leaders in each of the businesses who *own* those businesses. Eight years ago, we had to sell the idea of ownership. Today the challenge is to move that sense of ownership, that commitment to relentless personal interaction and immediate sharing of information, down through the organization. We're very early in this, and it's going to be anything but easy. But it's something we have to do.

From an organizational point of view, how are the 14 businesses changing? Are they going through a delayering process? Are their top people communicating as the CEC does?

In addition to locomotives, which I've already discussed, we've had major delayering and streamlining in almost all of our businesses, and they have made significant improvements in total cost productivity.

The CEC concept is flowing down as well. For example, each of the businesses has created its own executive committee to meet on policy questions. These committees meet weekly or monthly and include the top staff and line people from the businesses. Everyone in the same room, everyone with the same information, everyone buying into the targets. Each business also has an operations committee. This is a bigger group of maybe 30 people for each business: 5 staffers, 7 people from manufacturing, 6 from engineering, 8 from marketing, and so on. They get together every quarter for a day and a half to thrash out problems, to get people talking across functions, to communicate with each other about their prospects and programs. That's 30 people in 14 businesses, more than 400 people all together, in a process of instant communication about their businesses and the company.

You see, I operate on a very simple belief about business. If there are six of us in a room, and we all get the same facts, in most cases, the six of us will reach roughly the same conclusion. And once we all accept that conclusion, we can force our energy into it and put it into action. The problem is, we don't get the same information. We each get different pieces. Business isn't complicated. The complications arise when people are cut off from information they need. That's what we're trying to change.

That brings us to Work-Out, which you've been championing inside GE since early this year. Why are you pushing it so hard?

Work-Out is absolutely fundamental to our becoming the kind of company we must become. That's why I'm so passionate about it. We're not going to succeed if people end up doing the same work they've always done, if they don't feel any psychic or financial impact from the way the organization is changing. The ultimate objective of Work-Out is so clear. We want 300,000 people with different career objectives, different family aspirations, different financial goals, to share directly in this company's vision, the information, the decision-making process, and the rewards. We want to build a more stimulating environment, a more creative environment, a freer work atmosphere, with incentives tied directly to what people do.

Now, the business leaders aren't particularly thrilled that we're so passionate about Work-Out. In 1989, the CEO is going to every business in this company to sit in on a Work-Out session. That's a little puzzling to them. "I own the business, what are you doing here?" they say. Well, I'm not there to tell them how to price products, what type of equipment they need, whom to hire; I have no comments on that.

But Work-Out is the next generation of what we're trying to do. We had to put in a process to focus on and change how work gets done in this company. We have to apply the same relentless passion to Work-Out that we did in selling the vision of number one and number two globally. That's why we're pushing it so hard, getting so involved.

What is the essence of Work-Out, the basic goal?

Work-Out has a practical and an intellectual goal. The practical objective is to get rid of thousands of bad habits accumulated since the creation of General Electric. How would you like to move from a house after 112 years? Think of what would be in the closets and the attic—those shoes that you'll wear to paint next spring, even though you know you'll never paint again. We've got 112 years of closets and attics in this company. We want to flush them out, to start with a brand new house with empty closets, to begin the whole game again.

The second thing we want to achieve, the intellectual part, begins by putting the leaders of each business in front of 100 or so of their people, eight to ten times a year, to let them hear what their people think about the company, what they like and don't like about their work, about how they're evaluated, about how they spend their time. Work-Out will expose the leaders to the vibrations of their business—opinions, feelings, emotions, resentments, not abstract theories of organization and management.

Ultimately, we're talking about redefining the relationship between boss and subordinate. I want to get to a point where people challenge their bosses every day: "Why do you require me to do these wasteful things? Why don't you let me do the things you shouldn't be doing so you can move on and create? That's the job of a leader—to create, not to control. Trust me to do my job, and don't make me waste all my time trying to deal with you on the control issue."

Now, how do you do get people communicating with each other with that much candor? You put them together in a room and make them thrash it out.

These Work-Out sessions, and I've already done several of them, create all kinds of personal dynamics. Some people go and hide. Some don't like the dinner in the evening because they can't get along with the other people. Some emerge as forceful advocates. As people meet over and over, though, more of them will develop the courage to speak out. The norm will become the person who says, "Dammit, we're not doing it. Let's get on with doing it." Today the norm in most companies, not just GE, is not to bring up critical issues with a boss, certainly not in a public setting, and certainly not in an atmosphere where self-confidence has not been developed. This process will create more fulfilling and rewarding jobs. The quality of work life will improve dramatically.

It's one thing to insist that the people who report directly to you, or who work one or two layers below you, become forceful advocates and criticize the status quo. They've got your support. But what about people lower in the organization, people who have to worry how their bosses will react?

You're right on the hottest issue—when a boss reacts to criticism by saying, "I'll get that guy." Now, hopefully, that guy is so good he quits that same week and shows the boss where that attitude gets him. That's not the best result for GE, of course, but that's what it may take to shake people up.

It's not going to be easy to get the spirit and intent of Work-Out clear throughout the company. I had a technician at my house to install some appliances recently. He said, "I saw your videotape on Work-Out. The guys at my level understand what you're talking about: we'll be free to enjoy our work more, not just do more work, and to do more work on our own. But do you know how our supervisors interpreted it? They pointed to the screen and said, 'You see what he's saying, you guys better start busting your butts.'" We have a long way to go!

The potential for meanness in an organization, for a variety of reasons, is often in inverse proportion to level. People at the top have more time and resources to be fair. I wasn't trained to be a judge, but I spend a lot of time worrying about fairness. The data I get generally favor the manager over the employee. But we have two people at headquarters, fairness arbitrators so to speak, who sift the situation. So when I get a problem, I can smell it and feel it and try to figure out what's really happening. Managers down in the organization don't have the time or help for that. They too often say, "This is how we do it here, go do it." Work-Out is going to break down those attitudes. Managers will be in front of their people, challenged in a thousand different ways, held to account (see Appendix for a case illustration of Work-Out).

To change behavior, you must also change how people are compensated and rewarded. Are those systems being changed at GE?

We let every business come up with its own pay plan. It can create bonus plans in any way that makes sense. We're also doing all kinds of exciting things to reward people for their contributions, things we've never done before. For example, we now give out $20 to $30 million in management awards every year—cash payments to individuals for outstanding performance. We're trying desperately to push rewards down to levels where they never used to be. Stock options now go to 3,000 people, up from 400 ten years ago, and that's probably still not enough.

Another way to influence behavior is to promote people based on the characteristics you want to encourage. How can you evaluate executives on qualities as subjective as candor and speed?

Not only can we do it, we *are* doing it. Again, we're starting at the top of the company and, as the new systems prove themselves, we'll drive them down. We took three years to develop a statement on corporate values, what we as a company believe in. It was a brutal process. We talked to 5,000 people at our management development center in Crotonville. We sweated over every word. This will be the first year that our Session C meetings, the intensive process we use to evaluate the officers of the company, revolve around that value statement. We've told the business leaders that they must rank each of their officers on a scale of one to five against the business and individual characteristics in that statement (see Exhibit). Then I, Larry Bossidy, and Ed Hood, our other vice chairman, will rate the officers and see where we agree or disagree with the business leaders.

We had a long discussion about this in the CEC. People said just what you said: "How can you put a number on how open people are, on how directly they face reality?" Well, they're going to have to—the best numbers they can come up with, and then we'll argue about them. We have to know if our people are open and self-confident, if they believe in honest communication and quick action, if the people we hired years ago have changed. The only way to test our progress is through regular evaluations at the top and by listening to every audience we appear before in the company.

All corporations, but especially giant corporations like GE, have implicit social and psychological contracts with their employees— mutual responsibilities and loyalties by which each side abides. What is GE's psychological contract with its people?

Like many other large companies in the United States, Europe, and Japan, GE has had an implicit psychological contract based

Exhibit *GE Value Statement*

Business Characteristics	Individual Characteristics

Lean
What: Reduce tasks and the people required to do them.
Why: Critical to developing world cost leadership.

Agile
What: Delayering.
Why: Create fast decision making in rapidly changing world through improved communication and increased individual response.

Creative
What: Development of new ideas—innovation.
Why: Increase customer satisfaction and operating margins through higher value products and services.

Ownership
What: Self-confidence to trust others. Self-confidence to delegate to others the freedom to act while, at the same time, self-confidence to involve higher levels in issues critical to the business and the corporation.
Why: Supports concept of more individual responsibility, capability to act quickly and independently. Should increase job satisfaction and improve understanding of risks and rewards. While delegation is critical, there is a small percentage of high-impact issues that need or require involvement of higher levels within the business and within the corporation.

Reward
What: Recognition and compensation commensurate with risk and performance—highly differentiated by individual, with recognition of total team achievement.
Why: Necessary to attract and motivate the type of individuals required to accomplish GE's objectives. A #1 business should provide #1 people with #1 opportunity.

Reality
What: Describe the environment as it is—not as we hope it to be.
Why: Critical to developing a vision and a winning strategy, and to gaining universal acceptance for their implementation.

Leadership
What: Sustained passion for and commitment to a proactive, shared vision and its implementation.
Why: To rally teams toward achieving a common objective.

Candor/Openness
What: Complete and frequent sharing of information with individuals (appraisals, etc.) and organization (everything).
Why: Critical to employees knowing where they, their efforts, and their business stand.

Simplicity
What: Strive for brevity, clarity, the "elegant, simple solution"—less is better.
Why: Less complexity improves everything, from reduced bureaucracy to better product designs to lower costs.

Integrity
What: Never bend or wink at the truth, and live within both the spirit and letter of the laws of every global business arena.
Why: Critical to gaining the global arenas' acceptance of our right to grow and prosper. Every constituency: shareowners who invest; customers who purchase; community that supports; and employees who depend, expect, and deserve our unequivocal commitment to integrity in every facet of our behavior.

Individual Dignity
What: Respect and leverage the talent and contribution of every individual in both good and bad times.
Why: Teamwork depends on trust, mutual understanding, and the shared belief that the individual will be treated fairly in any environment.

on perceived lifetime employment. People were rarely dismissed except for cause or severe business downturns, like in Aerospace after Vietnam. This produced a paternal, feudal, fuzzy kind of loyalty. You put in your time, worked hard, and the company took care of you for life.

That kind of loyalty tends to focus people inward. But given today's environment, people's emotional energy must be focused outward on a competitive world where no business is a safe haven for employment unless it is winning in the marketplace. The psychological contract has to change. People at all levels have to feel the risk-reward tension.

My concept of loyalty is not "giving time" to some corporate entity and, in turn, being shielded and protected from the outside world. Loyalty is an affinity among people who want to grapple with the outside world and win. Their personal values, dreams, and ambitions cause them to gravitate toward each other and toward a company like GE that gives them the resources and opportunities to flourish.

The new psychological contract, if there is such a thing, is that jobs at GE are the best in the world for people who are willing to compete. We have the best training and development resources and an environment committed to providing opportunities for personal and professional growth.

How deeply have these changes penetrated? How different does it feel to be a GE manager today versus five years ago?

It depends how far down you go. In some old-line factories, they probably feel it a lot less than we would like. They hear the words every now and then, but they don't feel a lot of difference. That's because the people above them haven't changed enough yet. Don't forget, we built much of this company in the 1950s around the blue books and POIM: plan, organize, integrate, measure. We brought people in buses over to Crotonville and drilled it into them. Now we're saying, "liberate, trust," and people look up and say, "What?" We're trying to make a massive cultural break. This is at least a five-year process, probably closer to ten.

What troubles you about what's happened to date?

First, there's a real danger of the expectation level getting ahead of reality. I was at Crotonville recently, talking about Work-Out, and someone said, "I don't feel it yet." Well, we're only a few months into it, it's much too early.

No matter how many exciting programs you implement, there seems to be a need for people to spend emotional energy criticizing the administration of the programs rather than focusing on the substance. I can sit in the Crotonville pit and ask, "How many of you are part of a new pay plan?" More than half the hands go up. "How many of you have received a management award in the last year?" More than 90% of the hands go up. "How many of you are aware of stock options?" All the hands go up. And yet many of these people don't see what we're trying to do with the programs, why we've put them in place. The emotional energy doesn't focus often enough on the objectives of the bonus plan or the excitement of the management award; it focuses on the details. The same is true of Work-Out. We'll have too much discussion on the Work-Out "process" and not enough on the "objective" to instill speed, simplicity, and self-confidence in every person in the organization.

When will we know whether these changes have worked? What's your report card?

A business magazine recently printed an article about GE that listed our businesses and the fact that we were number one or number two in virtually all of them. That magazine didn't get one complaint from our competitors. Those are the facts. That's what we said we wanted to do, and we've done it.

Ten years from now, we want magazines to write about GE as a place where people have the freedom to be creative, a place that brings out the best in everybody. An open, fair place where people have a sense that what they do matters, and where that sense of accomplishment is rewarded in both the pocketbook and the soul. That will be our report card.

Appendix

Work-Out: A Case Study

GE Medical Systems (GEMS) is the world leader in medical diagnostic imaging equipment, including CT scanners, magnetic resonance equipment, and X-ray mammography. Its more than 15,000 employees face formidable international competition. Despite positive financial results, GEMS is working to transform its human organization. Work-Out is designed to identify sources of frustration and bureaucratic inefficiency, eliminate unnecessary and unproductive work, and overhaul how managers are evaluated and rewarded.

Work-Out began last fall when some 50 GEMS employees attended a five-day offsite session in Lake Lawn, Wisconsin. The participants included senior vice president and group executive John Trani, his staff, six employee relations managers, and informal leaders from technology, finance, sales, service, marketing, and manufacturing. Trani selected these informal leaders for their willingness to take business risks, challenge the status quo, and contribute in other key ways to GEMS. We participated as Work-Out faculty members and have participated in follow-up sessions that will run beyond 1989.

The Lake Lawn session took place after two important preliminary steps. First, we conducted in-depth interviews with managers at all levels of GEMS. Our interviews uncovered many objections to and criticisms of existing procedures, including measurement systems (too many, not focused enough on customers, cross-functional conflicts); pay and reward systems (lack of work goals, inconsistent signals); career development systems (ambiguous career paths, inadequate performance feedback); and an atmosphere in which blame, fear, and lack of trust overshadowed team commitments to solving problems. Here are some sample quotes from our interviews:

"I'm frustrated. I simply can't do the quality of work that I want to do and know how to do. I feel my hands are tied. I have no time. I need help on how to delegate and operate in this new culture."

"The goal of downsizing and delayering is correct. The execution stinks. The concept is to drop a lot of 'less important' work. This just didn't happen. We still have to know all the details, still have to follow all the old policies and systems."

"I'm overwhelmed. I can and want to do better work. The solution is not simply adding new people; I don't even want to. We need to team up on projects and work. Our leaders must stop piling on more and help us set priorities."

Second, just before the first Work-Out session, Jack Welch traveled to GEMS headquarters for a half-day roundtable with the Work-Out participants. Here are some sample quotes from middle managers:

To senior management: "Listen! Think carefully about what the middle managers say. Make them feel like they are the experts and that their opinions are respected. There appear to be too many preconceived beliefs on the part of Welch and Trani."

To senior management: "Listen to people, don't just pontificate. Trust people's judgment and don't continually second-guess. Treat other people like adults and not children."

About themselves: "I will recommend work to be discontinued. I will try to find 'blind spots' where I withhold power. Any person I send to speak for me will 'push' peers who resist change."

About themselves: "I will be more bold in making decisions. I will no longer accept the status quo. I will ask my boss for authority to make decisions. In fact, I will make more decisions on my own."

The five-day Work-Out session was an intense effort to unravel, evaluate, and reconsider the complex web of personal relationships, cross-functional interactions, and formal work procedures through which the business of GEMS gets done. Cross-functional teams cooperated to address actual business problems. Each functional group developed a vision of where its operations are headed.

John Trani participated in a roundtable where he listened and responded to the concerns and criticisms of middle managers. Senior members of the GEMS staff worked to build trust and more effective communication with the functional managers. All the participants focused on ways to reorganize work and maximize return on organization time, on team time, and on individual time.

The five-day session ended with individuals and functional teams signing close to 100 written contracts to implement the new procedures. There were contracts between functional teams, contracts between individuals, contracts between function heads and their staffs, and businesswide contracts with John Trani and his staff.

Work-Out has picked up steam since Lake Lawn. Managers from different product lines have participated in workshops to review and implement the attitudes, values, and new work procedures discussed at Lake Lawn. A Work-Out steering committee has held cross-functional information meetings for field employees around the world. Managers throughout GEMS are reviewing and modifying their reward and measurement systems. And Welch continues to receive regular briefings on Work-Out's progress.

No two GE businesses approach Work-Out in the same way; a process this intensive can't be "cloned" successfully among vastly different businesses. But Work-Out at GEMS offers a glimpse of the change process taking place throughout General Electric.

—Noel Tichy and Ram Charan

2
Values Make the Company:
An Interview with Robert Haas

Robert Howard

As chairman and CEO of Levi Strauss & Co., Robert D. Haas has inherited a dual legacy. Ever since its founding in 1850, the San Francisco-based apparel manufacturer has been famous for combining strong commercial success with a commitment to social values and to its work force.

Achieving both goals was relatively easy throughout much of the postwar era, when the company's main product—Levi's jeans—became an icon of American pop culture and sales surged on the demographic wave of the expanding baby boom. But in the uncertain economic climate of the 1980s, Haas and his management team have had to rethink every facet of the business—including its underlying values.

Since his appointment as CEO in 1984, Haas has redefined the company's business strategy; created a flatter organization, including the painful step of cutting the work force by one-third; and invested heavily in new-product development, marketing, and technology. In 1985, he and his team took the company private in one of the most successful management-led LBOs of the 1980s. And in 1987, he oversaw the development of the Levi Strauss Aspirations Statement, a major initiative to define the shared values that will guide both management and the work force. (See Appendix for "Aspirations Statement.")

Many CEOs talk about values, but few have gone to the lengths Haas has to bring them to the very center of how he runs the business. The Aspirations Statement is shaping how the company defines occupational roles and responsibilities, conducts performance evaluations, trains new employees, organizes work, and makes business decisions.

The result is a remarkably flexible and innovative company, despite its age and size. Levi is a pioneer in using electronic networks to link the company more closely to its suppliers and retailers. The Dockers line of clothing, introduced in 1986, has been one of the fastest-growing new products in apparel industry history. And the company has made a successful major push into global markets. In 1989, international operations accounted for 34% of Levi's total sales and 45% of pretax operating profit.

Levi's financial results have also been extraordinary. From 1985 to 1989, sales increased 31% to $3.6 billion. And profits have risen fivefold to $272 million.

Meanwhile, the company has stayed true to its traditional commitment to social issues even as it has updated that commitment to reflect the economic and social realities of a new era. Levi Strauss has an exemplary record on issues ranging from work force diversity to benefits for workers dislocated by plant closings and technological change. Haas himself is the foremost corporate spokesperson on the responsibilities of business in the AIDS crisis.

Reinventing the Levi Strauss heritage has a special meaning for Haas. He is the great-great-grandnephew of the company founder, and his uncle, father, and grandfather all led the company before him. He joined Levi Strauss in 1973 and has served in a variety of leadership positions, including senior vice president of corporate planning and policy, president of the operating groups, and executive vice president and chief operating officer. He has also worked as an associate at McKinsey & Co. and spent two years as a Peace Corps volunteer in the Ivory Coast.

The interview was conducted by HBR associate editor Robert Howard.

HBR: Levi Strauss has long had a reputation for its social responsibility. Why are you placing so much emphasis on defining the company's values now?

Robert Haas: Levi has always treated people fairly and cared about their welfare. The usual term is "paternalism." But it is more than paternalism, really—a genuine concern for people and a recognition that people make this business successful.

In the past, however, that tradition was viewed as something separate from how we ran the business. We always talked about the "hard stuff" and the "soft stuff." The soft stuff was the company's commitment to our work force. And the hard stuff was what really mattered: getting pants out the door.

What we've learned is that the soft stuff and the hard stuff are becoming increasingly intertwined. A company's values—what it stands for, what its people believe in—are crucial to its competitive success. Indeed, values drive the business.

What is happening in your environment to bring you to that conclusion?

Traditionally, the business world had clear boundaries. Geographical or regional borders defined the marketplace. Distinctions between suppliers and customers, workers and managers, were well defined. Once you had a strong market position, you could go on for a long time just on inertia. You could have a traditional, hierarchical, command-and-control organization, because change happened so slowly.

People's expectations for work were also narrowly defined. They gave their loyalty and their efforts in exchange for being taken care of. They expected information and commands to come down from on high, and they did what they were told.

As a result of all the tumult of the 1980s—increased competition, corporate restructurings, the globalization of enterprises, a new generation entering the work force—those traditional boundaries and expectations are breaking down.

What do those changes mean for leadership?

There is an enormous diffusion of power. If companies are going to react quickly to changes in the marketplace, they have to put more and more accountability, authority, and information into the hands of the people who are closest to the products and the customers. That requires new business strategies and different organizational structures. But structure and strategy aren't enough.

This is where values come in. In a more volatile and dynamic business environment, the controls have to be conceptual. They can't be human anymore: Bob Haas telling people what to do. It's the *ideas* of a business that are controlling, not some manager with authority. Values provide a common language for aligning a company's leadership and its people.

Why isn't a sound business strategy enough to create that alignment?

A strategy is no good if people don't fundamentally believe in it. We had a strategy in the late 1970s and early 1980s that emphasized diversification. We acquired companies, created new brands, and applied our traditional brand to different kinds of apparel. Our people did what they were asked to do, but the problem was, they didn't believe in it.

The big change at Levi is that we have worked hard to listen to our suppliers, our customers, and our own people. We have redefined our business strategy to focus on core products, and we have articulated the values that the company stands for—what we call our Aspirations. We've reshaped our business around this strategy and these values, and people have started marching behind this new banner. In fact, they are running to grab it and take it on ahead of senior management. Because it's what they *want* to do.

At Levi, we talk about creating an "empowered" organization. By that, we mean a company where the people who are closest to the product and the customer take the initiative without having to check with anyone. Because in an organization of 31,000 people, there's no way that any one of us in management can be around all the time to tell people what to do. It has to be the strategy and the values that guide them.

What is the role of a manager in an empowered company?

If the people on the front line really are the keys to our success, then the manager's job is to help those people and the people that they serve. That goes against the traditional assumption that the manager is in control. In the past, a manager was expected to know everything that was going on and to be deeply involved in subordinates' activities.

I can speak from experience. It has been difficult for me to accept the fact that I don't have to be the smartest guy on the block—reading every memo and signing off on every decision. In reality, the more you establish parameters and encourage people to take initiatives within those boundaries, the more you multiply your own effectiveness by the effectiveness of other people.

So in a business world without boundaries, the chief role of managers is to establish some?

To set parameters. Those parameters are going to be different for different individuals. And for the same individual, they're going to be different for different tasks. Some people are going to be very inexperienced in certain things, so you need to be careful about setting the parameters of where they have authority and where they need to stop to seek clarification. Other people have experience, skills, and a track record, and within certain areas you want to give them a lot of latitude.

How does that compare with the traditional manager's job?

In many ways, it's a much tougher role because you can't rely on your title or unquestioning loyalty and obedience to get things done. You have to be thoughtful about what you want. You have to be clear about the standards that you're setting. You have to negotiate goals with your work group rather than just set them yourself. You have to interact personally with individuals whom you're dealing with, understand their strengths and shortcomings, and be clear about what you want them to do.

You also have to accept the fact that decisions or recommendations may be different from what you would do. They could very well be better, but they're going to be different. You have to be willing to take your ego out of it.

That doesn't mean abdication. Managers still have to make decisions, serve as counselors and coaches, be there when things get sticky, and help sort out all the tangles.

What else do managers in an empowered organization need to do?

They can clear away the obstacles to effective action that exist in any large organization. In most companies, including ours, there is a gap between what the organization says it wants and what it feels like to work there. Those gaps between what you say and what you do erode trust in the enterprise and in the leadership, and they inhibit action. The more you can narrow that gap, the more people's energies can be released toward company purposes.

Most people want to make a contribution and be proud of what they do. But organizations typically teach us bad habits—to cut corners, protect our own turf, be political. We've discovered that when people talk about what they want for themselves and for their company, it's very idealistic and deeply emotional. This company tells people that idealism is OK. And the power that releases is just unbelievable. Liberating those forces, getting the impediments out of the way, that's what we as managers are supposed to be doing.

What is happening in the apparel business that makes managing by values so important?

The same things that are happening in most businesses. For decades, apparel has been a very fragmented industry. Most producers were small. Typically, changes in manufacturing technology, the use of computers, and the application of marketing techniques came slowly if at all. Our customers were also highly fragmented. In the old days, we had some 18,000 domestic accounts of all sizes and in every town in the country.

In this environment, we considered ourselves a manufacturer. Our job was to design products, manufacture them, deliver them in accordance with our retailers' orders, and support the retailers with some consumer advertising to help the products sell. But the rest was up to the individual retailer.

Now all that is changing very rapidly. Today the top 50 accounts make up a large part of our domestic business. Style changes happen more rapidly because of innovations in fabric finishes and also because customers adopt new fashions more quickly. Technology is transforming sewing work and our relationships with our suppliers and customers. And we are operating in a global marketplace against international competition. As a result, the way we see our business has also changed.

What's the new vision?

First, we are a marketer rather than a manufacturer. And second, we are at the center of a seamless web of mutual responsibility and collaboration.

Take our relationships with our retailers: to secure the availability of a product, apparel retailers have traditionally had to order it as much as four to five months in advance. That's crazy. It forces retail buyers to guess four and five months down the road what a consumer who is 15 years old is going to want in jeans. During that time, a new movie can come out, and the trend goes from blue denim to black denim. And suddenly that inventory commitment is obsolete, causing costly markdowns.

One answer to this new circumstance is technology. Our electronic data-interchange system, LeviLink, was a pioneering effort in apparel to communicate with our customers and manage the order-replenishment cycle faster and more accurately than conventional systems could (see Exhibit I). As a result, we have customers operating with 20% to 30% less inventory and achieving 20% to 30% increased sales. Their return on their investment with us is much greater than it was in the past. And these retailers also serve their customers better because the desired product is in stock when the consumer goes to purchase it.

Exhibit I.   How Values Shape Technology

According to Chief Information Officer Bill Eaton, the Levi Strauss & Co. technology strategy is a direct reflection of the company's Aspirations Statement. "Empowerment is meaningless unless people have access to information," says Eaton. "The goal of our technology strategy is to make sure that the information is available on the desktop of the person who is doing the job."

To that end, Levi Strauss has embarked on a three-part program for the global integration of its business through information technology. The most visible part of this strategy is LeviLink, the electronic data-interchange system that ties retailers to the company's distribution network. The system collects point-of-sale information from cash registers at the company's major accounts, then uses the information to generate reorders, invoices, packing slips, and advance notifications to retailers of future shipments. It also provides company sales representatives with far more information on the activity of individual retailers than was available in the past. Currently, about 40% of the company's business comes through LeviLink—a figure that the company hopes to double over the next five years.

Although less visible, Levi Strauss has also made major strides in computerizing its manufacturing operations. In 10 of the company's

32 factories worldwide, every sewing station now comes equipped with a hand-sized computer terminal. As a bundle of fabric moves through the plant, each employee who works on it passes the bundle's bar-coded label through a scanner built into the terminal. The result is a "real-time production control" system that allows the company to track work-in-process as it moves through the factory. The system also provides workers with information on their own performance, which they can use to increase productivity.

The ultimate goal is to link these two systems, allowing the company to issue production orders for new products immediately as existing products are sold in retailers' stores. This capacity will be provided by the Levi's Advanced Business System (LABS), which the company will be implementing over the next three years. LABS will be able to track a product from its conception—including orders, inventory, and financial information. Based on a new "relational database" software architecture, LABS will allow employees to perform more powerful and more flexible searches of company databases and to get rapid access to information typically limited in the past to managers.

The way Levi Strauss manages the development of new systems also reflects its commitment to using technology to support people. CIO Eaton serves on the company's executive management committee, ensuring the integration of technology and business strategies. And close ties between the information systems and human resources departments—one HR staff member now works in information systems—help connect the development of the company's new information technology platform to the creation of new business processes, organization designs, and people skills.

We're also forming closer relationships with our suppliers. We used to have ten or twelve U.S. denim suppliers. Now we're down to four or five. There is a seamless partnership, with interrelationships and mutual commitments, straight through the chain that would've been unimaginable ten years ago. You can't be responsive to the end-consumer today unless you can count on those kinds of collaborations at each step along the way.

What are the implications of that seamless partnership for your work force?

Our employees have many new responsibilities. For example, because of our computer linkages to our customers, our account representatives have more information on what's selling at the store level than the retailer does—not only products but sizes, fabrics, and styles. The rep has to know how to analyze that information and interpret it for the customer. What's more, since the computer does all the mundane record-keeping now, the rep can concentrate on planning and projecting the store's needs and being a marketing consultant.

What our employees do for the retailers is also much broader. In addition to the account representative, we have merchandising coordinators who make sure the stock is replenished and train salesclerks so they know how to sell our products more effectively. We have specialists in "visual merchandising" who work with our accounts to improve the ways they display our products. We have promotions experts who help stores tailor promotions to their clientele. And we run consumer hot lines to help customers find the products they want.

The work is much more creative, more entrepreneurial. It's as if these people are in business for themselves. They're doing what human beings do best—think, plan, interact, see trends, humanize the business to make it more successful.

What does that have to do with values?

To do that kind of work effectively requires a whole new set of attitudes and behaviors. The passivity and dependence of traditional paternalism—doing what you're told—doesn't work anymore. People have to take responsibility, exercise initiative, be accountable for their own success and for that of the company as a whole. They have to communicate more frequently and more effectively with their colleagues and their customers.

In a traditional command-and-control organization, acting in this way is difficult, even risky. The Aspirations encourage and support the new behaviors that we need. For example, in an empowered organization there are bound to be a lot more disagreements. Because we value open and direct communication, we give people permission to disagree. They can tell a manager, "It doesn't seem aspirational to be working with that contractor because from what we've seen, that company really mistreats its workers." Or they can say, "It may help us conserve cash to be slow in paying our bills, but that company has been a supplier for a long time, and it's struggling right now. Wouldn't it be better in terms of the partnership we're trying to create with our suppliers to pay our bills on time?"

Those are very challenging discussions for peers to have—let alone for somebody to have with his or her boss. But if we can "sanctify" it by reference to commonly held standards that we all share, it makes it all right to disagree.

So the values help bring about the kind of business behavior you need to stay competitive.

Values are where the hard stuff and the soft stuff come together. Let me give another example: in the new, more dynamic business environment, a company has to understand the relationship between work and family. It used to be that what happened to your employees when they went home at the end of the day was their business. But today that worker's sick child is your business, because if she's worrying about her child or calling in sick when she isn't—and probably feeling resentful because she's had to lie—she isn't going to be productive.

By contrast, if employees aren't worrying about things outside the workplace, if they feel supported—not just financially but "psychically"—then they are going to be more responsive to the needs of customers and of the business. That support needs to come in a whole set of managerial areas: supervisory practices, peer relations, training, work organization, access to information, and the like.

What is Levi doing about this particular issue?

We've established a companywide task force that's looking at how to balance work and family commitments. In itself, that's no big deal. A lot of companies are studying the issue. But even the way we manage the task force reflects our values. For instance, I'm on the task force, but I don't run it. We have everyone from secretaries and sewing machine operators to senior managers on the task force—as part of our commitment to diversity.

And that too makes perfect business sense. After all, my family situation is about as traditional as it gets. I have a wife at home who looks after our daughter. What do I know about the problems of a sewing machine operator—expected to punch in at a certain time and punch out at another and with a half-hour lunch break—

whose child's day-care arrangements fall through that morning? Obviously, a better result is going to come out of a broad task force that represents a diversity of opinions, family situations, and points of view (see Exhibit II).

Exhibit II.   The Making of an Aspiration

In 1985, a small group of minority and women managers asked for a private meeting with Levi Strauss & Co. CEO Robert Haas. The company had always been committed to equal employment opportunity; compared with other corporations, its numbers were good. But the managers felt strongly that they had reached a plateau. There were invisible barriers keeping women and minorities from advancing in the organization.

In response to their concerns, Haas organized an off-site retreat. Ten senior managers, all white men, were paired with either a woman or minority manager from their work group. The senior managers believed the company had been doing a good job hiring and promoting women and minorities. They were surprised to discover the depth of frustration and anger their subordinates felt. After two-and-a-half days of often painful discussion, the group concluded that equal opportunity was not just a matter of numbers but of attitudes, and that considerable unconscious discrimination still existed at the company. Something more needed to be done.

Since that 1985 meeting, Levi Strauss has renewed its commitment to full diversity at all levels. It has also broadened the definition of diversity beyond equal employment opportunity to the active encouragement of different points of view and their inclusion in company decision making.

Between 1985 and 1988, 16 more off-site sessions paired white, male managers with women or minorities who work for them to reflect on unexamined assumptions about diversity and stereotypes about particular groups. In 1987, diversity became one of the six Aspirations defined in the company's Aspirations Statement. That same year, members of the company's executive management committee—the top 8 people in the company—began holding monthly forums for small groups of 15 to 20 employees. By 1989, 20 ongoing forums were taking place. And while the original focus of the meetings was on questions of race and gender, the forums have expanded to consider a broad range of workplace issues.

The forums have been the catalyst for a number of new initiatives:

Recognizing that women and minority employees often have special problems and needs, the company has inaugurated four new career-development courses—one each for women, blacks, Hispanics, and Asians.

These courses have led to the creation of ethnic support networks for blacks, Asians, and Hispanics. Representatives of these networks have direct feedback to top management through quarterly meetings with the senior personnel committee.

In 1989, Levi Strauss established a companywide task force to recommend new policies to support a more effective balance between work and family life. Its 18 members are drawn from all levels of management and the work force—from sewing operators and secretaries to a division president and the CEO. This past summer, the task force sent a 25-page questionnaire to 15,000 of Levi's 21,000 U.S. employees to survey their family needs.

In 1989, the company also inaugurated a three-day course on "Valuing Diversity." About 240 top managers will have taken the course by the end of 1990. Eventually, all Levi Strauss employees will take diversity training.

How does a CEO manage for values?

The first responsibility for me and for my team is to examine critically our own behaviors and management styles in relation to the behaviors and values that we profess and to work to become more consistent with the values that we are articulating. It's tough work. We all fall off the wagon. But you can't be one thing and say another. People have unerring detection systems for fakes, and they won't put up with them. They won't put values into practice if you're not.

You said it's tough. What are the common kinds of breakdowns?

It's difficult to unlearn behaviors that made us successful in the past. Speaking rather than listening. Valuing people like yourself over people of different gender or from different cultures or parts of the organization. Doing things on your own rather than collaborating. Making the decision yourself instead of asking different people for their perspectives. There's a whole range of behaviors that were highly functional in the old hierarchical organization that are dead wrong in the flatter, more responsive, empowered organization that we're seeking to become.

Once your own behavior is in line with the new values, how do you communicate the values to others?

One way is to model the new behaviors we are looking for. For example, senior managers try to be explicit about our vulnerability and failings. We talk to people about the *bad* decisions we've made. It demystifies senior management and removes the stigma traditionally associated with taking risks. We also talk about the limitations of our own knowledge, mostly by inviting other people's perspectives.

When I talk to employees about the development of the Aspirations Statement, I describe the stark terror I felt when I took over this company, just having turned 43 years old. We were a company in crisis. Our sales were dropping, our international business was heading for a loss, our domestic business had an eroding profit base, our diversification wasn't working, and we had too much production capacity. I had no bold plan of action. I knew that values were important but didn't have the two granite tablets that I could bring down from Mount Sinai to deliver to the organization. I talk about how alone I felt as a senior manager and how tough it is to be held up as a paragon to the organization. It helps people realize that senior management is human, that we can't be expected to know everything, and that we're inviting them in as partners in the organization.

Another important way to communicate values is through training. We've developed a comprehensive training program that we call the core curriculum. The centerpiece is a week-long course known as "leadership week" that helps managers practice the behavior outlined in the Aspirations Statement. We run about 20 sessions a year for a small group of about 20 people at a time. By the end of this year, the top 700 people in the company will have been through it. And at least one member of the executive management committee—the top 8 people in the company—or some other senior manager participates in every week-long session, just to send a signal of how important this is to us.

Can you really train people in new values?

You can't train anybody to do anything that he or she doesn't fundamentally believe in. That's why we've designed leadership week to give people an opportunity to reflect on their own values and to allow them to say what they want to get from work. In most cases, people learn that their personal values are aligned with those of the company. Of course, not everybody will buy into it. We've had some very honest discussions where managers say, "Look, I'm 53 years old, I've managed one way all my life and been successful, and now the company wants me to change. I don't know if I can do it."

But two things happen during leadership week. Because the groups are small, people build up a support network. They realize that others have the same problems that they have. Suddenly, they don't feel so alone.

Second, the training makes clear what's expected of them and what the consequences of succeeding or failing to adapt will be. It gives people the freedom to opt out. The real success of our core curriculum will be if it convinces some people that our environment is simply not right for them.

We also try to make sure that the core curriculum isn't just some nice experience that stops as soon as people get back to their jobs. For instance, there is a section of leadership week called "unanswered questions" where people voice concerns inspired by the course. Our human resources people collect these unanswered questions and report on them every quarter to the executive management committee. Sometimes, these questions can be handled by a particular individual. In other cases, we've set up a company-wide task force to study the issue and come back with suggestions for changes in the way we do things. This creates a dialogue within the company among the people who have to make things happen.

Do the company's values influence the way you evaluate managers?

One-third of a manager's raise, bonus, and other financial rewards depends on his or her ability to manage aspirationally—the "how" of management rather than the "what." That goes for decisions about succession planning as well.

In some areas of the company, they're weighting it even more strongly. The point is, it's big enough to get people's attention. It's real. There's money attached to it. Giving people tough feedback and a low rating on aspirational management means improvement is necessary no matter how many pants they got out the door. Promotion is not in the future unless you improve.

How important is pay for pushing the company's values through the organization?

It's an influence but not the most important one. The key factors determining whether the values take or not will be individual commitment and desire and the peer pressure in the environment that we create. To me, the idea of a person as a marionette whose arms and legs start moving whenever you pull the pay string is too simplistic a notion of what motivates people in organizations.

That goes against the trend in recent years to fine-tune compensation incentives and tie them more closely to performance.

What happens there is you end up using pay to manage your company. But pay shouldn't manage your company; managers should. Managers should set the example, create the expectations, and provide the feedback. Managers should create an environment where people want to move in a constructive direction—not because there's money tied to the end of it, but because they feel it's right and they want to do it. That's why the way we conduct performance evaluations is probably more important than the pay we attach to aspirational management.

What's the process?

The typical performance evaluation in business has a manager set goals for a subordinate at the start of the year, and then at the end of the year make a subjective judgment about how well he or she has fulfilled them. That tends to create rabid "upward serving" behavior. People play to the person who's buttering their bread.

But what constitutes effective performance for a manager, anyway? Not necessarily pleasing your boss. Rather, good managers mobilize the talents of subordinates, peers, and clients to further the group's goals.

So what I started doing years ago—long before we developed the Aspirations Statement—was to talk with the direct reports of the people I manage, as well as with their peers and others they interact with. To evaluate one individual, I might interview anywhere from 10 to 16 people. The discussions are anonymous and confidential. And I report only trends, not isolated incidences.

This is an extremely powerful process that promotes ongoing

feedback. The quotes may be anonymous, but they are very direct. "Here's what a group of people who work for you feel: You're much too controlling. You don't give them the latitude they need to show you how much they could do. People feel scared to take risks with you or to say controversial things because you act like you don't believe them."

I also ask the people who contribute to somebody's evaluation to say the same things to the person's face. If we can encourage regular dialogue among people so that they give their bosses or peers feedback on their performance, managers begin to realize that they have to pay attention to their people. If they create an unwholesome, unproductive environment and can't change it, we're not going to tolerate it.

Has the Aspirations Statement had any impact yet on the quality of major business decisions?

I'm the first to say our journey is incomplete. But compared with, say, five years ago, there definitely is a change. Suddenly, this $4 billion company feels like an owner-operated company, which is the goal.

Take the example of our Dockers product line. Dockers was like a new invention—a brand new segment in the casual pants market. The concept started in Argentina. Our Japanese affiliate picked it up under another name. Our menswear division adapted the idea to the U.S. market under the name of Dockers. Then the other domestic divisions saw its potential, and now it's in womenswear and kidswear. We also have a Shirts Dockers line and in selected international markets, we're seeing the startup of a Dockers product. In 1986, we sold 35,000 units. This year, we'll be doing a half-a-billion-dollar business in the United States.

We didn't have a business plan for Dockers. We had managers who saw an opportunity. They created a product and went out and made commitments for production that were greater than the orders they had in hand, because they believed in the product and its momentum. They got corporate support for an investment in advertising that was not justified on a cost-per-unit basis and created a product that anybody else in the market could have done.

And five years later, it's a staple in the American wardrobe. None of this would have happened before this more collaborative, open style of management.

We've talked about getting managers to accept and live the company's values. But more than 75% of Levi's work force consists of operators in your sewing and finishing plants. Isn't the real challenge to make the company's values meaningful for them?

Empowerment isn't limited to just white-collar workers. By utilizing our people more fully than the apparel industry traditionally has, we can organize sewing work in ways that are much more in keeping with our Aspirations. About a year ago, we initiated an experiment at our Blue Ridge, Georgia plant, where we set up a gain-sharing program. We said to the employees, "You are the experts. If you meet predetermined production goals and predetermined absenteeism and safety standards, we'll split 50-50 with you any savings that result from economies or productivity improvements."

Sewing machine operators are now running the plant. They're making the rules and in some cases changing them because they understand why the rules are there and which rules make sense and which don't. They're taking initiatives and making things work better because it's in their interest and they don't have to be told.

This was not an unproductive plant. It was among the top 10% in the company. Today it's one of the top two plants—after only nine months in the new program. The financial payoff has been considerable, and there's certainly more potential there. But to me, the most exciting thing is to see the transformation in the workplace. People who felt that they weren't valued despite maybe 20 years of work for the company have a completely different attitude about their work.

In my judgment, we can restructure the workplace far beyond what we've done in Blue Ridge. I see us moving to a team-oriented, multiskilled environment in which the team itself takes on many of the supervisor's and trainer's tasks. If you combine that with some form of gain sharing, you probably will have a much more productive plant with higher employee satisfaction and commitment.

During the same period in which Levi has been defining its values, you've also been downsizing the company. Is it possible to get a high-commitment work force without offering some kind of employment security?

You can't promise employment security and be honest. The best you can do is not play games with people. You can't make any guarantees.

Through the 1950s, 1960s, and 1970s, Levi was growing so dramatically that unless you committed a felony, you weren't going to lose your job. But that was a special era stimulated by economic expansion and tremendous demographic growth. Now we're in a real-world situation where market forces are less favorable, external competitive pressures are more intense, and change is more rapid. You have to help people appreciate the need to deal constructively with the changing environment. If we're doing our job, we need to understand the rapidity and magnitude of the changes taking place and provide people with all the tools we can to cope with change.

But isn't it disingenuous to be championing values like empowerment in an environment where workers are worried about losing their jobs?

There is an apparent contradiction but not a real one, because our most basic value is honesty. If we have too much capacity, it's a problem that affects the entire company. Sometimes, the only solution is to close a plant, and if we don't have the guts to face that decision, then we risk hurting a lot of people—not just those in one plant. We need to be honest about that.

We tie it to Aspirations by asking, "How are we going to treat people who are displaced by technology, by changes in production sources, or by market changes?" We are committed to making the transition as successful as possible and to minimizing the uprooting and dislocation. We give more advance notice than is required by law. We provide more severance than is typical in our industry, so the effect of displacement is cushioned. We extend health care benefits. We also support job-training programs and other local initiatives to help our former employees find new jobs. And in the community itself, which has been depending on us as a major employer, we continue for a period of time to fund community organizations and social causes that we've been involved with, so that our withdrawal isn't a double hit—a loss of employment and also a loss of philanthropic support.

But has the Aspirations Statement changed the way you make decisions about capacity and plant closings in the first place?

The Aspirations make us slow down decisions. We challenge ourselves more explicitly to give some factors more weight than we did before—especially the impact of a plant closing on the community. There have been plants we have decided not to close, even though their costs were higher than other plants we did close. The reason was the community impact.

The Aspirations also provide a way to talk about these difficult trade-offs inside the company. People now have the freedom and authority to say, "Is it aspirational to be closing a plant when we're having a good year?" Or, "If we must close this plant, are we meeting our responsibilities to the employees and their community?" That forces us to be explicit about all the factors involved. It causes us to slow up, reflect, and be direct with one another about what's happening.

If the company's values cause you to slow up, doesn't that make it more difficult to respond to fast-changing markets?

Only if you assume it's still possible to separate the hard stuff from the soft stuff. Most managers say they want to optimize their business decisions. My personal philosophy is to suboptimize business decisions. Too often, optimizing really means taking only one dimension of a problem into account. Suboptimizing means looking at more than one factor and taking into account the interests and the needs of all the constituents. When you do that, suddenly the traditional hard values of business success and the nontraditional soft values relating to people start blending. The result is a better business decision—and it can still be done quickly if your employees understand the company's values and are empowered to take action without layers of review.

You mentioned collecting "unanswered questions" from employees about the role of values in the business. What's the most difficult for you to answer?

One of the most frequent things I hear is: "When the next downturn in the business happens, is top management going to remain committed to Aspirations?" The only answer to that one is, "Test us." We hope we won't have a downturn, but even if we do, I have no doubts about what management's commitment is. Only the experience of going through that kind of a situation, however, will convincingly demonstrate that commitment.

Where is that commitment to let values drive the business leading?

We've launched an irreversible process. Now we have to support the commitment that the Aspirations Statement is creating and be willing to deal with the tough issues that it raises. Two years ago, I gave a speech about the Aspirations at one of our worldwide management meetings. At the end, I held up the Aspirations Statement and ripped it to shreds. And I said, "I want each of you to throw away the Aspirations Statement and think about what you want for the company and what kind of person you want to be in the workplace and what kind of a legacy you want to leave behind. If the result happens to be the Aspirations, that's fine. But if it happens to be something else, the important thing is that you think deeply about who you are and what you stand for. I have enough confidence in your judgment and motivations that I'll go with whatever you come up with."

The point is, the Levi Strauss of the future is not going to be shaped by me or even by the Aspirations Statement. It's going to be shaped by our people and their actions, by the questions they ask and the responses we give, and by how this feeds into the way we run our business.

Appendix

Aspirations Statement

We all want a company that our people are proud of and committed to, where all employees have an opportunity to contribute, learn, grow, and advance based on merit, not politics or background. We want our people to feel respected, treated fairly, listened to, and involved. Above all, we want satisfaction from accomplishments and friendships, balanced personal and professional lives, and to have fun in our endeavors.

When we describe the kind of Levi Strauss & Co. we want in the future, what we are talking about is building on the foundation we have inherited: affirming the best of our company's traditions, closing gaps that may exist between principles and practices, and updating some of our values to reflect contemporary circumstances.

What type of leadership is necessary to make our Aspirations a Reality?

New Behaviors: Leadership that exemplifies directness, openness to influence, commitment to the success of others, willingness to acknowledge our own contributions to problems, personal accountability, teamwork, and trust. Not only must we model these behaviors but we must coach others to adopt them.

Diversity: Leadership that values a diverse work force (age, sex, ethnic group, etc.) at all levels of the organization, diversity in experience, and diversity in perspectives. We have committed to taking full advantage of the rich backgrounds and abilities of all our people and to promoting a greater diversity in positions of influence. Differing points of view will be sought; diversity will be valued and honesty rewarded, not suppressed.

Recognition: Leadership that provides greater recognition—both financial and psychic—for individuals and teams that contribute to our success. Recognition must be given to all who contribute: those who create and innovate and also those who continually support the day-to-day business requirements.

Ethical Management Practices: Leadership that epitomizes the stated standards of ethical behavior. We must provide clarity about our expectations and must enforce these standards through the corporation.

Communications: Leadership that is clear about company, unit, and individual goals and performance. People must know what is expected of them and receive timely, honest feedback on their performance and career aspirations.

Empowerment: Leadership that increases the authority and responsibility of those closest to our products and customers. By actively pushing responsibility, trust, and recognition into the organization, we can harness and release the capabilities of all our people.

3
Red Auerbach on Management

Alan M. Webber

Former Boston Celtics star Bob Cousy calls him "Arnold." But most diehard basketball fans know him as "Red." Hanging from the rafters of the Boston Garden are 16 green-and-white championship banners, testimony to his managerial genius.

He is Arnold "Red" Auerbach—inspiration and leader of the most successful sports franchise in America. For 36 years, as coach, general manager, and now president of the Boston Celtics, Mr. Auerbach has practiced his style of management in an enterprise in which the difference between winning and losing is very clear and very public. His management philosophy, based on the values of loyalty, pride, teamwork, and discipline, is applicable to managers in any field. And the results he has attained—measured in athletic and economic terms, or even just in the number of victory cigars he has savored—demonstrate his ability to make this philosophy work.

Mr. Auerbach is the author of *On and Off the Court* (Macmillan, 1985), written with Joe Fitzgerald. This interview was conducted by Alan M. Webber, managing editor at HBR.

HBR: When you started here in 1950, there was no such thing as "Celtics pride."

Auerbach: Right.

Thirty-six years later, everybody talks about it. It's at the heart of the Celtics' mystique. What is it?

It's the whole idea of caring. I'm in contact with the Frank Ramseys and Ed McCauleys and Bones McKinneys who played for me 35 years ago. I know where they are, what they do. If they want something, they call me and if I want something, I call them.

There's a family feeling. Two people in particular evidenced it for me. One was Wayne Embry, who played at Cincinnati for nine years and came here to finish his career. He never talks about Cincinnati. He talks about Celtics pride and the Celtics organization.

The other was Paul Silas. One of the best compliments I ever got was from Paul Silas. One day he came over to me and said, "I heard a lot about this Celtics pride and I thought it was a bunch of crap"—because he was an old veteran when he came here. "But," he said, "I was wrong. I feel a part of it and this has been the happiest part of my career." It was super. When you hear it from the players, it really makes you feel nine feet tall.

What are some of the things that explain this special feeling?

Well, it started way back, when Walter Brown owned the team. I had this theory, which we still use. And that is, a player's salary is determined by what the coaches see and what I see. What determines a player's salary is his contribution to winning—not his statistical accomplishments.

I don't believe in statistics. There are too many factors that can't be measured. You can't measure a ballplayer's heart, his ability to perform in the clutch, his willingness to sacrifice his offense or to play strong defense.

See, if you play strong defense and concentrate and work hard, it's got to affect your offense. But a lot of players on a lot of teams, all they point at is offense. Like in baseball they say, "I hit .300 so I should get so much money."

I've always eliminated the statistic of how many points a guy scores. Where did he score them? Did he score them during garbage time? Did he score them when the game was on the line? Did he score them against good opponents? There are so many factors.

So part of the Celtics' system is the way you set up the salaries?

Well, it's not just the money reward, it's more than that. It's like Larry Bird always says before a big game: "I'll be ready and the other guys will be ready and we're going to win this thing." Not "I'm going to win it." He says, "We're going to win it." Larry Bird gets as big a thrill out of making the pass as he does making the shot.

What are the other factors?

One important thing is trust within our organization. I really believe that loyalty is a two-way street. Unfortunately, in most businesses managers expect loyalty from employees but are very reluctant to give loyalty.

We've built up an organization where we care about our people. That doesn't mean that you can't make trades. You must have a certain amount of flexibility so if you feel you can improve your club, you go ahead and make a trade. But over the years we've made very few trades. Anybody who's been with us for more than five or six years will usually finish his career here. And when a player is on the tail end of his career, we don't just say, "We paid you, you played. See you later."

Most of our players have self-retired. They tell me when they don't think they can play anymore. The Jones boys, Cousy, Russell, Havlicek, Sanders, Nelson, Heinsohn—they all announced their retirements with no pressure from me whatsoever. People who come here realize that if they produce and do the job as they should and are happy here, we'll do our best for them. And we're interested in what they do when they leave here, when their careers are over.

What else goes into the relationship with the players?

I think the players know that if I make a decision, we're all going to stand with it. The players won't con me because I don't con them. They don't give me what we call false hustle, when a guy just goes through the motions but he's not really putting out much effort.

How do you discipline your athletes?

We like our players to play for fun and to be happy rather than afraid. It's like that in any business. If you have employees who work through fear, you're not going to get any ingenuity out of them. You're not going to get any employees who will take a gamble or come up with ideas. All you'll have are robots that are going to do their jobs, have a low-key approach, stay out of trouble. They'll put in their hours and go home. But I'd rather have it the other way.

So we talk to people. We don't fine them indiscriminately. A lot of teams have rules that say if you're late or miss a plane, you get fined. We have rules, but we temper them with mercy. We talk to people. And we never threaten employees specifically.

What I used to do when I coached was this: I wouldn't say that if they did something I'd fine them a thousand dollars or I'd suspend them; I'd just say that if they did something I'd bust their hump. So then they'd wonder, what is he going to do?

How do you motivate the players?

Pride, that's all. Pride of excellence. Pride of winning. I tell our guys, "Isn't it nice to go around all summer and say that you're a member of the greatest basketball team in the world."

Of course, we used to do funny things. I mean, how many times can you go in there and say, "Hey, let's win one for the Gipper?" So one day I said to one of the players, Frank Ramsey, "Ramsey, give them a motivating talk." So he walked up to the board and he put down on it, "If you win, $8,000. If you lose, $4,000." And they all broke up.

But the biggest motivating force you can have is the championship ring.

And the Celtics players have always responded to this kind of approach?

You see, in sports you have so many things that aren't expected. There's so much uncertainty. So when players find themselves in a situation where management has a great deal of integrity and they can depend on my word or anybody else's word in the organization, they feel secure. And if the players feel secure, they don't want to leave here. And if they don't want to leave here, they're going to do everything they can on the court to stay here.

I've turned down a lot of trades where I might have gotten a better player, but I wasn't totally sure of the chemistry of that new player coming in. Even though he might possess golden ability, his personality and the way he gets along with teammates might be things you just don't want to cope with.

When you are thinking of making a trade or acquiring a new player, do you consult the players?

Sometimes, sure. Our players are quite intelligent and they want the Celtics to be as good as possible. So I'd talk to a Cousy, a Havlicek, or Russell, or Bird and say, "Hey, we've got a chance to get so and so. What do you think?" Why not ask them? I've never had the ego to think that I know it all.

The coaching staff is also involved in every decision. I would never take it upon myself to force any player down the coach's throat. Because if I give a player to the coach and the coach doesn't want him, he'll resent it and the production of the whole team will suffer.

Now that you're president of the Celtics, what is your relationship with the coaching staff?

It's simple. I don't interfere with the coaches of the team. If they have a problem or something is on their minds, they come to me and we discuss it. But it's only when they ask. Because the worst thing a guy in my position can do is interfere. You see it on so many other teams, where the general managers feel they know more than the coaches and the scouts and they really interfere. I think the players sense that, and it breeds discord. It affects the team's chemistry.

You have a reputation as a tough negotiator.

Not really.

No?

Yeah, I have a reputation for being a tough negotiator, but it's not like that. I just don't like it when a guy comes in with a player who's worth $100,000 and he wants a million, figuring we'll negotiate and he'll walk away with $500,000.

What I'd say is, "Now look, this is what the guy is worth, based on his abilities and his contribution to the ball club. We might give or take a few thousand, but I'm not interested in a million dollars. That's it. And there's nothing you can do to change my mind. So don't come in at one million. Come in at two million. Come in at three million. It won't do you any good." I'd say, "We're fair. Now if the player pays his dues and performs, we'll pay him more. But he's got to earn it first."

And you don't deal in perks with your players?

Not at all. I tell them, "Look, I'm not in the car business. I'm not in the real estate business or the banking business. How much does it cost for you to play basketball? Let's set a figure and do that. You want a car, buy a car."

I could tell you stories of guys who make a million dollars and want a $10,000 bonus for making the All-Rookie team. I tell them, "I'm paying you the highest money a rookie ever got and if you don't make the All-Rookie team I have to be dumb."

You place such a great emphasis on teamwork and Celtics pride. Does it bother you that there's a players' union?

It did at first, sure. I think they've done some good things for the players, no question about that. But they don't concern themselves with ownership. They want this, they want that, and you realize that if you give them all of it, you'll lose money. But they don't care. They don't want to know about your problems. They're interested in feathering their own nests. They figure, what's the difference? So the owner sells out. There's always someone with the ego out there who'll buy another franchise, mainly because of this ego factor and the idea of national recognition.

Well, eventually that could stop too. A lot of these super-wealthy people who indulge themselves in sports say they've got so much money they don't care if they lose five million dollars a year. Then as soon as they lose five million dollars they want to get out. They all want to get out, they run like thieves. It's not really the money. It's the fact that they spent the money, they lost the money, and they still didn't win.

But there's got to be a happy medium. There's got to be a meeting point where the players realize that if they get everything they want, the owner can't stay in business.

Speaking of owners, you've worked for two, both named Brown—Walter and John Y. Brown.

They're like day and night. Walter Brown was one of the finest human beings I've ever been associated with. I learned a lot from him. Hell, I worked for him for 16 years and never had a contract.

You never had a contract? How did you do business?

At the end of every year I'd say, "What's the deal for next year, Walter?" He'd say, "What do you want?" Sometimes I'd tell him I didn't want anything. We didn't make any money and the club was just pretty good. Sometimes I'd come in and say that I wanted more money. He'd say, "Fine, what else do you want?" I'd say, "Nothing." We'd have a discussion of no more than a minute.

We'd end up making the deal in the washroom every time. His office door was always open and there was always somebody in there. I used to get mad. I'd say, "For crying out loud, can't we sit and talk?" And he'd say, "All right, let's go to the bathroom and get the thing done."

What about the other Mr. Brown, John Y.?

The other Brown, he had a tremendous ego, like he knew it all. He used to call up different general managers around the league to pick their brains, and they'd lie to him. They'd feed him all this information and then they'd call me up and ask, "Hey, what does that guy really want?"

And he'd make deals. Well, he made one great big deal that could have destroyed the team, without even consulting me.

You worked for 30 years to build the team and the franchise. Could one owner really destroy it?

He did ruin it. We just happened to put it back together again, luckily. One wrong guy can ruin it so fast your head will swim.

How does one person ruin the whole franchise?

For instance, you make a wrong move that costs you a few million dollars. If you make a trade for a player who's getting a million dollars a year and he doesn't produce, all of a sudden you're stuck paying three or four million dollars for an unproductive situation. That happens all the time in the league, and most of these guys shrug it off. To me, a player like that is a distraction.

What was your approach to putting the team back together again?

I had to start from scratch. I picked out the best team in the league and said, "We've got to put a team together that's competitive with that team." Well, there was no way we could do it right away. You set a goal, you try for two or three years, and you say the hell with it, if we've got to suffer another year, let's do that. So we took Larry Bird, even though he wasn't eligible to play for another year. Then we made the deal for Kevin McHale and Robert Parrish. And the owner, Harry Mangurian, knew what had to be done and was behind me. He had a private plane in those days, and we flew out to Minnesota just to take a look at Kevin McHale, so Harry was with it.

With all the money involved, the owners, the big contracts, do you look at professional basketball as a business or a sport?

At the back of your mind, you can't help but think that it's a business. But basically I've always felt that it's a labor of love. I've always put the chemistry and the performance of the ball club first. My prime concern has always been to have a competitive basketball team.

If you have a team that people like to see because the players are charismatic and they hustle, they play hard, they play as if they enjoy it—when you've got that, you draw people and you make money. Then the business practices fall into place.

You've gone from being coach of the Celtics to general manager and now to president. Have you changed your thoughts on how to run the organization?

Not at all. I still try to answer all the letters I get because that's the way I always did it. I would always tell the people in the front office that I didn't want to see any special treatment of the rich people buying box seats, any more than the guy buying a $3 seat upstairs. I don't want to see any meanness toward the lesser customers. They're the backbone of our business. One thing we have here is manners. That person buying the tickets is our bread and butter, and we don't forget it.

Too often, when people become executives they think that gives them a key to the toilet nobody else has. All of a sudden their heads get bigger than their shirt size. I've never operated that way. My door is open. Guys come in to shoot the bull and we talk.

That doesn't mean you can let them get so close that they lose respect. You have to have some sort of distance without being a snob. Too many executives become snobs, their egos are so big. They lose touch, they forget what got them there. After a while they don't even care about names. All they do is get the reports every morning and look at the bottom line.

Do you think managing the Celtics is like managing any other business?

I do. People say that I could run any other business. They used to put in the paper that I should take over the Red Sox or manage the Patriots. But that doesn't make sense. My knowledge of the product isn't there.

That's one of the big problems in sports today. The old adage is true, a little knowledge is a dangerous thing. Lots of owners who have been successful in one thing think they can pick up something new in a few months. Then they can't understand why they're not successful in the new business. They don't realize that they don't have a complete knowledge of the product.

How did you get a knowledge of the product?

Well, I paid my dues. I started as a coach, and while I was coaching I was also the general manager, the road secretary, and the scout. I was working 16, 17 hours a day. We'd play in New York on Thursday and in Boston on Saturday. I'd tell somebody to handle practice and I'd go scout, because I had no scouts. We had no movies, no video. Today we have six guys doing what I used to do.

You've been part of the Celtics for more than 36 years. Is there Celtics pride after Red Auerbach? Are you the center of the whole thing?

No, it's a team. Everybody right now is a cog in the machine. If you take out one part, you just do the best you can until you can replace it. There was a Celtics team before Larry Bird, there will be a Celtics team after Larry Bird. There was a Celtics team before me, and there will be a Celtics team after me. How good, I don't know. But it'll be there.

So what is Red Auerbach's secret recipe for creating America's most successful sports franchise?

I think it all stems from the fact that the players' livelihoods depend on their contribution toward the Celtics, not toward themselves. And after a while they believe in this.

Take Bill Walton. He contacted me when he was a free agent and asked if I could possibly get him. So I asked him why he wanted to play with the Celtics. He said it was not only because we had a team that was a contender and he could get along tremendously with the guys we had. On top of that, the Celtics' chemistry and reputation made it a team he'd always dreamed of playing for—which I felt was very kind. In fact, when he was with San Diego, he came up here to my office to see me. He wanted some Celtics T-shirts for his kids because to him this was what a sports franchise should be.

So it worked out that we got him. And one day he told me that he was down in the dumps. I asked him what was wrong, and he said he didn't feel like he was contributing to the team. I told him, "Of course you're contributing." "But I'm not scoring," he said. "That's the trouble with you," I said. "You're worried about statistics."

I told him that we didn't care about what he scored. All we were interested in was what he contributed. Did he roll down? Did he play defense? Did he run the court? Did he pass?

He asked, "You mean you really don't care about scoring?" I told him, "Not at all. It won't affect you one iota."

You could see his face light up. And from that point on, he was a different guy. He was always great to begin with, but this made him even better. He became loose. And he never looked to see what he scored. All he looked at was, did we win. And it was "we," not "I."

PART
III
Global Leadership

1

The Logic of Global Business: An Interview with ABB's Percy Barnevik

William Taylor

Percy Barnevik, president and CEO of ABB Asea Brown Boveri, is a corporate pioneer. He is moving more aggressively than any CEO in Europe, perhaps in the world, to build the new model of competitive enterprise—an organization that combines global scale and world-class technology with deep roots in local markets. He is working to give substance to the endlessly invoked corporate mantra, "Think global, act local."

Headquartered in Zurich, ABB is a young company forged through the merger of two venerable European companies. Asea, created in 1890, has been a flagship of Swedish industry for a century. Brown Boveri, which took shape in 1891, holds a comparable industrial status in Switzerland. In August 1987, Barnevik altered the course of both companies when he announced that Asea, where he was managing director, would merge with Brown Boveri to create a potent new force in the European market for electrical systems and equipment.

The creation of ABB became a metaphor for the changing economic map of Europe. Barnevik initiated a wrenching process of consolidation and rationalization—layoffs, plant closings, product exchanges between countries—that observers agreed will one day come to European industries from steel to telecommunications to automobiles. And soon more than a metaphor, Barnevik's bold moves triggered a wholesale restructuring of the Continent's electrical power industry.

The creation of ABB also turned out to be the first step in a trans-Atlantic journey of acquisition, restructuring, and growth. ABB has acquired or taken minority positions in 60 companies representing investments worth $3.6 billion—including two major acquisitions in North America. In 1989, ABB acquired Westinghouse's transmission and distribution operation in a transaction involving 25 factories and businesses with revenues of $1 billion. That same year, it spent $1.6 billion to acquire Combustion Engineering, the manufacturer of power-generation and process-automation equipment.

Today ABB generates annual revenues of more than $25 billion and employs 240,000 people around the world. It is well balanced on both sides of the Atlantic. Europe accounts for more than 60% of its total revenues, and its business is split roughly equally between the European Community countries and the non-EC Scandinavian trading bloc. Germany, ABB's largest national market, accounts for 15% of total revenues. The company also generates annual revenues of $7 billion in North America, with 40,000 employees. Although ABB remains underrepresented in Asia, which accounts for only 15% of total revenues, it is an important target for expansion and investment. And ABB's business activities are not limited to the industrialized world. The company has 10,000 employees in India, 10,000 in South America, and is one of the most active Western investors in Eastern Europe.

In this interview, Percy Barnevik, 49, offers a detailed guide to the theory and practice of building a "multidomestic" enterprise. He explains ABB's matrix system, a structure designed to leverage core technologies and global economies of scale without eroding local market presence and responsiveness. He describes a new breed of "global managers" and explains how their skills differ from those of traditional managers. He reckons candidly with the political implications of companies such as ABB.

The interview was conducted by HBR associate editor William Taylor.

HBR: Companies everywhere are trying to become global, and everyone agrees that ABB is more global than most companies. What does that mean?

Percy Barnevik: ABB is a company with no geographic center, no national ax to grind. We are a federation of national companies with a global coordination center. Are we a Swiss company? Our headquarters is in Zurich, but only 100 professionals work at headquarters and we will not increase that number. Are we a Swedish company? I'm the CEO, and I was born and educated in Sweden. But our headquarters is not in Sweden, and only two of the eight members of our board of directors are Swedes. Perhaps we are an American company. We report our financial results in U.S. dollars, and English is ABB's official language. We conduct all high-level meetings in English.

My point is that ABB is none of those things—and all of those things. We are not homeless. We are a company with many homes.

Are all businesses becoming global?

No, and this is a big source of misunderstanding. We are in the process of building this federation of national companies, a multi-domestic organization, as I prefer to call it. That does not mean all of our businesses are global. We do a very good business in electrical installation and service in many countries. That business is superlocal. The geographic scope of our installation business in, say, Stuttgart does not extend beyond a ten-mile radius of downtown Stuttgart.

We also have businesses that are superglobal. There are not more than 15 combined-cycle power plants or more than 3 or 4 high-voltage DC stations sold in any one year around the world. Our competitors fight for nearly every contract—they battle us on technology, price, financing—and national borders are virtually meaningless. Every project requires our best people and best technology from around the world.

The vast majority of our businesses—and of most businesses—fall somewhere between the superlocal and the superglobal. These are the businesses in which building a multidomestic organization offers powerful advantages. You want to be able to optimize a business globally—to specialize in the production of components, to drive economies of scale as far as you can, to rotate managers and technologists around the world to share expertise and solve problems. But you also want to have deep local roots everywhere you operate—building products in the countries where you sell them, recruiting the best local talent from the universities, working with the local government to increase exports. If you build such an organization, you create a business advantage that's damn difficult to copy.

What is a business that demonstrates that advantage?

Transportation is a good one. This is a vibrant business for us, and we consider ourselves number one in the world. We generate $2 billion a year in revenues when you include all of our activities: locomotives, subway cars, suburban trains, trolleys, and the electrical and signaling systems that support them. We are strong because we are the only multidomestic player in the world.

First, we know what core technologies we have to master, and we draw on research from labs across Europe and the world. Being a technology leader in locomotives means being a leader in power electronics, mechanical design, even communications software. Ten years ago, Asea beat General Electric on a big Amtrak order for locomotives on the Metro-liner between New York and Washington. That win caused quite a stir; it was the first time in one hundred years that an American railroad bought locomotives from outside the United States. We won because we could run that track from Washington to New York, crooked and bad as it was, at 125 miles an hour. Asea had been pushing high-speed design concepts for more than a decade, and Brown Boveri pioneered the AC technology. That's why our X2 tilting trains are running in Sweden and why ABB will play a big role in the high-speed rail network scheduled to run throughout Europe.

Second, we structure our operations to push cross-border economies of scale. This is an especially big advantage in Europe, where the locomotive industry is hopelessly fragmented. There are two companies headquartered in the United States building locomotives for the U.S. market. There are three companies in Japan. There are 24 companies in Western Europe, and the industry runs at less than 75% of capacity. There are European companies still making only 10 or 20 locomotives a year! How can they compete with us, when we have factories doing ten times their volume and specializing in components for locomotives across the Continent? For example, one of our new plants makes power electronics for many of the locomotives we sell in Europe. That specialization creates huge cost and quality advantages. We work to rationalize and specialize as much as we can across borders.

Third, we recognize the limits to specialization. We can't ignore borders altogether. We recently won a $420-million order from the Swiss Federal Railways—we call it the "order of the century"—to build locomotives that will move freight through the Alps. If we expect to win those orders, we had *better* be a Swiss company. We had better understand the depth of the Swiss concern for the environment, which explains the willingness to invest so heavily to get freight moving on trains through the mountains to Italy or Germany and off polluting trucks. We had better understand the Alpine terrain and what it takes to build engines powerful enough to haul heavy loads. We had better understand the effects of drastic temperature changes on sensitive electronics and build locomotives robust enough to keep working when they go from the frigid, dry outdoors to extreme heat and humidity inside the tunnels.

There are other advantages to a multidomestic presence. India needs locomotives—thousands of locomotives—and the government expects its suppliers to manufacture most of them inside India. But the Indians also need soft credit to pay for what is imported. Who has more soft credit than the Germans and the Italians? So we have to be a German and an Italian company, we have to be able to build locomotive components there as well as in Switzerland, Sweden, and Austria, since our presence may persuade Bonn and Rome to assist with financing.

We test the borderlines all the time: How far can we push cross-border specialization and scale economies? How effectively can we translate our multidomestic presence into competitive advantages in third markets?

Is there such a thing as a global manager?

Yes, but we don't have many. One of ABB's biggest priorities is to create more of them; it is a crucial bottleneck for us. On the other hand, a global company does not need thousands of global managers. We need maybe 500 or so out of 15,000 managers to make ABB work well—not more. I have no interest in making managers more "global" than they have to be. We can't have people abdicating their nationalities, saying "I am no longer German, I am international." The world doesn't work like that. If you are selling products and services in Germany, you better be German!

That said, we do need a core group of global managers at the top: on our executive committee, on the teams running our business areas (BAs), in other key positions. How are they different? Global managers have exceptionally open minds. They respect how different countries do things, and they have the imagination to appreciate why they do them that way. But they are also incisive, they push the limits of the culture. Global managers don't passively accept it when someone says, "You can't do that in Italy or Spain because of the unions," or "You can't do that in Japan because of the Ministry of Finance." They sort through the debris of cultural excuses and find opportunities to innovate.

Global managers are also generous and patient. They can handle the frustrations of language barriers. As I mentioned earlier, English is the official language of ABB. Every manager with a global role *must* be fluent in English, and anyone with regional general management responsibilities must be competent in English. When I write letters to ABB colleagues in Sweden, I write them in English. It may seem silly for one Swede to write to another in English, but who knows who will need to see that letter a year from now?

We are adamant about the language requirement—and it creates problems. Only 30% of our managers speak English as their first language, so there is great potential for misunderstanding, for misjudging people, for mistaking facility with English for intelligence or knowledge. I'm as guilty as anyone. I was rushing through an airport last year and had to return a phone call from one of our managers in Germany. His English wasn't good, and he was speaking slowly and tentatively. I was in a hurry, and finally I insisted, "Can't you speak any faster?" There was complete silence. It was a dumb thing for me to say. Things like that happen every day in this company. Global managers minimize those problems and work to eliminate them.

Where do these new managers come from?

Global managers are made, not born. This is not a natural process. We are herd animals. We like people who are like us. But there are many things you can do. Obviously, you rotate people around the world. There is no substitute for line experience in three or four countries to create a global perspective. You also encourage people to work in mixed-nationality teams. You *force* them to create personal alliances across borders, which means that sometimes you interfere in hiring decisions.

This is why we put so much emphasis on teams in the business areas. If you have 50 business areas and five managers on each BA team, that's 250 people from different parts of the world—people who meet regularly in different places, bring their national perspectives to bear on tough problems, and begin to understand how things are done elsewhere. I experience this every three weeks in our executive committee. When we sit together as Germans, Swiss, Americans, and Swedes, with many of us living, working, and traveling in different places, the insights can be remarkable. But you have to force people into these situations. Mixing nationalities doesn't just happen.

You also have to acknowledge cultural differences without becoming paralyzed by them. We've done some surveys, as have lots of other companies, and we find interesting differences in perception. For example, a Swede may think a Swiss is not completely frank and open, that he doesn't know exactly where he stands. That is a cultural phenomenon. Swiss culture shuns disagreement. A Swiss might say, "Let's come back to that point later, let me review it with my colleagues." A Swede would prefer to confront the issue directly. How do we undo hundreds of years of upbringing and education? We don't, and we shouldn't try to. But we do need to broaden understanding.

Is your goal to develop an "ABB way" of managing that cuts across cultural differences?

Yes and no. Naturally, as CEO, I set the tone for the company's management style. With my Anglo-Saxon education and Swedish upbringing, I have a certain way of doing things. Someone recently asked if my ultimate goal is to create 5,000 little Percy Barneviks, one for each of our profit centers. I laughed for a moment when I thought of the horror of sitting on top of such an organization, then I realized it wasn't a silly question. And the answer is no. We can't have managers who are "un-French" managing in France because 95% of them are dealing every day with French customers, French colleagues, French suppliers. That's why global managers also need humility. A global manager respects a formal German manager— Herr Doktor and all that—because that manager may be an outstanding performer in the German context.

Let's talk about the structures of global business. How do you organize a multidomestic enterprise?

ABB is an organization with three internal contradictions. We want to be global and local, big and small, radically decentralized with centralized reporting and control. If we resolve those contradictions, we create real organizational advantage.

That's where the matrix comes in. The matrix is the framework through which we organize our activities. It allows us to optimize our businesses globally *and* maximize performance in every country in which we operate. Some people resist it. They say the matrix is too rigid, too simplistic. But what choice do you have? To say you don't like a matrix is like saying you don't like factories or you don't like breathing. It's a fact of life. If you deny the formal matrix, you wind up with an informal one—and that's much harder to reckon with. As we learn to master the matrix, we get a truly multidomestic organization.

Can you walk us through how the matrix works?

Look at it first from the point of view of one business area, say, power transformers. The BA manager for power transformers happens to sit in Mannheim, Germany. His charter, however, is worldwide. He runs a business with 25 factories in 16 countries and global revenues of more than $1 billion. He has a small team around him of mixed nationalities—we don't expect superheroes to run our 50 BAs. Together with his colleagues, the BA manager establishes and monitors the trajectory of the business.

The BA leader is a business strategist and global optimizer. He decides which factories are going to make what products, what export markets each factory will serve, how the factories should pool their expertise and research funds for the benefit of the business worldwide. He also tracks talent—the 60 or 70 real standouts around the world. Say we need a plant manager for a new company in Thailand. The BA head should know of three or four people— maybe there's one at our plant in Muncie, Indiana, maybe there's one in Finland—who could help in Thailand. (See Appendix "Power Transformers—The Dynamics of Global Coordination.")

It is possible to leave the organization right there, to optimize every business area without regard for ABB's broad collection of activities in specific countries. But think about what we lose. We have a power transformer company in Norway that employs 400 people. It builds transformers for the Norwegian market and exports to markets allocated by the BA. But ABB Norway has more than 10,000 other employees in the country. There are tremendous benefits if power transformers coordinates its Norwegian operation with our operations in power generation, switchgear, and process automation: recruiting top people from the universities, building an efficient distribution and service network across product lines, circulating good people among the local companies, maintaining productive relations with top government officials.

So we have a Norwegian company, ABB Norway, with a Norwegian CEO and a headquarters in Oslo, to make these connections. The CEO has the same responsibilities as the CEO of a local Norwegian company for labor negotiations, bank relationships, and high-level contacts with customers. This is no label or gimmick. We *must* be a Norwegian company to work effectively in many businesses. Norway's oil operations in the North Sea are a matter of great national importance and intense national pride. The government wouldn't—and shouldn't—trust some faraway foreign company as a key supplier to those operations.

The opportunities for synergy are clear. So is the potential for tension between the business area structure and the country structure. Can't the matrix pull itself apart?

BA managers, country managers, and presidents of the local companies have very different jobs. They must understand their roles and appreciate that they are *complementing* each other, not competing.

The BA managers are crucial people. They need a strong hand in crafting strategy, evaluating performance around the world, and working with teams made up of different nationalities. We've had to replace some of them—people who lacked vision or cultural sensitivity or the ability to lead without being dictators. You see, BA managers don't own the people working in any business area around the world. They can't order the president of a local company to fire someone or to use a particular strategy in union negotiations. On the other hand, BA managers can't let their role degrade into a statistical coordinator or scorekeeper. There's a natural tendency for this to happen. BA managers don't have a constituency of thousands of direct reports in the same way that country managers do. So it's a difficult balancing act.

Country managers play a different role. They are regional line managers, the equivalent of the CEO of a local company. But country managers must also respect ABB's global objectives. The president of, say, ABB Portugal can't tell the BA manager for low-voltage switchgear or drives to stay out of his hair.

He has to cooperate with the BA managers to evaluate and improve what's happening in Portugal in those businesses. He should be able to tell a BA manager, "You may think the plant in Portugal is up to standards, but you're being too loose. Turnover and absenteeism is twice the Portugese average. There are problems with the union, and it's the managers' fault."

Now, the presidents of our local companies—ABB Transformers in Denmark, say, or ABB Drives in Greece—need a different set of skills. They must be excellent profit center managers. But they must also be able to answer to two bosses effectively. After all, they have two sets of responsibilities. They have a global boss, the BA manager, who creates the rules of the game by which they run their businesses. They also have their country boss, to whom they report in the local setting. I don't want to make too much of this. In all of Germany, where we have 36,000 people, only 50 or so managers have two bosses. But these managers have to handle that ambiguity. They must have the self-confidence not to become paralyzed if they receive conflicting signals and the integrity not to play one boss off against the other.

Isn't all this much easier said than done?

It does require a huge mental change, especially for country managers. Remember, we've built ABB through acquisitions and restructurings. Thirty of the companies we've bought had been around for more than 100 years. Many of them were industry leaders in their countries, national monuments. Now they've got BA managers playing a big role in the direction of their operations. We have to convince country managers that they benefit by being part of this federation, that they gain more than they lose when they give up some autonomy.

What's an example?

Finland has been one of our most spectacular success stories, precisely because the Finns understood how much they could gain. In 1986, Asea acquired Strömberg, the Finnish power and electrical products company. At the time, Strömberg made an unbelievable assortment of products, probably half of what ABB makes today.

It built generators, transformers, drives, circuit breakers—all of them for the Finnish market, many of them for export. It was a classic example of a big company in a small country that survived because of a protected market. Not surprisingly, much of what it made was not up to world-class standards, and the company was not very profitable. How can you expect a country with half the population of New Jersey to be profitable in everything from hydropower to circuit breakers?

Strömberg is no longer a stand-alone company. It is part of ABB's global matrix. The company still exists—there is a president of ABB Strömberg—but its charter is different. It is no longer the center of the world for every product it sells. It still manufactures and services many products for the Finnish market. It also sells certain products to allocated markets outside Finland. And it is ABB's worldwide center of excellence for one important group of products, electric drives, in which it had a long history of technology leadership and effective manufacturing. Strömberg is a hell of a lot stronger because of this. Its total exports from Finland have increased more than 50% in three years. ABB Strömberg has become one of the most profitable companies in the whole ABB group, with a return on capital employed of around 30%. It is a recognized world leader in drives. Strömberg produces more than 35% of all the drives ABB sells, and drives are a billion-dollar business. In four years, Strömberg's exports to Germany and France have increased ten times. Why? Because the company has access to a distribution network it never could have built itself.

This sounds enormously complicated, almost unmanageable. How does the organization avoid getting lost in the complexity?

The only way to structure a complex, global organization is to make it as simple and local as possible. ABB is complicated from where I sit. But on the ground, where the real work gets done, all of our operations must function as closely as possible to stand-alone operations. Our managers need well-defined sets of responsibilities, clear accountability, and maximum degrees of freedom to execute. I don't expect most of our people to have "global mind-sets," to do things that hurt their business but are "good for ABB." That's not natural.

Take Strömberg and drives in France. I don't want the drive company president in Finland to think about what's good for

France. I want him to think about Finland, about how to sell the hell out of the export markets he has been allocated. Likewise, I don't expect our profit center manager in France to think about Finland. I expect him to do what makes sense for his French customers. If our French salespeople find higher quality drives or more cost-effective drives outside ABB, they are free to sell them in France so long as ABB gets a right of first refusal. Finland has increased its shipments to France because it makes economic sense for both sides. That's the only way to operate.

But how can an organization with 240,000 people all over the world be simple and local?

ABB *is* a huge enterprise. But the work of most of our people is organized in small units with P&L responsibility and meaningful autonomy. Our operations are divided into nearly 1,200 companies with an average of 200 employees. These companies are divided into 4,500 profit centers with an average of 50 employees.

We are fervent believers in decentralization. When we structure local operations, we always push to create separate legal entities. Separate companies allow you to create *real* balance sheets with *real* responsibility for cash flow and dividends. With real balance sheets, managers inherit results from year to year through changes in equity. Separate companies also create more effective tools to recruit and motivate managers. People can aspire to meaningful career ladders in companies small enough to understand and be committed to.

What does that mean for the role of headquarters?

We operate as lean as humanly possible. It's no accident that there are only 100 people at ABB headquarters in Zurich. The closer we get to top management, the tougher we have to be with head count. I believe you can go into any traditionally centralized corporation and cut its headquarters staff by 90% in one year. You spin off 30% of the staff into free-standing service centers that perform real work—treasury functions, legal services—and charge for it. You decentralize 30% of the staff—human resources, for example—by pushing them into the line organization. Then 30% disappears through head count reductions.

These are not hypothetical calculations. We bought Combustion

Engineering in late 1989. I told the Americans that they had to go from 600 people to 100 in their Stamford, Connecticut headquarters. They didn't believe it was possible. So I told them to go to Finland and take a look. When we bought Strömberg, there were 880 people in headquarters. Today there are 25. I told them to go to Mannheim and take a look at the German operation. In 1988, right after the creation of ABB, there were 1,600 people in headquarters. Today there are 100.

Doesn't such radical decentralization threaten the very advantages that ABB's size creates?

Those are the contradictions again—being simultaneously big and small, decentralized and centralized. To do that, you need a structure at the top that facilitates quick decision making and carefully monitors developments around the world. That's the role of our executive committee. The 13 members of the executive committee are collectively responsible for ABB. But each of us also has responsibility for a business segment, a region, some administrative functions, or more than one of these. Eberhard von Koerber, who is a member of the executive committee located in Mannheim, is responsible for Germany, Austria, Italy, and Eastern Europe. He is also responsible for a worldwide business area, installation materials, and some corporate staff functions. Gerhard Schulmeyer sits in the United States and is responsible for North America. He is also responsible for our global "industry" segment. Naturally, these 13 executives are busy, stretched people. But think about what happens when we meet every three weeks, which we do for a full day. Sitting in one room are the senior managers collectively responsible for ABB's global strategy and performance. These same managers individually monitor business segments, countries, and staff functions. So when we make a decision—snap, it's covered. The members of the executive committee communicate to their direct reports, the BA managers and the country managers, and the implementation process is under way.

We also have the glue of transparent, centralized reporting through a management information system called Abacus. Every month, Abacus collects performance data on our 4,500 profit centers and compares performance with budgets and forecasts. The data are collected in local currencies but translated into U.S. dollars to allow for analysis across borders. The system also allows you to work with the data. You can aggregate and disaggregate results by business segments, countries, and companies within countries.

What kind of information does the executive committee use to support the fast decision making you need?

We look for early signs that businesses are becoming more or less healthy. On the tenth of every month, for example, I get a binder with information on about 500 different operations—the 50 business areas, all the major countries, and the key companies in key countries. I look at several parameters—new orders, invoicing, margins, cash flows—around the world and in various business segments. Then I stop to study trends that catch my eye.

Let's say the industry segment is behind budget. I look to see which of the five BAs in the segment are behind. I see that process automation is way off. So I look by country and learn that the problem is in the United States and that it's poor margins, not weak revenues. So the answer is obvious—a price war has broken out. That doesn't mean I start giving orders. But I want to have informed dialogues with the appropriate executives.

Let's go back to basics. How do you begin building this kind of global organization?

ABB has grown largely through mergers and strategic investments. For most companies in Europe, this is the right way to cross borders. There is such massive overcapacity in so many European industries and so few companies with the critical mass to hold their own against Japanese and U.S. competitors. My former company, Asea, did fine in the 1980s. Revenues in 1987 were 4 times greater than in 1980, profits were 10 times greater, and our market value was 20 times greater. But the handwriting was on the wall. The European electrical industry was crowded with 20 national competitors. There was up to 50% overcapacity, high costs, and little cross-border trade. Half the companies were losing money. The creation of ABB started a painful—but long overdue—process of restructuring.

That same restructuring process will come to other industries: automobiles, telecommunications, steel. But it will come slowly. There have been plenty of articles in the last few years about all the cross-border mergers in Europe. In fact, the more interesting issue is why there have been so *few*. There should be *hundreds* of them, involving *tens of billions* of dollars, in industry after industry. But we're not seeing it. What we're seeing instead are strategic alliances and minority investments. Companies buy 15% of each other's shares. Or two rivals agree to cooperate in third markets but not merge their home-market organizations. I worry that many European alliances are poor substitutes for doing what we try to do—complete mergers and cross-border rationalization.

What are the obstacles to such cross-border restructuring?

One obstacle is political. When we decided on the merger between Asea and Brown Boveri, we had no choice but to do it secretly and to do it quickly, with our eyes open about discovering skeletons in the closet. There were no lawyers, no auditors, no environmental investigations, and no due diligence. Sure, we tried to value assets as best we could. But then we had to make the move, with an extremely thin legal document, because we were absolutely convinced of the strategic merits. In fact, the documents from the premerger negotiations are locked away in a Swiss bank and won't be released for 20 years.

Why the secrecy? Think of Sweden. Its industrial jewel, Asea—a 100-year-old company that had built much of the country's infrastructure—was moving its headquarters out of Sweden. The unions were angry: "Decisions will be made in Zurich, we have no influence in Zurich, there is no codetermination in Switzerland."

I remember when we called the press conference in Stockholm on August 10. The news came as a complete surprise. Some journalists didn't even bother to attend; they figured it was an announcement about a new plant in Norway or something. Then came the shock, the fait accompli. That started a communications war of a few weeks where we had to win over shareholders, the public, governments, and unions. But strict confidentiality was our only choice.

Are there obstacles besides politics?

Absolutely. The more powerful the strategic logic behind a merger—the greater the cross-border synergies—the more powerful the human and organizational obstacles. It's hard to tell a competent country manager in Athens or Amsterdam, "You've done a good job for 15 years, but unfortunately this other manager has done a better job and our only choice is to appoint your colleague to run the operation." If you have two plants in the same country running well but you need only one after the merger, it's tough to explain that to employees in the plant to be closed. Restructuring operations creates lots of pain and heartache, so many companies choose not to begin the process, to avoid the pain.

Germany is a case in point. Brown Boveri had operated in Germany for almost 90 years. Its German operation was so big—it had more than 35,000 employees—that there were rivalries with the Swiss parent. BBC Germany was a technology-driven, low-profit organization—a real underperformer. The formation of ABB created the opportunity to tackle problems that had festered for decades.

So what did you do?

We sent in Eberhard von Koerber to lead the effort. He made no secret of our plans. We had to reduce the work force by 10%, or 4,000 employees. We had to break up the headquarters, which had grown so big because of all the tensions with Switzerland. We had to rationalize the production overlaps, especially between Switzerland and Germany. We needed lots of new managers, eager people who wanted to be leaders and grow in the business.

The reaction was intense. Von Koerber faced strikes, demonstrations, barricades—real confrontation with the unions. He would turn on the television set and see protesters chanting, "Von Koerber out! Von Koerber out!" After a while, once the unions understood the game plan, the loud protests disappeared and our relationship became very constructive. The silent resistance from managers was more formidable. In fact, much of the union resistance was fed by management. Once the unions got on board, they became allies in our effort to reform management and rationalize operations.

Three years later, the results are in. ABB Germany is a well-structured, dynamic, market-oriented company. Profits are increasing steeply, in line with ABB targets. In 1987, BBC Germany generated revenues of $4 billion. ABB Germany will generate twice that by the end of next year. Three years ago, the management structure in Mannheim was centralized and functional, with few clear responsibilities or accountability. Today there are 30 German companies, each with its own president, manufacturing director, and so on. We can see who the outstanding performers are and apply their talents elsewhere. If we need someone to sort out a problem with circuit breakers in Spain, we know who from Germany can help.

What lessons can other companies learn from the German experience?

To make real change in cross-border mergers, you have to be factual, quick, and neutral. And you have to move boldly. You must avoid the "investigation trap"—you can't postpone tough decisions by studying them to death. You can't permit a "honeymoon" of small changes over a year or two. A long series of small changes just prolongs the pain. Finally, you have to accept a fair share of mistakes. I tell my people that if we make 100 decisions and 70 turn out to be right, that's good enough. I'd rather be roughly right and fast than exactly right and slow. We apply these principles everywhere we go, including in Eastern Europe, where we now have several change programs under way.

Why emphasize speed at the expense of precision? Because the costs of delay are vastly greater than the costs of an occasional mistake. I won't deny that it was absolutely crazy around here for the first few months after the merger. We *had* to get the matrix in place—we couldn't debate it—and we *had* to figure out which plants would close and which would stay open. We took ten of our best people, the superstars, and gave them six weeks to design the restructuring. We called it the Manhattan Project. I personally interviewed 400 people, virtually day and night, to help select and motivate the people to run our local companies.

Once you've put the global pieces together and have the matrix concept working, what other problems do you have to wrestle with?

Communications. I have no illusions about how hard it is to communicate clearly and quickly to tens of thousands of people around the world. ABB has about 15,000 middle managers prowling around markets all over the world. If we in the executive committee could connect with all of them or even half of them and get them moving in roughly the same direction, we would be unstoppable.

But it's enormously difficult. Last year, for example, we made a big push to squeeze our accounts receivable and free up working capital. We called it the Cash Race. There are 2,000 people around the world with some role in accounts receivable, so we had to mobilize them to make the program work. Three or four months after the program started—and we made it very visible when it started—I visited an accounts receivable office where 20 people were working. These people hadn't even *heard* of the program, and it should have been their top priority. When you come face-to-face with this lack of communication, this massive inertia, you can get horrified, depressed, almost desperate. Or you can concede that this is the way things are, this is how the world works, and commit to doing something about it.

So what do you do?

You don't inform, you *overinform*. That means breaking taboos. There is a strong tendency among European managers to be selective about sharing information.

We faced a huge communications challenge right after the merger. In January 1988, just days after the birth of ABB, we had a management meeting in Cannes with the top 300 people in the company. At that meeting, we presented our policy bible, a 21-page book that communicates the essential principles by which we run the company. It's no glossy brochure. It's got tough, direct language on the role of BA managers, the role of country managers, the approach to change we just discussed, our commitment to decentralization and strict accountability. I told this group of 300 that they had to reach 30,000 ABB people around the world within 60 days—and that didn't mean just sending out the document. It meant translating it into the local languages, sitting with people for a full day and hashing it out.

Cannes and its aftermath was a small step. Real communication takes time, and top managers must be willing to make the investment. We are the "overhead company." I personally have 2,000 overhead slides and interact with 5,000 people a year in big and small groups. This afternoon, I'll fly up to Lake Constance in Germany, where we have collected 35 managers from around the world. They've been there for three days, and I'll spend three hours with them to end their session. Half the executive committee has already been up there. These are active, working sessions. We talk about how we work in the matrix, how we develop people, about our programs around the world to cut cycle times and raise quality.

I'll give a talk at Lake Constance, but then we'll focus on problems. The manager running high-voltage switchgear in some country may be unhappy about the BA's research priorities. Someone may think we're paying too much attention to Poland. There are lots of tough questions, and my job is to answer on the spot. We'll have 14 such sessions during the course of the year—one every three weeks. That means 400 top managers from all over the world living in close quarters, really communicating about the business and their problems, and meeting with the CEO in an open, honest dialogue.

Let's discuss the politics of global business. For senior executives, the world becomes smaller every day. For most production workers, though, the world is not much different from the way it was 20 years ago, except now their families and communities may depend for jobs on companies with headquarters thousands of miles away. Why shouldn't these workers worry about the loss of local and national control?

It's inevitable that a global business will have global decision centers and that for many workers these decision centers will not be located in their community or even their country. The question is, does the company making decisions have a national ax to grind? In our case the answer is no. We have global coordination, but we have no national bias. The 100 professionals who happen to sit in Zurich could just as easily sit in Chicago or Frankfurt. We're not here very much anyway. So what does it mean to have a headquarters in Zurich? It's where my mail arrives before the important letters are faxed to wherever I happen to be. It's where Abacus collects our performance data. Beyond that, I'm not sure if it means much at all.

Of course, saying we have no national ax to grind does not mean there are any guarantees. Workers will often ask if I can can guarantee their jobs in Norway or Finland or Portugal. I don't sit like a godfather, allocating jobs. ABB has a global game plan, and the game plan creates opportunities for employment, research, exports. What I guarantee is that every member of the federation has a fair shot at the opportunities.

Let's say you're a production worker at ABB Combustion Engineering in Windsor, Connecticut. Two years ago, you worked for a company that you knew was an "American" company. Today you are part of a "federation" of ABB companies around the world. Should you be happy about that?

You should be happy as hell about it. A production worker in Windsor is probably in the boiler field. He or she doesn't much care what ABB is doing with process automation in Columbus, Ohio, let alone what we're doing with turbines outside Gdańsk, Poland. And that's fair. Here's what I would tell that worker: we acquired Combustion Engineering because we believe ABB is a world leader in power plant technology, and we want to extend our lead. We believe that the United States has a great future in power plants both domestically and on an export basis. Combustion represents 80 years of excellence in this technology. Unfortunately, the company sank quite a bit during the 1980s, like many of its U.S. rivals, because of the steep downturn in the industry. It had become a severely weakened organization.

Today, however, the business is coming back, and we have a game plan for the United States. We plan to beef up the Windsor research center to three or four times its current size. We want to tie Windsor's work in new materials, emissions reduction, and pollution control technology with new technologies from our European labs. That will let us respond more effectively to the environmental concerns here. Then we want to combine Combustion's strengths in boilers with ABB's strengths in turbines and generators and Westinghouse's strengths in transmission and distribution to become a broad and unique supplier to the U.S. utility industry. We also have an ambition for Combustion to be much more active in world markets, not with sales agents but through the ABB multidomestic network.

What counts to this production worker is that we deliver, that we are increasing our market share in the United States, raising exports, doing more R&D. That's what makes an American worker's life more secure, not whether the company has its headquarters in the United States.

Don't companies like ABB represent the beginning of a power shift, a transfer of power away from national government to supranational companies?

Are we above governments? No. We answer to governments. We obey the laws in every country in which we operate, and we don't make the laws. However, we do change relations *between* countries. We function as a lubricant for worldwide economic integration.

Think back 15 years ago, when Asea was a Swedish electrical company with 95% of its engineers in Sweden. We could complain about high taxes, about how the high cost of living made it difficult to recruit Germans or Americans to come to Sweden. But what could Asea do about it? Not much. Today I can tell the Swedish authorities that they must create a more competitive environment for R&D or our research there will decline.

That adjustment process would happen regardless of the creation of ABB. Global companies speed up the adjustment. We don't create the process, but we push it. We make visible the invisible hand of global competition.

Appendix

Power Transformers—The Dynamics of Global Coordination

ABB is the world's leading manufacturer of power transformers, expensive products used in the transmission of electricity over long distances. The business generates annual revenues of $1 billion, nearly four times the revenues of its nearest competitor. More to the point, ABB's business is consistently and increasingly profitable—a real achievement in an industry that has experienced 15 years of moderate growth and intense price competition.

Power transformers are a case study in Percy Barnevik's approach to global management. Sune Karlsson, a vice president of ABB with a long record in the power transformer field, runs the business area (BA) from Mannheim, Germany. Production takes place in 25 factories in 16 countries. Each of these operations is organized as an independent company with its own president, budget, and balance sheet. Karlsson's job is to optimize the group's strategy and performance independent of the national borders—to set the global rules of the game for ABB—while allowing local companies freedom to drive execution.

"We are not a global business," Karlsson says. "We are a collection of local businesses with intense global coordination. This makes us unique. We want our local companies to think small, to worry about their home market and a handful of export markets, and to learn to make money on smaller volumes."

Indeed, ABB has used its global production web to bring a new model of competition to the power transformer industry. Most of ABB's 25 factories are remarkably small by industry standards, with annual sales ranging from as little as $10 million to not more than $150 million, and 70% of their output serves their local markets. ABB transformer factories concentrate on slashing throughput times, maximizing design and production flexibility, and focusing tightly on the needs of domestic customers. In short, the company deploys the classic tools of flexible, time-based management in an industry that has traditionally competed on cost and volume.

As with many of its business areas, ABB built its worldwide presence in power transformers through a series of acquisitions. Thus one of Karlsson's jobs is to spread the new model of competition to the local companies ABB acquires.

"Most of the companies we acquired had volume problems, cost problems, quality problems," he says. "We have to convince local managers that they can run smaller operations more efficiently, meet customer needs more flexibly—and make money. Once you've done this 10 or 15 times, in several countries, you become confident of the merits of the model."

Karlsson's approach to change is in keeping with the ABB philosophy: show local managers what's been achieved elsewhere, let them drive the change process, make available ABB expertise from around the world, and demand quick results. A turnaround for power transformers takes about 18 months.

In Germany, for example, one of the company's transformer plants had generated red ink for years. It is now a growing, profitable operation, albeit smaller and more focused than before. The work force has been slashed from 520 to 180, throughput time has been cut by one-third, work-in-process inventories have decreased by 80%. Annual revenues have fallen $70 million per year to a mere $50 million—but profits are up substantially. Today the German manager who championed this company's changes is in Muncie, Indiana, helping managers of a former Westinghouse plant acquired by ABB to reform their operation.

ABB's global scale also gives it clout with suppliers. The company buys up to $500 million of materials each year—an enormous presence that gives it leverage on price, quality, and delivery schedules. Karlsson has made strategic purchasing a priority. ABB expects zero-defect suppliers, just-in-time deliveries, and price increases lower than 75% of inflation—major advantages that it is in a position to win with intelligent coordination.

Sune Karlsson believes these and other "hard" advantages may be less significant, however, than the "soft" advantages of global coordination. "Our most important strength is that we have 25 factories around the world, each with its own president, design manager, marketing manager, and production manager," he says. "These people are working on the same problems and opportunities day after day, year after year, and learning a tremendous amount. We want to create a process of continuous expertise transfer. If we do, that's a source of advantage none of our rivals can match."

Creating these soft advantages requires internal competition and coordination. Every month, the Mannheim headquarters distributes detailed information on how each of the 25 factories is performing on critical parameters, such as failure rates, throughput times, inventories as a percentage of revenues, and receivables as a percentage of revenues. These reports generate competition for outstanding performance within the ABB network—more intense pressure, Karlsson believes, than external competition in the marketplace.

The key, of course, is that this internal competition be constructive, not destructive. Since the creation of ABB, one of Sune Karlsson's most important jobs has been to build a culture of trust and exchange among ABB's power transformer operations around the world and to create forums that facilitate the process of exchange. At least three such forums exist today:

The BA's management board resembles the executive committee of an independent company. Karlsson chairs the group, and its members include the presidents of the largest power transformer companies—people from the United States, Canada, Sweden, Norway, Germany, and Brazil. The board meets four to six times a year and shapes the BA's global strategy, monitors performance, and resolves big problems.

Karlsson's BA staff in Mannheim is not "staff" in the traditional sense—young professionals rotating through headquarters on their way to a line job. Rather, it is made up of five veteran managers each with worldwide responsibility for activities in critical areas such as purchasing and R&D. They travel constantly, meet with the presidents and top managers of the local companies, and drive the coordination agenda forward.

Functional coordination teams meet once or twice a year to exchange information on the details of implementation in production, quality, marketing, and other areas. The teams include managers with functional responsibilities in all the local companies, so they come from around the world. These formal gatherings are important, Karlsson argues, but the real value comes in creating informal exchange throughout the year. The system works when the quality manager in Sweden feels compelled to telephone or fax the quality manager in Brazil with a problem or an idea.

"Sharing expertise does not happen automatically," Karlsson emphasizes. "It takes trust, it takes familiarity. People need to spend time together, to get to know and understand each other. People must also see a payoff for themselves. I never expect our operations to coordinate unless all sides get real benefits. We have to demonstrate that sharing pays—that contributing one idea gets you 24 in return."

—William Taylor

2

A European Platform for Global Competition: An Interview with VW's Carl Hahn

Bernard Avishai

Volkswagen AG is arguably the most daring company in Europe today. Since becoming chairman of the board of management in 1982, Carl H. Hahn has spearheaded a breathtaking program of expansion, acquiring the Spanish carmaker Seat in 1986 and Czechoslovakia's Skoda in 1990. Today Volkswagen is building or refitting new plants from East Germany to China, from Spain to Mexico.

Hahn has made federation the operative word in Wolfsburg, Germany—Volkswagen's company town. Hahn's challenge is to offer a much wider variety of cars and build them in much reduced cost structures. His vision is a pan-European company whose autonomous divisions—Volkswagen, Audi, Seat, and Skoda—are more flexible than the old, centralized Volkswagen, closer to customers, and operating in comparatively low-wage regions. The price of expansion: nearly $35 billion—on average, $7 billion a year, which is $3 billion more than the company's reported annual cash flow.

The question is, how will Volkswagen pay for this? Volkswagen AG's sales have been rising to an estimated $47 billion in 1991; it boasts the largest European market share of any automaker—around 15%. Yet its 1991 profits are expected to be well under $1 billion. And there is concern over the company's mass-production operations in Germany, especially the Wolfsburg auto plant, the largest in the world. Managing such complexity is hardly conducive to reducing cost structures: the company's plants have to be at 90% capacity just to break even. Wages are $25 to $28 an hour.

Hahn's federal vision mirrors and embodies the transformation that Europe itself is going through. Volkswagen's goal is to grow along with a united Europe and create in its burgeoning, integrated market a base of operations for global competition. The local competition is intense, however, and will get more so as Japanese companies move in. Volkswagen will face particular difficulties if global competitors such as Toyota use their financial advantages to cut prices. European producers have the capacity to make two million more cars than they are selling. The top six European and U.S. automakers each have roughly 10% to 15% of the market; the combined Japanese presence is another 12% and growing.

Before becoming Volkswagen's management board chairman in 1982, the deceptively soft-spoken Hahn had been, most notably, CEO of Volkswagen of America. Later he became Volkswagen AG's head of world sales. He left the company in 1972 to become the chairman of Continental Gummi-Werke AG, a leading tire and rubber manufacturer. He was brought back as chairman when sales in Europe were flat—Volkswagen Group's European market share was barely 12% even by 1984—and U.S. sales were plummeting. In 1970, Volkswagen sold approximately 600,000 vehicles in the United States; in 1990, 150,000.

In this interview, Hahn argues forcefully for his strategic vision and speculates about Volkswagen's prospects for regaining lost ground in the U.S. market through a Mexican strategy. He also discusses the virtues of Japanese manufacturing. A member of the foreign trade advisory committee of the Federal Economics Ministry, Hahn considers the future of German, and European, unification, and discusses the competitive efficacy of Germany's system of codetermination.

The interview was conducted by a former HBR associate editor, Bernard Avishai.

HBR: Volkswagen has undertaken the most ambitious investment program in Europe, committing some DM 50 billion—$35 billion— to expansion and acquisition. Why?

Carl Hahn: Some have called the Europe of 1992 a potential fortress. I see Europe not as a fortress but as a platform for global competition. It is by concentration on the European market that Volkswagen will establish the corporate structures and generate the enormous resources needed for world markets.

Aside from being the most lucrative market in the world right now, Europe is also the world in microcosm: it has higher and lower cost regions, more and less developed countries, true cultural diversity, 330 million people who have suddenly become 500 million. What works in Europe will equip us to reach beyond it.

Our effort to expand is actually part of an even more ambitious effort to reorganize within the new European platform. We seek to turn Volkswagen AG into a "federated" European company: a true multinational emerging from the European theater, gaining the capacities to compete across the board worldwide. Poking fun at Lenin, I have told my people, "All power to the marques." I want us to pursue a vision of divisional autonomy: Volkswagen, Audi, Seat, and Skoda.

Why a federated structure?

In the automobile industry, profits nowadays come mostly by satisfying narrower and narrower groups of customers. We want to be able to customize closer to where European drivers acquire and express their tastes. Norway is not Spain. We want integrated factories and design centers to offer consumers the touches they really want. We want a network of various dealer organizations, in various locations, selling makes of various character, addressing various markets. If the young drivers of Europe, for example, show an increased taste for Mediterranean styling, we can approach them through Seat, our Spanish division.

At the same time, we want every marque in the group to emphasize Volkswagen's traditional strength: solid engineering, drivability. So we intend to maintain our research and development center in Germany. The management board of Volkswagen Group is there to provide the leadership and coordination and to allocate the funds.

Is your vision becoming an organization?

We are currently in transition. Three of the marques—Audi, Seat, and Skoda—are essentially independent corporate entities. The fourth, Volkswagen, has recently been established as a division with its own separate management—not an easy task, since its operations dwarf those of the other marques. Volkswagen's large

R&D organization renders services, advice, and coordination to the engineering groups of the other marques.

Each marque has its own chief executive, who participates in the board of management of Volkswagen AG. We expect the managers of these entities to cooperate and take advantage of available synergies. Consequently, no division can make unilateral decisions.

The individual entities are, by intent, largely national but part of a totally integrated international group. Seat, for example, has remained a Spanish company while enjoying access to our worldwide resources and participating in the various decision-making committees of the Group. Skoda is just getting started along similar lines.

How are the divisions faring?

Seat's performance is especially encouraging. Its factories are fully integrated: they ship components to us and we to them. Some of Seat's cars compete with cars bearing the Volkswagen marque. In April, for example, Seat presented a new car called the Toledo, which was developed in just three years by a team whose members were from Barcelona, Wolfsburg, and Torino, all connected by satellite—coordinated R&D, divisional autonomy, German thoroughness, Mediterranean touch.

And we are starting to feel friendly competition from the new parts of the corporate federation. Spanish designers want to show German designers that they are better. Czechs want to prove that it will take no time for them to lead in automobile engineering, as they did before 1939. By harnessing national rivalry, we can customize cars more successfully.

Why does Volkswagen pursue a pan-European and inherently global strategy when most European carmakers are so "national"?

From the very beginning, Volkswagen thought beyond Germany and even beyond Europe. We planned accordingly, acted accordingly.

In coping with our highly fragmented and segmented European market, private companies such as Fiat have depended on national manufacturing structures supported by protected national sales. Most European companies were nationally oriented.

But Volkswagen has never been an automobile company in the

ordinary sense. We have been a monument and driver of the post-war German recovery. Next to making profits, our mandate was to motorize our country and large parts of Europe, to provide employment for tens of thousands of people. Even today, we provide 20% of the employment in Lower Saxony and 50% of its exports.

This responsibility meant that early on we were forced to concentrate on developing markets abroad. We could not be restricted to a protected home market. The Beetle had to become a world car. Our van business was born, for example, when a Dutchman told us how nice it would be if our indestructible, indefatigable vehicle had a box on the top of it so that he could transport eggs around Holland.

In retrospect, this imperative to globalize has been advantageous to us. We are number one in Europe. We are number one in Italy after the Italian companies, number one in France after the French companies. We were the first European carmaker to penetrate the U.S. market, where we were the number one importer for many years.

Although we did not do well in the United States during the late 1980s—we are down to just 1.5% of the market—when you look at other markets where we go head to head with global competitors—Switzerland, or Norway, or whatever—we have hardly ever lost market share. We have more than held our own in Canada. We are number one by far in Mexico, as well as in Brazil. By investing in several ventures in China, where we have also become the number one car manufacturer, we have established an important starting position in Asia, which will help create more export possibilities for our European operations. We are also doing rather well in Japan: we are the number one importer there, though this still amounts to about 50,000 cars a year.

Does the impending intensification of competition in Europe from other global companies, especially Japanese automakers, explain why your reorganization of Volkswagen is so ambitious?

All Europeans are now vulnerable to some extent. That is why we, and all Europeans, have to be more aggressive about offering and learning to cope with variety. Our more autonomous divisions have to practice niche marketing and manufacturing. Just think of the Karmann Ghia of the 1960s and of our present Golf Convertible, a real cult car.

Can Europeans compete with the Japanese at their own game?

Is it really *their game?* Is it "Japanese" manufacturing or just plain common sense? The Japanese are accustomed to playing the underdog, dwelling on their "poor environment," their lack of natural resources. So they bring a sense of urgency to all economic problems. Perhaps we cannot compete with this. But for years, we have misinterpreted their progress, and we have spoken about MITI or slave wages—all sorts of excuses for falling behind.

Actually, the Japanese have simply reexamined the rules of manufacturing. They have had to overcome a reputation they have had for making junk, so they applied the lessons of certain American experts that most everybody else was ignoring. We have to realize their achievement, grapple with it, and change our attitudes. We have to go and learn, we Germans, we Europeans. I think our trade union people, our workers, are all beginning to be aware of this. We have been so accustomed to teaching engineering to the world that we've lost some of our receptiveness to learning.

Does Volkswagen have competitive disadvantages?

Our most serious problem by far is a cost structure in our German operations that is too high. Those German companies that manufacture by continuous processes—steel and chemicals, for instance—are the most efficient in the world. They bring to bear the German genius for automation and engineering. Labor costs are not decisive there. But companies that manufacture and assemble complex finished products suffer if they are dependent on German labor alone.

Wolfsburg, for example, is the biggest car plant in the world: 5,000 cars and CKD sets a day, as many as 100,000 varieties; more than 60,000 people—about two-thirds on the factory floor and some 7,000 in R&D—in the most expensive region of the world.

The Beetle engendered a corporate "monoculture" around it. We built a factory of enormous scale to turn them out. The plant grew because Europe is so compact. Transportation costs were never of paramount importance, so we always found that it paid to add a bit here rather than to build somewhere else. While the Japanese were revamping the concept of manufacturing to cope with rising labor costs, we tried to avoid unpleasant confrontations with trade unions. We aimed for productivity gains by installing machines that would replace direct labor but would not require us to reduce the labor force.

We have begun to address our problems. We now build plants that make 1,000 to 1,500 cars a day rather than 4,000, plants in which our managers can know all of their employees.

If you go to Barcelona, where we are building a new plant, you will see us coming along in a very organized way, following intelligent, up-to-date procedures. The point is to de-emphasize capital and automation and to reemphasize the flexibility of human beings.

But then, European and U.S. automakers have to manage a substantially older work force. A Japanese transplant in Britain, which is becoming the center for Japanese operations in Europe, will hire 200 people—as a rule, all young and healthy—out of 100,000 applicants. They will not have to worry much about old-age pensions, sick leaves, or reeducation problems for quite some time.

What are you doing to compensate for your disadvantages?

I would stress that we get important *advantages* from the skills cultivated in the German labor force. We do have to apply these skills better, but we would not want to dismantle any German plants. However, it is true that improving the organization of our German operations will not by itself solve our cost problem. Rather, by expanding into the lower wage areas of Europe and the world, we can create a wider and wider division of labor and lower cost subsidiaries.

Our best solution to contain costs is consistent with other imperatives to federate the company. No automaker has more new factories under construction or in planning today in various parts of Europe and beyond: Martorel in Spain, Mosel in East Germany, Bratislava in Czechoslovakia, Changchun in China. They are of optimal size, are tied into our production network, and are located in comparatively low-wage areas.

As for Wolfsburg itself, we do not intend it to grow. But we believe that the demand for Golfs will continue to be so significant in the future that scale of this size can be justified.

We expected the German market for new cars to be 2.8 million this year. Because of the demand for cars now in former East Germany, however, the market for new cars will be closer to 3.5 million. Last year, a lot of that pent-up demand was satisfied with used vehicles brought in from West Germany. Some East Germans have even been importing used Golfs from Chicago.

Isn't so much expansion risky?

Indeed. We are financing our huge investments out of our cash flow at a time when competition is bound to intensify. But each of these investments must be seen in context, one at a time.

The capacity we are establishing in Mosel is replacing capacity that is already falling to pieces. How much risk is there in expanding production in Germany? Our country has just gained a 25% increase in population, and we enjoy a stable 30% of market here.

In our Changchun venture, we hold 40% equity; in Shanghai, we hold 50%. In the emerging European minivan market, we are a 50% partner with Ford. Our Spanish facilities leave us the freedom to increase capacity or not. We invested DM 10 billion in Seat—not all in one day, of course, the plan was for ten years. We are halfway down the road, and Seat is already paying its way.

The risks are highest in Czechoslovakia, since we do not know how quickly and with how much pain the Czechs will make the transition to a free-market economy. But we know that the government is determined, and we trust the government. The car market in Central Europe has been heavily subsidized. We cannot be sure what the market will be like when people have to pay a realistic price for a car.

Do you have other ways of hedging risks?

The venture in Chemnitz, one of the few stable places of employment in former East Germany right now, is supplying us with 1,340 engines a day. We are extending the engine plant to build 2,000 engines a day in the second half of the decade. People say, well, in this venture, and in the assembly plant at Mosel, they are investing DM 4 billion. But *one-third of the investment is subsidies* from various quarters.

We are entitled to very substantial funds from the European Community. The EC has a law that when companies invest in an area where the standard of living is 70% lower than the average standard of living in the community, they may draw from a common development fund. Substantial amounts will go to East Germany, as they do to Portugal or some parts of Spain.

Will liquidity be a problem? During the first three quarters of 1990, you showed nearly a 7% gain in sales but only a 2% gain in earnings.

We have no reason to be satisfied with our earnings. But liquidity is not likely to be a problem. You simply cannot compare the profit and loss statement of a German company with that of a North American corporation. Different accounting laws and traditions play a significant role.

Look at Volkswagen. Here is a company that has shown relatively low profit, has high investment in relation to sales, yet has inconsequential debt. During the last ten years, in spite of our meager earnings, our capital increased from some DM 6 billion to DM 16 billion, even though we raised only about DM 4 billion from sale of stock. Most large German companies have been so adept at building up reserves that their traditional dependency on German banks disappeared during the 1980s.

And Volkswagen has had certain advantages, particularly in the way we have been able to manage depreciation allowances to build up our reserves. Normally, a German business may depreciate an investment 10% a year over ten years. But the German government has supported an accelerated pace of investments near the old East Germany—an advantage we were able to exploit because Wolfsburg is less than ten kilometers from the old border. So we were usually able to depreciate 50% of our investments here during the first year.

In spite of these precautions, won't it finally come down to a battle of financial resources? Toyota is two-thirds the size of GM, but its pockets are probably deeper. Isn't it in a position to cut prices dramatically in Europe and then outlast Volkswagen—much in the same way it captured market share from GM in America?

We have deep pockets too. We have contractual arrangements with a group of European and worldwide banks, who give us a standby facility of $1.5 billion. A group of German banks adds $1 billion—besides what is being provided by insurance companies. These are significant, guaranteed lines of credit. But most important, we know our products are strongly accepted by the European customer.

What have you learned from the slide you had in the U.S. market?

Our U.S. manufacturing venture proved to be quite problematic. Our basic mistake was to entrust the design adaptation of the Golf—you knew it as the Rabbit—to "American" thinking: too much attention to outward appearances, too little to engineering detail.

We were right to set up an assembly plant in Westmoreland, Pennsylvania in 1976. We knew we had to manufacture in dollars. We had every hope of building toward a 5% share in the United States.

But we were not true to our heritage. We gave American customers a car that had all the handling characteristics—one might say, the smell—of a U.S. car. We should have restricted ourselves to our traditional appeal, aiming at customers who were looking not for American style but for a European feel. Instead, we gave them plush, color-coordinated carpeting on the door and took away the utility pocket. We gave the seats that matched the door but were not very comfortable.

Were there other problems?

Our quality was not up to the reputation we had established with the Beetle. This was the result of another misjudgment. We did not try to transfer our production culture to U.S. manufacturing. To run our operations, we hired excellent American executives. But we did not *mesh* U.S. operations with German operations. It wasn't that anyone was incompetent or that the hardware was inconsistent. The problem was that the two groups of management were never really integrated. We made changes in design, so did they; we did not communicate or take responsibility for one another. If the parts didn't fit, it was the other person's problem.

American workers were not at fault; they did their best. We considered our Westmoreland facility one of our most productive assembly plants. Today there is no issue of cultural barriers anymore. Consequently, we have succeeded in making our Chinese and Mexican workers very finicky about quality, which is a part of the precision customers feel when they drive.

Can an automobile company ever be truly global if it claims only 1.5% of the U.S. market, the proving ground for global competition?

We realize that North America is a very important market not only because of its purchasing power but also because of what you can learn there. This is why we have now established a North American regional management to integrate all aspects of our business in Canada, the United States, and Mexico. We have a design center in California, where we can learn the most about American drivers.

But there is also the matter of timing. Some opportunities come only once; the window opens for only a short time. We are moving into Czechoslovakia; we are moving into China. Besides our operation in Shanghai, we will set up a plant in Changchun for only $1 billion. Both will, in time, be excellent platforms for Asia and the rest of the world.

Does Volkswagen have a strategy for making a comeback in the United States?

We are optimistic, largely owing to the strength of our engineering. The first generation of Japanese cars were miniaturized versions of American style—all chrome and bounce. Today the Japanese and Europeans are converging on what began as a tighter European design. Americans want, in handling and styling, a different car from the one Detroit has produced—and, for all the Japanese lessons, still produces.

So we are following a gradualist Mexican strategy, increasing our manufacturing in the dollar area but not in the United States. We have an ideal cost structure in Mexico, better than anything in Asia or Europe. It's a small but excellent platform for the whole North American market.

Mexico has an enormous growth rate: one hundred million Mexicans in the near future, one million vehicles a year. So even if we forgot the North American free-trade area, Mexico is big enough to support an automotive industry. Volkswagen has a 40% market share in passenger cars that gives it a strong dealer organization.

We have also grown to over 4% of the Canadian market. All in all, it's a good base to regain position in the United States.

Some say that European automakers have another way of hedging risks, which is to seek restrictions on foreign competition from the European Community. What is your response?

It is true that some of our neighbors, especially Italy and France, have been advocating transitional periods. We agree that abrupt changes in current trade policy are counterproductive. A transitional period is appropriate; however, a new Europe *is* quickly taking shape. Europeans have an integrated and compact communications infrastructure, advanced engineering, science, design, and managers who understand strategy and marketing. We will not shy away from becoming an open market because European companies will take full advantage of our blessings in global competition.

But isn't the European Community planning to limit the growth of Japanese automakers' market share for at least the next eight years?

This plan should not be interpreted as a policy of restricting competition. Even the U.S. government has negotiated voluntary restraints, especially with the Japanese, in many products.

The Community is discussing a proposal for a six-year transition in which Japanese automakers will be allowed to increase their market share in Europe from 11.5% to 15%, a faster increase than anything we have observed in the United States. Our intention is to buffer the hardship that people suffer when change comes too quickly. In contrast, look at what has happened in the United States: not only short-term damage to the auto industry but also long-term structural damage to industry in the United States as a whole.

As the new European market takes shape, will various European automakers have to combine?

I have my doubts. When you put companies together, they do not necessarily get stronger. They can even become very much weaker. We have had some successes, thank God. Seat is now airborne. But think of the experience of Dunlop and Pirelli, which turned out to be a flop. Renault and Volvo have agreed to join forces, but both companies may find it difficult to find synergies.

Where companies might get together is in joint ventures. For instance, we have an agreement with Ford to build the new European multipurpose vehicle in Portugal. We have learned to work together successfully in Brazil.

Will European automakers at least have to get substantially bigger?

Bigger does not necessarily mean smarter and more flexible. Growth has to be in structures that allow for great flexibility—our federated structure, for example. Except for Mercedes and BMW, most European automakers now make somewhere between one million and two million units a year. Given today's technology, that seems an acceptable size.

Moreover, consolidation of the car industry into fewer, somewhat bigger European companies means even greater opportunity for our Japanese competitors. The Japanese were scared of Europe as long as Europe was segmented. The Europeans have to get organized to deal with increased competition in the united European market.

How does your European strategy, which entails moving into low-wage areas outside Germany, sit with your German work force? Didn't you have to prove to your union, the Industrial Union of Metal-Workers, that buying Seat would not result in fewer German jobs?

I proved to them that it would *create* German jobs—in transmission plants, engine plants, and axle plants, where our automation plays a higher role than labor does. We can hold employment in Germany, increase productivity, and support new operations abroad and get stronger.

A global strategy means fine-tuning an international division of labor, segmenting work, taking advantage of the wage differentials—the different price sensitivities of products, the different contributions products make to our overall profitability, and so on. It does not mean diminishing the contribution of German engineering and skill. Now that the Seat experiment is such a success, our workers' council has seen this to be a very interesting and plausible strategy. It can create not only blue-collar jobs but also white-collar jobs—dozens more senior management positions worldwide every year. We are more attractive than ever to talented people from all over the world.

Can you be as nimble as you have to be in the global economy when your union is represented on your supervisory board?

Emphatically, yes. The velocity of our decision making is second to none. It has been my experience that when labor representatives, who are highly accomplished in their own jobs, come on the supervisory boards, they can come to agreement with boards of management over complex and painful business decisions, as long as they know all of the facts. When you consider that our labor people were willing to buy Seat, go into Czechoslovakia, where they know there are low wages, and approve several substantial investments even during the Middle East crisis—well, management can hardly complain. Labor participation may even speed up strategic decisions, if the employees understand the issues. The important thing is to maintain the spirit of understanding with open communication and continuous information.

What must managers do particularly well to make codetermination work?

We must be on top of our business. Codetermination works when persuasive information becomes the basis for agreement. Workers' representatives on our supervisory board are apprised of the facts of life—Korean and Japanese competition, the state of all our factories. They know we have problems, like everybody else.

We make some of the finest automotive robots—1,000 a year. However, we do not intend to go into the robotics business. We stick to our knitting. My colleagues and I are close to the shop floor, we walk around. We can feel the vibrations from the stamping presses in our offices. We are oriented toward customers, in touch with markets and with the competition—this is our strength. Electronic mail and other forms of instant worldwide communication help, obviously. But most important, we are carmakers, "auto educated."

Is your political environment different from a U.S. manager's? People describe you as more statesman than CEO.

With respect to the government, the public authorities, German managers are absolutely free. There is no Japanese- or French-style intervention. As for corporate governing structures, compared with an Anglo-American board of directors—and I know how they work, since I am a member of one—the supervisory board gives the board of management an enormous degree of freedom.

On the other hand, directors of multinational companies have quite an impact on the economic and political life of a region or country in which they become active. How can one separate us from the politics of a society—its social problems or its environment?

Indirectly or directly, whether we want it or not, our enormous impact on society means responsibility. Recently, one of my colleagues organized an assembly of Czech vendors in Prague. Over 400 people came, 100 from the West, 300 from Czech territories. And the next day, he had 300 in Bratislava from Slovakia. The entire armaments industry was there, looking for Western partners and new products. About 30 years ago, 30 German industrialists went to Brazil. We brought Krupp for steel making, Bosch for electrics, electronics, and injection pumps—everything you can imagine to make cars. This had enormous repercussions. The risk of making mistakes under these circumstances should not make you crazy, but it should at least make you humble.

Consider the responsibilities you've shouldered in the East. Will integration with East Germany work as well as planned?

There are some disturbances now. More than 800,000 people are out of work and are candidates for political manipulation. DM 100 billion is earmarked for transfer to the East, in addition to a new civil service, a Western-style social security system, and a stable currency. But the Communists had always said the unemployment was the scandal of capitalism. Now people are too frightened to think about how long it takes for investments to become working enterprises—even DM 100 billion a year will not change the picture overnight—or about how economic breakdown would have been more disastrous under Communism.

But I come from the East, I knew the people would be waiting for us. West Germany has the capital and the know-how to bring about integration. And when you take responsibility for overhauling an entire economy of 16 million East Germans—what an enormous boost this has given West Germany!

Are there lessons here for Europe as a whole?

If ever the Europeans determine to take care of Eastern and Central Europe, considering the potential of the people and economies, we will all eventually enjoy rewarding results. Europe could do much to manage the problems of Central Europe at a far lower price than what West Germans are spending on East Germany, where we had to introduce the deutsche mark to keep people from emigrating.

I think Czechoslovakia, Poland, and Hungary should be treated with urgency by Western Europe as a whole. We should offer an economic association with these neighbors soon, membership in the Community later.

The people in all of these countries have lived at a miserably low standard of living, which nevertheless was beyond their means. They were not earning enough to pay for the depreciation of their capital stock, their housing, their infrastructure. So before their incomes can rise, they are going to have to go through tough times.

Are you heartened by the people you've been working with in Central Europe?

You cannot but be optimistic when you think of how utterly European these people are in their cultural and industrial heritage, when you think of, say, Czechoslovakia's engineering skills or the Czechs' and Slovaks' political ordeal, which—when you survive it—is a positive thing for democratic process. Czechoslovakia presents a particularly wonderful opportunity. It is so impressive the way the Czechs and the Slovaks survived Communism.

Statistics have indicated that East German living standards were number one in the Communist bloc and Czechoslovakia's were number two. East Germany was actually number one in falsifying statistics. And it was probably fine with the Czechoslovakians— better to have a low profile and live better. They also maintained better factories, roads, cities. And they made better products. Skoda's factory is on a level with what we found in Seat. In contrast,

Zwickau, the old East German automobile factory, will eventually have to be scrapped. That's quite a difference.

What about the Soviet Union?

The disintegration, stagnation, and overall crisis in the Soviet Union is very dangerous for the world and not just Central Europe. The Russian Republic of the USSR may become the leader in making the transition—not necessarily to a pure, free-market economy but to industrial progress. We consider the conditions in the Soviet Union totally unstable and do not see any basis for industrial engagement at this time.

Thus we concentrate on the Central European countries that still have people with entrepreneurial experience and knowledge. They will be transmitters and eventually even a showcase for the countries farther East, who will buy their products and receive help in redesigning economic structures. They speak, directly or indirectly, our language. We're sure they will learn fast.

3

A Japanese Giant Rethinks Globalization: An Interview with Yoshihisa Tabuchi

Michael Schrage

In 1985, Yoshihisa Tabuchi became president and CEO of Nomura Securities Co., Ltd.—now the largest and most profitable financial institution in the world. Nomura has more than five million customers in Japan and manages more than $430 billion in assets. Its 1988 revenues were nearly $8 billion, and its net income exceeded $1.7 billion—more than the combined profits of Bear, Stearns, Merrill Lynch, Morgan Stanley, PaineWebber, and Salomon Brothers. Putting it simply, no nongovernmental organization anywhere in the world can rival the financial scale of Nomura Securities.

A hard-driving salesman and sales manager, Mr. Tabuchi, a 33-year Nomura veteran, is very much a product of the aggressive, high-pressure enterprise he now heads. According to company legend, he made 100 calls a day and wore out a pair of shoes a week selling stocks and bonds to Japanese investors. Company records document that he turned every branch office he managed into Nomura's most profitable office in Japan. Once asked to describe the central lesson he learned as a Nomura salesman and manager, Mr. Tabuchi replied, "To work to your utmost, make money, win fame, beat the competition—I realized just how great those things are."

HBR recently explored the tensions between Japan's wealth and its limited capacity for world financial leadership. (See R. Taggart Murphy, "Power Without Purpose: The Crisis of Japan's Global Financial Dominance," HBR March–April 1989.) Nomura Securities is the principal vehicle through which Japan channels its resources around the world. As Mr. Tabuchi engineers his company's evolution from a Japanese brokerage house to a diversified financial institution with a global presence, he faces many of the questions that confront Japan itself. What is Nomura's appropriate and most effective role in the world? What kind of leadership should it exercise? How should it allocate its great and growing resources?

This interview was conducted by Michael Schrage, visiting scholar at MIT's Media Lab and contributing editor to *Manhattan, inc.* For four years he reported on technology and finance for the *Washington Post.*

[Ed.'s Note: Mr. Tabuchi is currently senior adviser to Nomura Securities.]

HBR: Japan is the world's wealthiest country. Nomura is Japan's most powerful investment house. What role do you want Nomura to play in the world?

Yoshihisa Tabuchi: This is the first time that Japan's role in global economics and finance has been so important. But Nomura's strength is our influence throughout Asia, not just in Japan. We are at the center of the country that leads the fastest growing region in the world. If we can continue to help this region grow, we can contribute to the health of the entire world economy. This is our competitive positioning in the global financial structure.

Let me put it another way. We have tremendous research capabilities, examining every sector of Asian industry, and we have active offices in Hong Kong and Singapore. But I don't think that we, at any time in the foreseeable future, can improve on the research that the people on Wall Street are doing on Latin America. And I don't think Nomura can do better research on Europe than Deutsche Bank. But that doesn't mean we're just concentrating on Asia.

So is Nomura becoming a global company or a Japanese company with international operations?

We are seeing the emergence of regional economies and regional investment houses that have global links. People once thought globalization meant a simple integrated financial market. That sounds good, and perhaps if everybody agreed on deregulation and standardized rules, we would have that simple integrated market. But in the real world—the world where real business is done—globalization is neither simple nor integrated. Our corporate strategy and structure must reflect this reality, not just our ambitions.

Our basic strategy hasn't changed. Globalization is like putting together a jigsaw puzzle. Nomura may be very large and have tremendous resources, but we can't do everything all by ourselves everywhere in the world. So we have been very aggressive about striking alliances with top-tier boutiques in local markets. We invest in and collaborate with firms that are the best in their fields. No one would question the expertise of Wasserstein Perella in mergers and acquisitions. Eastdil Realty has few peers in large commercial real estate deals. Babcock & Brown is the top quality name in commercial leasing. We think these relationships give us the pieces of the puzzle to assemble a truly global financial services company. We will continue pursuing this strategy.

You see, we have no choice but to operate globally. Nomura is fundamentally a client-driven firm. And our best clients operate around the world. As long as we have Japanese clients that need our products and databases in their non-Japanese markets, we have to be there. We know what's best for Japanese business. And, of course, as long as American clients need service in Japan, we can provide that as well.

It sounds as if you're rethinking what it means to be a global company. Perhaps financial services are not as "global" as Nomura and others once thought.

Some businesses are inherently domestic, so why try to make them global? Retail brokerage is a good example. The style and structure we use to sell securities in Japan can't work in America, and we would be foolish to try. Unless you have a significant market share, retail is a very competitive, low-margin business. So we are not that interested in retail in America.

Other lines of business that are inherently domestic, like mergers and acquisitions or real estate, do offer the twin opportunities of growth and margin. We are going to invest in those businesses, but we are going to invest with the finest local partner available. There's no reason to do it ourselves.

We also expect to acquire expertise from our local partners. A firm such as Wasserstein Perella represents a very high level of skill in a very high value-added service. It is absolutely vital that our people be exposed to the institutional frameworks, the legal frameworks, the culture, even the emotions of that business. Of course, Wasserstein Perella also accumulates expertise by working with Japanese customers. So these investments work both ways. They really are partnerships.

How does that fit with what your predecessor, Setsuya Tabuchi, once said: "We'd like to be like Deutsche Bank domestically, Citibank in our penetration of the international market, and Salomon Brothers in our trading capability"?

When our current chairman and former president said that, the world was significantly different. It's not as easy to make those comparisons today.

Does that explain why you were smiling during my question?

Yes.

Japan's industrial export strategy has been to imitate the innovations of Western market leaders at higher quality and lower cost. Is this Nomura's approach?

Look, if Japanese securities houses were capable of only imitating others, American securities houses would be the leaders in the Japanese market. They are not. Likewise, European securities houses are rarely leaders on Wall Street. Each market has its own unique characteristics and needs.

My belief is that the Japanese do not tend to emulate what others do. Of course, over our long history, Japanese companies have imitated the products of others. But there is an old saying by a wise French poet that "Genius is the product of imitation." What's the correct ratio between genius and imitation? You tell me. I'm not sure that's a very useful question in our business.

Do you expect that American companies will begin to emulate Nomura?

Most likely, American corporations will emulate the Japanese. They already are in many respects. But because our relationships will be much more interdependent, one-sided imitation in either direction won't be adequate. We are forging a new level of market relationships that will shape innovation—innovations of interdependence.

What does that mean in practice?

New relationships between local markets will create tremendous growth opportunities—but only if we really understand those local markets. It's important that our operations in London, New York, or Paris become part of the local woodwork. This is called *dochaku-ka,* or becoming deeply rooted. In London, that means everything from helping fund museums to hiring more Oxford and Cambridge graduates than Britain's Foreign Office.

We also plan to bring back to Japan many of the new products and techniques developed in these local markets. Interest-rate swaps are an example. We developed our expertise in the very competitive European market and successfully transplanted that expertise to Tokyo. And new products that we introduce in Japan can be sold around the world. We just formed an export committee with representatives from Europe, America, and Japan to identify opportunities for cross-border product development and distribution. That's how we will become an effective global company. For this form of globalization to be managed effectively, we need a Japanese executive in the center to act as an intermediary between cultures.

That raises an important point. Nomura is a Japanese company that's now managing thousands of non-Japanese professionals. It's no secret that there have been problems in Europe and America. How do you reconcile such different professional cultures and compensation systems?

It's one of the critical management issues we face. We actually have two or three different employment systems. For example, the American employment system at Nomura is by contract. Under that system, we are prepared to pay the best possible price now. The Japanese employment system, in contrast, is very traditional—step-by-step. Our Japanese employees give up part of today's salary to enjoy guarantees of future employment and income. Every few years, everyone gets promoted at the same time. If our American employees would accept the Japanese system, we would be glad to offer it. But as of today, no American has signed up for it.

Does accommodating other cultures mean Nomura must become less Japanese?

The day is over when people should think of Nomura only as a Japanese brokerage house. Certainly, our traditional culture is as a Japanese brokerage house. We've been described as very aggressive salesmen, and I would not dispute that. But as we expand throughout the world, that style, by itself, isn't adequate. We must become multicultural. Each market has its own characteristics and is now part of a global network. We have to create internal structures and styles to match the diverse cultures of markets. And when I say markets, I'm not speaking just in terms of geography. A multicultural Nomura must also have investment banking and merchant banking subcultures within our operations in Japan.

Is that why Nomura has been establishing so many subsidiaries in Japan—Nomura Investment Management Co. in pension funds, JAFCO in venture capital, Nomura Finance in real estate?

The spin-offs are a form of internal diversification for whatever our clients need, wherever they need it. Financial services are and will remain our core. But we also recognize that our primary market in Japan can't grow at the rate that it has in the past; the dynamics of the business have changed. So we are fundamentally changing Nomura's corporate structure, shifting to group management. We have to stop thinking about the growth of Nomura as Nomura and start thinking about our growth as a collection of these spin-offs. Not as a *zaibatsu;* that's not Nomura's style. A zaibatsu wants to control its industries; we want our collection of businesses to flourish independently.

Group management allows us to find leadership roles for our best people. We're taking some of the brightest managers at Nomura and putting them in charge of these new companies. Having so many talented people creates problems. We need to find places for them to grow. I would like to promote every Nomura person capable of being a president to the position of president, but that's just not possible. So we have to create opportunities for them to lead.

What is Nomura's greatest weakness?

If you look over our history, you'll see that we have succeeded in everything we have tried. We haven't had a failure. To me that is a weakness. I think Nomura needs a failure.

Why would you want a failure?

Past success can be as much a trap as a guide. Markets today are very volatile; the world can change in a day. But some people at Nomura believe that the way we succeeded in the past is the way to succeed in the future. It's natural to want to believe that. But unless you tear yourself away from that kind of thinking, you cripple your ability to cope with change and, more important, to create change.

There should be no limits in our organization as far as creativity is concerned. We refer a great deal to *mugin soi,* which means "limitless creativity." But before creativity must come the destruction of the old order. In this sense, I believe in Joseph Schumpeter's famous concept of creative destruction. Innovation comes from creative destruction. So too will Nomura's future. We have to destroy to apply our *mugin soi.* We need more courage to break from the past.

How much money are you prepared to lose in such a failure?

Please don't misunderstand. I'm not arguing for a disaster. If the organization as a whole is alert, we will be able to detect problems before they become too serious. I am talking about tolerating the problems that arise from experimentation and risk taking. The point is that we are creating a new Nomura, where creativity and innovation occur in a global context.

What is your major weakness as a manager?

This is very difficult for me to answer. I don't usually comment on this type of question. I don't intend to escape from my weak points, but I don't talk about them in public.

Nomura's greatest source of profit, and its platform for global expansion, is fixed commissions on trading Japanese stocks. Will deregulation in Japan, which the Ministry of Finance insists is coming, undermine your international expansion plans?

First of all, deregulation is no longer the Holy Grail it once was—in Japan or elsewhere. The winds have shifted a bit because the problems have proven to be more serious than many deregulators anticipated. If we look at the discussions in the U.S. Congress about LBOs and the savings and loans, or what's happened in Canada since commercial banks have entered the securities industry, we see that deregulation has a bright side and a dark side. People should worry more about the dark side.

As for fixed commissions, Nomura may be in an even better position than our competitors to deal with changes in the current structure. As the largest brokerage firm in Japan, we have economies of scale that our competitors can't match. So cutthroat competition in our business brought on by too much deregulation might lead to an oligopoly or even a monopoly. We wouldn't like that. Japan's equity markets couldn't exist under those circumstances.

America's regulatory climate is very different from Japan's. Do you worry about the effect of government restrictions on Nomura's continuing expansion in the United States?

We are very sensitive to both American law and American perception. We are very concerned about the emotional reaction that Americans may have to Japanese acquisitions.

Is that one reason Nomura chose not to make any Wall Street acquisitions in the wake of the October 1987 stock market crash?

Yes, you're right. I have a basic philosophy about this. We must be as open and up-front as possible about our relationships. A specific example was our effort to obtain a primary dealership for U.S. Treasury securities. We went through the front door. We applied to the Federal Reserve through the proper channels. We could have gotten a primary dealership much sooner, as some other Japanese firms did, by going through the side entrance—buying a firm that already had primary dealer status. That's not the way Nomura wants to participate in the U.S. marketplace.

How do you evaluate leveraged buyouts? After all, Japanese banks have become major participants in the U.S. marketplace by financing these multibillion-dollar transactions.

I'm ambivalent. The trend certainly interests me, but it also worries me. On the one hand, LBOs can be a rational and logical way to stimulate lackluster businesses. On the other hand, they can be extremely risky. You're right, Japanese banks are lending for LBOs. Many Japanese banks have also had experience lending to South American countries. At the time, they thought these loans would be very profitable. Nobody knows whether LBOs will recreate the problems of the LDCs. But given the tremendous assets of Japanese banks, the LBO loans are a drop in the bucket. And Japanese banks are very, very careful in their lending.

Do you think governments should therefore move to limit LBOs?

It's my belief that as long as we do business in free markets, doing deals just because they are viable, well structured, and profitable isn't enough. There's more to a business than its cash flow. I think there has to be an ethical dimension—some morality—to the deals that are done. But I don't want government legislating ethics and morality. These ethical standards should be set by the market participants themselves. Some LBO participants will go too far, and there will be problems. But the errors will yield more self-discipline and self-regulation.

In general, do you expect the political complications surrounding global finance to increase?

I think things will become more political around the world. There are two faces to financial services. One is the face of globalization; money knows no borders. At the same time, financial services are still domestic. Each market has its own characteristics and unique elements. America is not Japan, and Japan is not Europe. Sometimes these differences create synergies. Other times, the two faces of globalization are at odds. We have to manage the business and political implications of both faces.

When it comes to finance, politics and technology are like the wheels of a bicycle. Each is indispensable, and when they work together, they can create a momentum that propels economies forward. The globalization of financial markets should have the desirable effect of stimulating the domestic financial sector and improving customer service.

What if the wheels begin to pull apart?

That's not going to happen. Governments do not want to undermine their national markets. They don't want to put their countries at a disadvantage in world markets. But precisely because financial services are so vital to the infrastructure of the national economy, politics will always play a role. I don't think any country would accept too much influence from foreign companies.

What do Americans misunderstand about Japan?

Many things, primarily because there have been so many fundamental changes between our two countries in so short a time. Our real interdependence has just started. The United States has gone from a net creditor country to a net debtor country, and Japan has gone from a net debtor to a net creditor. I don't know whether this is healthy, but Japanese capital finances about 30% of America's deficit. Therefore, it's only natural that we're in the process of structural change between our two nations. This has caused some misunderstandings and some tensions.

Wall Street has changed as well and is still changing. In that respect, it is a microcosm of America. The United States is looking, thinking, wondering what direction it should go in the world. We need more time to promote mutual understanding.

As a country and as a company, we have not fully adjusted to our new wealth and role in the world. And as we make adjustments, they must be explained to and understood by all the relevant parties. Only then will we be able to pursue new, creative business opportunities. But as long as we behave like intelligent businessmen, I think we can resolve the difficult issues posed by this new interdependence in a relatively short time. We really are at a turning point.

4

From National Champion to Global Competitor: An Interview with Thomson's Alain Gomez

Janice McCormick and Nan Stone

As chairman and CEO of Thomson S.A., Alain Gomez runs a company committed to competing in what may be the world's toughest market—electronics. In part, that commitment is a legacy. But in two critical domains—consumer electronics and semiconductors—Thomson's presence reflects recent decisions as unusual as they are daring.

Just when many Western companies were abandoning these businesses or retreating to niches, Thomson signaled its commitment to stand and fight. In 1987, Gomez swapped Thomson's medical equipment business, CGR, plus $800 million for GE's RCA consumer electronics business. The same year, he merged Thomson's semiconductor business with IRI's to form SGS-Thomson, a 50-50 joint venture that competes in every segment of the chip business. In short, Thomson is betting not just on its ability to compete but on its ability to overtake stronger, mostly Asian, rivals who already hold a commanding lead.

As Gomez himself is the first to point out, that contest is far from over. But Thomson is running an impressive race, particularly in light of the distance it has had to come.

In 1981, the socialist government nationalized five of the largest French industrial groups, including Thomson S.A. When Gomez was named by the government in 1982 to head the company, it was an industrial conglomerate on the verge of bankruptcy. He moved quickly to cut general expenses, introduce consistent management systems, and restructure. In a break with tradition, he brought in new managers (most under age 40) to head the subsidiaries and key staff functions. Expansion into foreign markets became a prime objective. So did the ongoing rationalization of operations. Even Thomson's headquarters reflected the company's new look: the staff moved from an elegant nineteenth century building on the Boulevard Haussmann to a modern office tower at the suburban complex, La Défense.

Amidst all this change, constants emerge: respect for systems, order, and numbers; flexibility to use whatever options come to hand; perseverance; regard for hard work and the ability to learn. For Thomson, as for Gomez personally, these are guiding principles in the race for global competitiveness.

Although a government appointee, Gomez is first and foremost a manager. From 1970 until he came to Thomson, he was at Saint-Gobain, the French glass and construction-products giant, where he rose from deputy vice president of finance to chairman and CEO of the glass and packaging divisions. Educated at the École Nationale d'Administration, the prestigious training ground for the elite of the French civil service, Gomez spent only a few years at the Finance Ministry before moving to Saint-Gobain.

The interview was conducted by Janice McCormick and Nan Stone. Janice McCormick is associate professor of organizational behavior and human resource management at the Harvard Business School. An expert on French political economy, she is completing a book on the management of human resources in global companies. Nan Stone is HBR's senior editor.

HBR: Ten years ago, Thomson was not a player in world consumer electronics markets. Now you are among the leaders. How did that happen?

Alain Gomez: The first thing we did was commit to being in the business. That meant making hard choices about what we would not be in, like telephone exchanges, medical equipment, connectors, and light bulbs. It also meant being hardheaded about what we had to work with, which was not very much. Historically, Thomson was a white-goods manufacturer that produced washing machines, refrigerators, and other household appliances. Then, about 25 years ago, it happened to develop some very, very small capacity, not in "consumer electronics"—no one thought of it that way yet—but in a few products like radios, record players, and

TVs. For years and years, RCA was far and away the world leader. We were merely an underdog. If there had been horse races in consumer electronics, there is no way anyone would have bet on us. Now we own RCA consumer electronics.

Before that happened, we swallowed up a goodly percentage of our European competitors: French companies first and then, as the industry went through a shaking-out process, others like Telefunken and Saba in Germany and Ferguson in the United Kingdom. (See Exhibit.)

So the basic strategy in consumer electronics was to buy market share?

Yes, at least initially. Because as you know, one needs a certain scale and market presence to compete. But market share is one thing and managing it is another. External growth puts a heavy burden on your balance sheet and P&L statement. Thomson Consumer Electronics (TCE) has always been racing after profitability and financing. And growth alone says nothing about how you are going to control costs, go on the markets with the right products, and develop the required technology.

We grew our capacity as well as growing by acquisition. We took a very long-term view in measuring our return on investments. And when we had to, we licensed technologies and created joint ventures. But we always had the objective of attaining an in-house capacity in strategic technologies.

How do you decide what technology to keep in-house, what to do yourself?

That question applies more specifically to defense electronics. Let me give you the example of what we did in semiconductors. In the 1970s, we were lousy in semiconductors—we bungled and missed everything. With experience we improved a lot, but we were still too small, we still had insufficient market share to compete even in the European market. So in 1987, we merged our semiconductor group with SGS, a subsidiary of the Italian group IRI, to form SGS-Thomson Microelectronics. Together we represent about 3% of the world semiconductor market. But we did not merge all our semiconductor capacity. We thought we had to keep certain components within Thomson-CSF to protect some other products

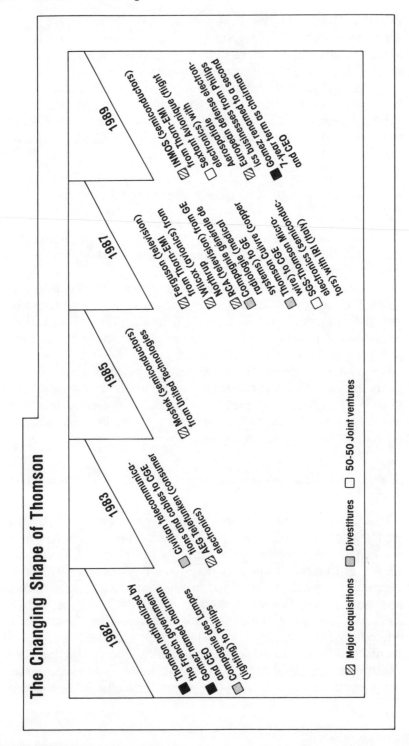

The Changing Shape of Thomson

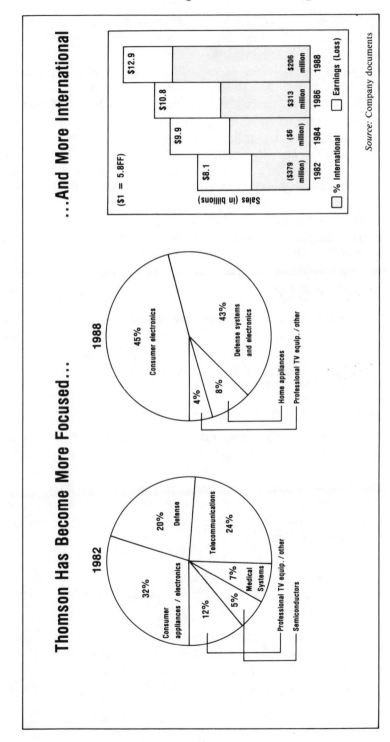

Thomson Has Become More Focused...

1982

- 32% Consumer appliances / electronics
- 20% Defense
- 24% Telecommunications
- 12% Professional TV equip. / other
- 5% Semiconductors
- 7% Medical Systems

1988

- 45% Consumer electronics
- 43% Defense systems and electronics
- 8% Home appliances
- 4% Professional TV equip. / other

...And More International

($1 = 5.8FF)

Sales (in billions)

	1982	1984	1986	1988
	$8.1	$9.9	$10.8	$12.9
Earnings (Loss)	($379 million)	($6 million)	$313 million	$206 million

☐ % International   ☐ Earnings (Loss)

Source: Company documents

and systems. So we had a technology decision to make. We had to decide what those key components were, what we had to do ourselves to stay in business.

That decision is not so very difficult to make if you keep three criteria in mind. One, does this component represent a critical part of our products or system, not so much in terms of cost but in terms of performance? Two, if we do not control this component, are we at risk of depending on competitors? And three, if we control this component, will we have a lot more freedom? It is a rule of the game that you can always buy more from other companies if you can develop and produce yourself what they might be selling. If you are out of the game, they will blackmail you.

The hard part of the decision is the management part, the in-house negotiation. In semiconductors, we have the "buyers" on one side of the table and the "vendors" on the other. The buyers, who are the systems and products division people, say we should go outside for everything because it would be cheaper. Their preoccupation with costs is legitimate, but isn't it also egotistical, blinding them to what is necessary for the company overall to survive long term? As for the vendors, they argue that maintaining our independence has a price. But isn't that point also a disguised plea for internal subsidies? The final decision is a management one.

Can you give us an example of a critical technology?

Gallium arsenide semiconductors. We know that this particular technology is very important in the new detection and countermeasures defense systems. The next generation of airborne and ground radars will be organized around it. We think we have to develop and master that technology in-house and subordinate the question of its impact on the P&L. It is the price of autonomy in our defense electronics businesses.

As technology decisions get more and more complicated, and the consequences get more and more costly, will CEOs need to be technical specialists themselves?

They would if it were possible to be an "all techniques" technical specialist. Remember, as CEO you have to look across the entire organization, not just down into the lab. What is a CEO, after all? A CEO has no specialty. Your job is to help the organization function by itself, to produce on its own. An organization is neither an island nor inert. It is a living system interrelated to a set of wider systems. The CEO's task is to monitor how the company is attuned to the outside world and how it is renewing itself internally.

What are the most important decisions the CEO and top management in a technology-driven company have to make?

Getting the timing right is one of those important decisions. You have to feel the moment, and that takes a lot of analysis and discussion, a lot of intuition. Industrial graveyards are littered with the corpses of European and U.S. companies that chose the wrong technology or overextended their development efforts or mistimed innovations. Telefunken ventured imprudently in a VCR development that was beyond its means. Grundig did the same thing in several domains. A very premature foray into the videodisc business was one of the factors in the demise of RCA consumer electronics.

Timing, intuition, is something the people at TCE are very good at and one of the things I love them for. So far we have always managed to be on the right side in our competitive battles with non-Japanese companies. There are two reasons for that. One is that we have always had good manufacturing and overall cost management. The other is that deeply rooted in TCE's culture is the capacity to detect the relevant technologies and choose the right ones. On Betamax versus VHS, for instance, we chose VHS from the very first day. Not everybody did that.

Suppose you've made a mistake—chosen the wrong technology, for instance, or failed to develop a product in time. What do you do in that situation?

Sometimes you can rejoin the first rank by being a shrewd follower. The trick is being willing to learn from your competitors. TCE has done that twice in an important way, first with RCA in picture tubes, then with the Japanese in VCRs. Both times the reason was the same—we had no other option if we wanted to stay in business. With picture tubes and VCRs, you are talking about major components and major products. And in both cases, at the time, TCE was nowhere technologically.

Take TVs. The picture tube accounts for about 30% of the cost of a TV. Less than 20 years ago, we did not know how to produce picture tubes. Now we are among the leaders. We had to learn how from RCA through a licensing agreement and a joint venture that lasted most of the 1970s. Finally, by the end of that decade, we were autonomous. Now ten years later, we've launched a new movie-screen format tube called the 16:9 that represents an important step on the road to high-definition TV. Other companies are making it too. But Thomson was the first to develop and produce it.

In the case of RCA, you were learning from Americans. Can the same kind of learning take place when you are working with the Japanese?

We played the same game when it came to VCRs. At the beginning of the 1980s, the Japanese were already producing and selling millions of sets, and Thomson Consumer Electronics could not produce one. So again we had catching up to do, and again we started by distributing our competitors' products. In fact, for years and years, all we heard was that we were the people sticking labels on Japanese sets. But we had entered into technical agreements with JVC. Next we developed our own in-house production capacity. Now we have both a 50–50 venture with JVC in Berlin and a plant in Singapore where this year we will produce one million sets based on proprietary technology.

The Japanese have a high regard for their own capacity, and rightly so. They are unbelievable managers. They have great companies. And their technology is superb. But that does not mean that other companies in other countries cannot catch up. Look at what happened in Korea. Whole technologies were brought into that country by the Japanese through licensing agreements out of which the Koreans were clever enough to free themselves.

Even so, not many Western companies have learned enough from their collaborations with the Japanese to strike off and compete on their own. What lessons would you draw from TCE's experience?

To start with, we had a very clear idea about our strategy, our objectives. We knew what we wanted to learn, and we structured and managed the joint venture so that we could achieve it. The most important thing is not to fall victim to the entrapping comfort of the licensee-distributor position. On the contrary, you must know that the receiving end of a technology transfer agreement is the one that requires the most activity and initiative. Also, accept that emerging from full dependence takes a long time. Throughout our collaboration, we were heavily criticized both for working with the Japanese and for being so slow.

Who criticized TCE and why?

We were criticized by some of our competitors and by some of the French. As the only French consumer and defense electronics company, we were supposed to be the national champion. And since the French love leapfrogging—we built Concorde, after all—we were expected to jump over the abyss, to achieve technological preeminence without ever having ensured that our muscles were strong enough and that the ground was prepared.

It is quite a different world from America, where no one criticizes a CEO's policy. We had to shut our ears and keep our course in what was hopefully a coherent, step-by-step way. Like the parrot when it climbs a ladder; it never leaves one rung until it has its other claw strongly fixed on the next.

A story like that suggests that state ownership is more a hindrance than a help. Has that been the case for Thomson?

State ownership provided Thomson with the funds it needed for its comeback. It was what allowed us to move up into the first division of consumer electronics companies by acquiring General Electric's GE/RCA consumer electronics business. Backing that bet required a very brave, very long-term investor. Those are not necessarily the main attributes of private investors and the public capital markets. The state can integrate a purely financial decision into a wider set of considerations. It can say, "I want that company to be in consumer electronics for such and such reasons."

But there is one major problem with being a state-owned company. Their CEOs are named by the state. This does not mean that the choices will necessarily be bad. But it does mean that the process is feudal and bureaucratic. It carries the risk of breaking down the immunological barriers between the state and the companies, between entities that have to be separate. And in the long term, that disease has every chance of being fatal.

Do you see similar political problems infecting European research consortia like Eureka and JESSI?

Forming an R&D consortium is like balancing a pyramid on its tip. Sooner or later it will collapse because the logic is not purely a business logic.

When you start a joint venture with another company, you do not start with R&D. You start with your manufacturing facilities and/or products and/or distribution systems. Then you might put together your balance sheets, your P&Ls, and perhaps your shareholders. The goal is to rationalize, to develop synergies. Only then could you develop R&D.

There is something artificial in long-term R&D ventures between competing companies that have no other links. They are useful for a time, then you have to think of something else.

Consortia are expensive: some say the costs are multiplied by the square of the number of participants. They are slow. And the results are not always better than those of a one-company project. Compare the European fighter plane project, EFA, with the French fighter plane project, Rafale. The development of EFA is slow, it has many cross-national political problems, and the plane does not look any better than the one the French are building alone.

If the product development process takes longer and costs more, and the product is no better than available alternatives, do consortia have any advantages?

One criterion is financial. Consortia may provide an important source of external funding. Because of the cost of R&D and the pace at which markets are changing, the competitive threshold is rising all the time. Also, consortia have helped us begin to reshuffle our industries by teaching us how to cooperate with one another, how to develop a sort of togetherness that is essential for our survival.

But R&D consortia are a very partial and therefore imperfect response to the problem European companies in many industries face: the fragmentation of Europe into national markets. There is no wholly unified, deregulated European market in telecommunications, data processing, defense-related products, even automobiles and food products. Consumer electronics is an exception— and that is why the industry has been consolidated for half a dozen years.

Yet the reasons for consolidating European companies already exist: national markets represent only about 3% to 5% of the world market in many industrial sectors, and that is no longer enough to ensure the financing of R&D and other investments. Thus European companies have a choice: consolidate—through acquisitions or ventures—or die by attrition. Getting together in a technical or commercial agreement is a preliminary phase. So is participation in an R&D consortium. They are way stations on the road to expanding to full European size. For that reason, we need consortia more in Europe than you might in the United States, where there has been a huge, unified domestic market for more than 100 years and the size of companies reflects that.

You say that U.S. companies may not need consortia. Is the same true of industrial policy generally?

Let me talk first about France, where there has also been debate about the effectiveness of industrial policy. In some specific cases, it worked well. The restructuring of the French telecommunications, steel, chemical, and pharmaceutical industries has been accomplished through an "industrial policy" approach. Ariane is clearly a success. Airbus may be more controversial, but it too looks like a success. On the other hand, classic shortcomings were not avoided: huge waste in the relentless subsidizing of antiquated, hopeless sectors and bureaucrats having fun poking their noses into postmodern industrial zoning and construction.

Historically, Great Britain and the United States attained industrial and economic preeminence through 100% free-market mechanisms. But we sometimes forget that they were the only countries that did. Surely, perfect markets work perfectly well when perfect information is perfectly available to everyone. But not everybody and everything is perfect except the Japanese, who are more perfect than others. Adam Smith and David Ricardo, please meet Messieurs Ishihara and Morita!

For me, the question of industrial policy is not so much a matter of theory as a matter of process. When you have an industrial policy, you are basically deciding that some organization or authority is more clever than the market and allowing it to propose its own aims and objectives. That worries me because when you get away from the constraints of the market, anything is possible: the success of the countries that practice "development capitalism" on the one hand; the wastefulness of the gulags on the other.

What makes the difference? Why does industrial policy work so well for some countries and so poorly for others?

A great deal depends on the comprehensiveness and logic of the guidance systems that replace the feedback managers would otherwise get from "the market"—their customers, vendors, employees, shareholders, and so on. A guidance system whose magnetic pole is "strive to dominate world markets" is very simple to make work. And if you are among the first to adopt it, you have a great competitive advantage. For one thing, the standard it sets is quantitative, so it is easy to monitor results and hold organizations accountable. It is also a purely microeconomic system, so you can discount other considerations like the adequacy of housing or transportation. Finally, it is self-correcting because you are always adding volume to volume. Even if you have missed something or made mistakes, you are working in a virtuous circle, so you will still be gaining overall.

The question for us in the West is how to react to the effects of such a policy. Invariably, the discussion comes down to trying to find some qualitative measures, some criteria by which you can define the national interest. Industrial policy can attain near perfection in a small, socially cohesive country like Singapore, be very efficient in Japan, and work well in Germany. But the larger and more diverse your country is, the more complicated it becomes. For that reason, if I were an American I would probably question the wisdom of "industrial policy" too. But even in America, where industrial policy is probably not desirable 90% of the time, there is still the other 10%—for instance, protecting strategically disruptive technologies like biotech or superconductivity that may be the jugular vein of your economic life ten years from now.

Does that make protectionism an essential part of Europe's catch-up strategy against Southeast Asia?

When you have few options, you use the ones you have. In the last decade, Europe has improved its performance overall. Even so, if we extrapolate the trend lines in high-tech industries, we are still washed up. And by we, I mean the West—not just Europe. Japan is so far ahead on the experience curve that it is poised for victory. We cannot possibly catch up unless there is some kind of rupture, some sharp break with the past.

Historically, ruptures always happen. "Catastrophe" is at the end of linear processes. But when? We do not have the luxury of time. So why not anticipate? At this point, Europe is probably not grown-up enough not to have to wait for the United States to send a protectionist signal first.

Nevertheless, the state can do only so much. There is no question that the center of the world is moving toward Southeast Asia. Not only are the costs much lower but the workers are very good, as are the engineers and professionals. It is a function of social coherence and education and valuing hard work and family. The question for the West is how you instill that. I know you do not answer it through the state.

Some 500 of the managers and engineers in TCE's Asian operations are Asians, many of them part of the Chinese diaspora. They are good in everything they do. But the Chinese diaspora is a product of centuries of hard times in which only the very best managed to get away. To develop that kind of drive and coherence you have to undergo the throes and terrors of bad times—which may mean that we in Europe are in for it in the future.

You sound pessimistic about the outcome of the competitive battles between West and East. Do Western companies have any hidden cards, any unexpected assets that might come into play?

Our multiculturalism—and our ability to nurture it, develop it, and thrive on it. Culturally, the United States and Europe are melting pots. That is an asset, not a liability.

Every human grouping has its strengths and weaknesses as well as its own culture. Putting those differences together can give you a sum that is much more than one plus one. As businesspeople, we recognize such possibilities all the time when it comes to research specialties. One of the reasons we acquired RCA consumer electronics was that we knew our labs were complementary, that the Europeans were better in electronics and micromechanics and the Americans were stronger in software.

The principle works in management too. TCE was very French in its management culture—flexible and fast moving, but also a little too intuitive, not systematic or organization-oriented enough. GE/RCA, on the other hand, had all the American management strengths and systems that are indispensable in a big organization—as well as a decision process that was overly full of procedures. The two cultures mixed up rather well. The Americans are learning to accelerate their pace, and the French are learning to be more systematic in their decisions.

That is where I believe we have an advantage against our Japanese friends. In the 1960s, the Japanese learned American management techniques. From that standpoint, there is no difference among any of us, except that they applied those techniques with superior thoroughness, dedication, and seriousness. But there is also that propensity to rigidity that comes when you are so cautious, so dedicated to preparation and analysis. You run the risk of falling prisoner to your own proprietary work. You may lose the openness of mind that comes with the knowledge that, indeed, anything can happen and that you must always keep something in reserve, some flexibility to adapt to a situation that is new.

Are there instances where the Japanese have been taken by surprise, where their own success has worked against them?

In a way, that is what happened with HDTV in Europe. The Japanese launched what they deemed to be their final offensive in the TV business. We responded, but on a rather small scale, partly as a final life reflex, partly as a bluff. We said, "The proposed Japanese standard is not in the interest of the consumers because it is not compatible. We, Europeans, will demonstrate a compatible standard two years from now." Two years later, it was a reality— a complete prototype system was presented at Brighton, England. Three years ago, the battle was supposed to be over and done with: there would be one Japanese standard for Europe and the United States. Now they can forget about Europe, and the United States has become an open question.

Had we been Japanese, it would already be all over because, according to the book, chapter 1 through chapter 25, we did not stand a chance. The battle for HDTV is far from being over, of course. But I suspect that at the end of the day, when you are talking about global companies in global markets, Japan's homogeneity could be its Achilles' heel.

What about Thomson? Is it a global company, or is it a French company doing business throughout the world?

In its defense electronics business, Thomson is not global at all. Until the beginning of this year, it was nearly all French. But the defense market is changing. Its timetables are speeding up, and it is becoming a much more cost-competitive world. So the patterns of competition that drove the consolidation of the consumer electronics and semiconductor industries are now coming into play in defense electronics as well. That is why in January we bought Philips's European defense businesses. And why Thomson-CSF will become more European, more international, if not necessarily more global. You do not choose to become global. The market chooses for you; it forces your hand. And the day has not yet come when defense-related products will be wholly global.

TCE is global. We operate in all three parts of the triad. Our products are completely fungible. And there are no impediments to worldwide distribution. We must have an organization that can install and move the links of the business chain to any part of the world. Ten years ago, that meant moving assembly and production to low-cost areas such as Malaysia and Taiwan. Now it also means moving marketing and R&D to places like Singapore. Years from now, the wisest decision might be to bring production plants back to Europe and move the headquarters wherever the brightest, most hardworking people are.

How will you know that TCE is managing its multiculturalism successfully?

Product development will be one measure. Multiculturalism will be a competitive advantage when we can quickly and routinely adapt global products to national market characteristics without the heavy apparatus of big marketing, engineering, and R&D procedures steamrolling along. Even if products do converge completely—and I am not at all sure that they will, that Americans, for instance, will give up their wooden TV cabinets for European high-tech—we will still have to search for ways to satisfy national characteristics.

Management is the other metric I watch. We must develop a natural system of promotion that will produce leaders in proportion to the nationalities that are part of Thomson. Right now we have two Americans and one German national among our top eight management positions. That is not bad, but it is not good enough. When you drop down in the management ranks, the proportion is even lower.

To address that, we insist on the internationalization of in-house training. We have instituted seminars for senior managers in which half of the seminar takes place in Europe and half takes place in the United States. Next year, those seminars will include our Asian managers, and half the time will be spent in the Far East, with the other half in either Europe or the United States. Each year we also hold several sessions that bring together groups of 150 or so young engineers and executives who have been with the company for three years. They come to France from all over Thomson and all over the world.

What does globalizing Thomson mean for individual managers?

A tough personal life. No one can afford to be lazy in any business anymore, and that is particularly true in electronics. It is the toughest market in the world because the technology changes at such an accelerated rhythm. It also leaves you no choice but to become global fast, and that is hard work.

Look at Pierre Garcin, the CEO of Thomson Consumer Electronics. He spends at least one week in the United States every month, plus a week in Asia every second month, plus, of course, commuting inside Europe. Two of the executive vice presidents in charge of the four world product groups are based in Indianapolis, while the other two are in Paris. They have to meet regularly as well as travel to their sales organizations. Contrast that with what life used to be in a national or traditional "international" company, where nationally based executives had the responsibility for a single country, and the corporate staff worked on the basis of functional reporting.

What about younger managers? What will characterize the future leaders of global companies?

Performance and character. I usually look first for character. Do they have stamina and dedication? Do they have the physical and mental balance to be leaders? Not everybody makes the same choice in weighing work and personal life, and that is legitimate. But for leaders you need the people who are willing to work hard and get results. Then, of course, that judgment always has to be tested against the record, what their bosses say about their performance.

Leadership also demands an open mind and the willingness to engage with different points of view. That is something Americans could relearn. Americans used to be the greatest travelers and adventurers in the world. Then, in the 1970s, they stopped traveling so much and learning about everyone else. They hid behind their language barrier—the fact that English is the "universal" language.

It is time for Americans to reopen themselves to real international exposure, to regain the flair for international affairs. One has to remove the ideological blinders and accept that life has a lot of messy realities, that the world is not perfect—it is unstable and, sometimes, dangerous. Then get on with it.

5

Citicorp Faces the World: An Interview with John Reed

Noel Tichy and Ram Charan

John S. Reed, chairman and CEO of Citicorp, has never been reluctant to make waves. During his 25-year career with the most powerful bank in the United States, Reed has engineered radical change in a major operating group, built a lucrative new business from scratch, and played a high-visibility role in the pivotal issue of Third World debt. Reed made his first real mark at Citicorp in the early 1970s, when he overhauled the company's back office. Later, he was the architect of Citicorp's consumer bank—a global empire of credit cards, retail branches, and home mortgages that will earn more than $1 billion in 1990.

Reed, now 51, became chairman on September 1, 1984. His ambition is clear: to create the world's first truly global financial institution. Clear too are the tensions and challenges under which he operates.

Citicorp may be the only U.S. bank with the potential to become a dominant global force. It is not only the largest bank in the United States, with assets of more than $230 billion, but also the ninth largest in the world, the only U.S. bank among the top ten. Chase Manhattan, the second largest U.S. bank in terms of assets, ranks only thirty-second in the world.

Despite its scale, Citicorp operates under considerable financial constraints. Its precarious balance sheet, with $4 billion of loan-loss reserves mainly on Third World debt, limits its capacity to acquire large, healthy institutions in the United States and Europe. On nearly every commonly accepted financial ratio, Citicorp lags most of its smaller domestic rivals—as well as some larger foreign competitors.

Reed faces human and organizational challenges as well. Many of Citibank's operations are world-class. Its consumer bank is a model of nearly seamless global enterprise—perhaps the best model anywhere. It has 35 million outstanding charge and credit cards around the world and more than 700 branches in Europe. Citicorp's commercial banking and finance activities in the developing countries are well positioned and extremely profitable, as are its worldwide businesses both with other financial institutions, organized under the Financial Institutions Group, and with multinational companies, under the World Corporation Group.

On the other hand, the JENA corporate bank—a sophisticated lending, trading, and deal-making organization in the interlinked markets of Japan, Europe, and North America—has struggled. It has experienced growing pains and strategic setbacks, including an aborted effort to become a major stockbroker in London. Along with other lenders, it has experienced a series of embarrassing reversals on high-profile transactions in LBOs and commercial real estate in the United States.

In this interview, Reed explores how he is reckoning with these tensions. He sketches an alluring set of strategic options that can revolutionize the structure of global banking. He elaborates on the management lessons of Citicorp's consumer bank. He promises a thorough overhaul of the corporate bank and describes his role in the change process.

The interview was conducted by Noel Tichy and Ram Charan. Noel Tichy is a professor at the University of Michigan's School of Business Administration and director of its Global Leadership Program. Ram Charan is a Dallas-based consultant who advises companies in the United States, Europe, and Asia on implementing global strategies.

HBR: Citicorp may be the only U.S. financial institution that can be a global leader in both consumer and corporate banking. How do you evaluate your competitive position?

John Reed: Global competition in banking is strategic as opposed to tactical. Competition among the top 30 players around the world is about occupying space. It's about positioning yourself wisely over time, not wiping out the other guys on specific products. I approach competition a little like the Chinese board game Go. You see where other players have put their chips, figure out why, and decide where to put your chips.

When Walt Wriston became chairman in 1970, we were the third largest bank in the United States after Chase Manhattan and Bank of America. When I took over from Walt in 1984, we were number one. You can't point to any one reason; Walt just occupied space in the global marketplace more effectively than our competitors. Our commitment to the consumer bank was one dramatically different play. The rest of the industry thought we had made a mistake. They weren't competing with us because they thought we were wasting a lot of energy on a business that would be a dead end. It turns out they were wrong.

This is quite different from the manufacturing world. One of the things that strikes me about industrial competition is how real, how visceral it can be. I'm on the board of United Technologies. Pratt & Whitney knows when General Electric sells a jet engine; every sale for GE is a sale that Pratt didn't get. I'm also on the board of Philip Morris. I was very impressed by what Philip Morris did after it bought Miller Beer. It asked: What are the most popular beers? It found them, adopted a very savvy strategy to confront them head-on, and increased its market share from less than 5% to almost 20% in just a few years. One-on-one competition clarifies your alternatives. You can measure what your opponent is doing, then choose to compete on that basis or to try something completely different. The business we're in isn't like that.

As you look around the world, who is occupying space most effectively?

The French banks are doing well. They aren't taking any business from us, and I'm sure their execution isn't perfect, but they are developing an effective strategic posture that will make it difficult for me to occupy space in their marketplace. Deutsche Bank is a formidable competitor. I don't think their acquisition of Morgan Grenfell, the British investment bank, will be financially fruitful, but I certainly noticed it. On the other hand, the Japanese banks are heavily domestic. They haven't concentrated on occupying space in the way we use the phrase.

How do the dynamics of global competition affect how you think about strategy?

It creates lots of options for the future. There's no secret about what we're trying to accomplish. We want to occupy much more space, both domestically and outside the United States. We want to build a more diverse business engine, with broader channels of distribution that embrace on-line information technologies. If we're successful, the institution I leave behind will have a more robust, and therefore more predictable, business.

The real questions are in the strategic how-to category. Two of the alternatives I've been imagining would involve big changes in the institutional structure of banking. One scenario is to evolve toward a structure similar to the energy business. I'm no expert on the oil industry, but it strikes me that competitive success has a lot to do with long-term positioning. Do you own part of the North Sea when it's worth owning, and are you out of it when it's not worth owning? That's why Shell and Exxon and Chevron are willing to do joint development, own fields together, make bids together. They don't see themselves in head-to-head tactical competition.

You can think about similar relationships in banking. We could web the world together. Imagine a scenario in which 10 or 12 international banks—much like the 5 or 6 giant oil companies—share the capital and risk associated with different parts of the business. The most effective way for us to become a big corporate bank in Germany might be to own 10% or 15% of one of the big German banks' corporate business. Since it might be hard for that bank to replicate our presence in Asia, we could swap 5% or 10% of that business in return. Somewhere else, we could go to a whole-sale bank and say, "How would you like 25% of our consumer business in exchange for a piece of your corporate business?" This relationship could become very stabilizing, a better capital structure for the whole banking industry.

I'm not saying we will go this way. I've thought about it, but since I'm not sure many of my industry colleagues would agree with me, we might not be able to pull it off.

What's the second alternative?

My guess is that the legal barriers between industry and banking in the United States will eventually dissolve. Giant industrial companies have immense capital. They could absorb a bank and essentially add no capital. The accounting would be complicated, but that's how it would work. There could be a large efficiency gain in having industry and banking use the same capital. After all, capital for a bank is used only in the event of potential bankruptcy; other than that you never touch it. So there are billions and billions of dollars of benefits.

These kinds of arrangements do raise some real social issues, like the perception of concentrated power. Some people might not like the idea of a big manufacturer owning a big bank; they'd worry that problems on the industrial side would destroy the bank. I've talked to the Fed about the idea; they don't like it very much. You've got to be careful. But Ford already owns $110 billion worth of financial assets, including a bunch of institutions with government insurance. They're in the federal safety net.

What's driving these kinds of strategic alternatives?

There is intense global pressure on the ten big players, in ways that people haven't fully identified yet. Our financial resources are limited right now. We're squeezed on a number of fronts, and so are lots of other people. Some of the squeeze is artificial. I don't believe the bulk of the $4 billion we have reserved for loan losses is needed; it's there to some extent for perfume. But because it's there, we can't touch it, and we don't want to go off and raise new money with it there.

You have to ask two questions: Is the banking industry short of capital? Does the industry need new ways to share and balance risks around the world? If the answers are yes, then you search for some new models.

Given these forces, what are Citicorp's advantages as you work to build a more diverse business engine?

Our most important advantage is our globality. There are few companies in the world that are truly global; we are the only global bank. Globalization has been firmly entrenched here at least since the 1920s. For 70 years, people have come here knowing they work for an international bank. Citibank lost money in the United States during the Depression; it was the dividend from the Shanghai branch that kept us going. We didn't get thrown out of China until 1950, and it was the Korean War, not the coming of the Communists, that made the difference. We've never closed our branch in Managua.

This global quality struck me as soon as I joined the bank in 1965. The colorful characters, the people with the most energy, seemed to be the international bankers. We had a cadre of people—and still do—called International Staff (IS), who were the transmitters of our culture around the world. IS people were permanent expatriates, the bank's foreign legionnaires. They had to be prepared to go any place, at any time, no questions asked—have your bags packed and don't tell us that your family doesn't want to go. In the 1950s, IS people even had to ask the bank's permission to get married, and a number of them were denied that permission. That doesn't happen anymore, of course. Later, when we opened domestic beachheads in places like Atlanta and Miami, we also put in Citicorp legionnaires.

Why is this a big advantage, particularly against rivals who are better financed?

It creates a worldview at the top of the company that shapes how we approach the business. Our global human capital may be as important a resource, if not more important, than our financial capital. Look at the Policy Committee, the top 30 or so officers in the bank. Almost 75% have worked outside the United States; more than 25% have worked in three or more countries. Half speak a language other than English; more than a quarter speak two or more languages other than English. Seven were born outside the United States. Compare that with single-culture competitors who are in a solid position financially.

The Japanese, for instance, are not global in the financial services business. Almost all of their earnings are domestic. They may be fine in commodity banking like foreign exchange, but when it comes to the customer interface, to origination, it's a little bit like computer logic chips—they don't have any. They don't feel comfortable in global-customer or originating interactions. They worry they're being taken advantage of. These are limiting factors, although they could well change over time.

How does Citicorp's global outlook affect how you run the business?

Let's talk about the consumer bank. We started the consumer bank in 1974 on a blank sheet of paper. From the very first day, we aspired to build a global organization. We never said, "Let's start in New York, go to St. Louis, and see what happens." It was "Let's do the whole world."

I still remember getting on a TWA flight in New York with Pam Flaherty, who was on the international side then and who now runs northeast U.S. branch banking, our biggest network. We flew to Belgium and all around Europe. We flew from London to Hong Kong and all around Asia. Then we flew to South America. At each stop, we studied what Citibank was doing, what was relevant to the consumer business, and how it could become part of a new business collective. We wound up identifying 11 countries with significant consumer operations.

We also made an important discovery that drove everything we did later. It became apparent that there were more similarities than differences among customers around the world. People's attitudes about their finances are a function of how they're raised, their education, and their values, not of their nationalities. What works in New York also works in Brussels, Hong Kong, and Tokyo. From day one, therefore, we built the consumer business independent of geography. We didn't distinguish style, business objectives, or anything else around the world—just customer characteristics.

That was 15 years ago. Today Citicorp has the greatest global reach in consumer banking. How do you leverage that presence to keep building on your lead?

To make it work, you need three things: a shared vision and common vocabulary around the world, an organization that can translate global scale into local advantage, and the capacity to transfer local innovations around the world.

The thing that separates us in the consumer business is our shared vision. Most bankers want to make loans, run branches, and sell credit cards, but they don't identify with customers. We do. We don't say, "Consumers need credit cards." We say, "Consumers need ways to buy things easily." That may mean credit cards, checks, or easy access to lots of cash. In Chile, for example, merchants accept checks because if you bounce a check, you go to jail. You don't build up a bunch of credit cards in that environment.

It still amazes me, but the philosophy of the consumer bank— the cultural claim of being a Citibanker—dominates almost everything else. We've institutionalized how we run the business around the world. The level of energy and the approach to problems are uniformly baked in—whether it's branch banking in Hong Kong, home mortgages in Europe, or auto loans in Puerto Rico. Without that shared vision and vocabulary, we couldn't leverage global economies of scale.

What's an example of the power of scale?

Our private bank is a good one. Globality is our most important advantage, even over the Swiss, who have been the world's best private bankers. We have competitors in every country, but we don't have a single, unified, worldwide competitor.

In 1985, we consolidated our private banking operations into a unified global business with offices in 68 cities in 32 countries and nearly $60 billion under management. We even have a private banking operation in Japan, and to the best of my knowledge, there is no such thing as a Japanese private bank. We want to be totally global and totally local. We want every source of market presence and credibility to reinforce the others. In other words, if we can successfully invest the assets of a French customer in France, that increases our credibility with an Argentine customer who is interested in French investments. If a Saudi customer wants to go into Japanese real estate, that customer should believe we know the market as well as anyone and that we have real experts on the ground in Tokyo.

Our uniform presence around the world also lets us do things no one else can do. You want a piece of a paper company in Chile? We can do it. You want to buy into a gold mine in Zambia? We can do it. When people finally recognize that investing in Mexican stocks is worthwhile, we'll be able to do it for them.

We haven't reached our goal yet; we're not even close. This is a fairly new effort, and private banking is a business with long time horizons. In some places, it's very hard to get business from older, wealthy people who have banked with a certain institution for decades. You have to wait for their kids or their kids' kids. But global scale also gives us staying power. We're willing to wait.

What about the third part of your equation, spreading local innovations around the world?

We call this process "success transfer." The term was coined by a Citibanker, Rana Talwar, who came out of our Indian branch system to head up our consumer business in Singapore. He developed a new collection of mutual funds, and they became a great success in Singapore. He had the notion of transferring that success throughout the Asia Pacific region, and it worked.

This has become a way of life in the consumer bank. Eight months after we rolled out our cash machines in New York, we had them in Hong Kong; now we're working on linking all our machines around the world. Success transfer doesn't always work as smoothly as we'd like. We're just now rolling out cash machines in Germany. We wanted to do it years ago, but our people in Germany resisted. They said Germans don't like cash machines and would never use them. Well, we tried them, they're working fine, and we're using our own machines just like everywhere else.

How do you make success transfer happen?

You create the demand for sharing with a strong and consistent drive from the top. In the early days, a few of us were catalysts, flying all over the world and urging people to work together. You create the supply by showing people what has been done elsewhere. Exposing people to success gives them the courage and drive to persist. It's a known fact in the scientific literature that if you tell one lab that another lab has succeeded at an experiment, the first lab is much more likely to succeed as well. The same dynamic works in the consumer bank.

But surely there are formal processes.

It's much less formal than you might imagine. One thing we do is transfer people. Early on, for example, we took people who understood the credit card business in Brazil and moved them to places where we needed them. The branch system in our Saudi Arabia affiliate, which is quite successful, is the work of Danny Li, who came out of our Hong Kong branch operation.

We've always had lots of meetings organized by function or lines of business. We might get all the credit card people in the world together and let them tell war stories—what works in Australia, what's working in Germany. We also carefully track performance around the world. We would take auto loans, for example, and organize a conference to compare revenues, expenses, write-offs, staffing levels, and so on. Puerto Rico was always one of our best markets for auto loans, as were the Philippines and Australia. We would learn from what they were doing and transfer those insights around the world.

But this was never an innovation. It was a natural by-product of the Citibank culture—the global outlook I talked about earlier—and how we built the consumer bank. And it gets stronger every year. I recently ran across some of our people in Germany and France who had just returned from Chile. Apparently, there was a conference in which people from various countries showed off "model branches." That's simply the way we do business in the consumer bank.

Which raises one of the great mysteries of Citicorp. How can you run such a world-class organization on the consumer side and have such problems on the corporate side?

First, let's be clear what business we're talking about. We have a uniquely successful business in the developing and newly industrialized economies, what we've traditionally called international banking—making loans and providing financial services to corporations and financial institutions. If you go to the Philippines, Indonesia, Bahrain, or Turkey, we inevitably have the best, most energized people, and the Citibank name is fantastic. You can say the same things globally about our Financial Institutions Group and the World Corporation Group. These groups are working well the way they are; any changes there are like changing the oil in a car every few thousand miles.

Our big challenge is in what we call JENA business—sophisticated corporate banking and market intermediation in the interlinked economies of Japan, Europe, and North America. That's where the competition has become the most fierce. That's where everything has changed. That's where the world keeps score, and that's where success requires global coordination across markets. Markets in the developing world aren't seamlessly interlinked. If you're in Mexico and you know what's going on in London, you just can't move smoothly between pesos and sterling. Capital within the JENA countries does move smoothly, which makes it a truly global market and a more complicated business.

We take your point. What's the major difference between the consumer bank, which is also a global operation, and the JENA corporate bank?

There's at least one big difference. In terms of what it takes to win, consumer banking is a little like building cars. Success comes when you routinize things to a point where a group of people at the top build the strategy, drive the creative work, and push the new products, while execution takes place relatively effortlessly, through good blocking and tackling. That's what success transfer is all about. It's about implementing new ideas quickly and uniformly around the world.

Corporate banking is more like delivering medicine. Your most expensive person, the doctor, is the guy who deals with the patients. The hospital administrators, the managers, are different from and not necessarily as talented as the doctors. But you can't let the doctors run the hospital. That creates chaos. That's the essence of the management challenge.

In the corporate bank, we don't have common products that we design and sell. We have relationships and transactions that are specialized and unique. Moreover, our professional competence sits down low in the corporate bank, with the people on the front lines who deal with customers and devise the transactions. We can't develop new products at the center and push them out. Good corporate bankers are walking product development departments.

What does that mean in terms of the kind of organization you have to build?

We have to build a *smart* organization, not just a responsive organization. A smart organization has shared wisdom and perspective, a textured competence that shapes the behavior of individual practitioners. We know how to hire smart people and put them in an organization; that doesn't automatically produce a smart organization.

How do you create perspective in an organization with thousands of professionals scattered across three continents?

Part of it has to do with the kinds of practitioners you value and promote. That's a problem for everyone in corporate banking. You can make such an ethic of management and deal making that you kill off the great bankers.

What do you mean?

You can devalue the truly knowledgeable industry experts, the people to whom others look for advice, in favor of people with big, bold management jobs or who are great number crunchers. You really need them all. Today we have to rebuild the bankers. Fred Bradley, who covers aerospace, knows everyone in the industry, and everyone knows him. When McDonnell and Douglas came together, and that was years ago, he was right in the middle of it. When Boeing thinks of doing something, they talk to him; when Airbus thinks of doing something, they talk to him. Now he is not a manager; he probably disappears for days without telling his secretary. He is a banker.

The Morgan impresses me as a place with great customer-contact bankers—not deal makers in the Wall Street sense but people who understand relationships. They'll do deals we won't touch on pricing because they seem to be able to get the returns later or in other ways. They seem to know how to buy into a business and how to be in a position to leverage themselves with customers over time.

How else do you create perspective?

You have to affect values. Are we in business to make money? Are we in business to serve customers? If all you want to do is make money, you do what the Wall Street guys do: convince your customers to do things that generate big fees right away.

That's not our business. It was not our best moment when we financed Campeau. We're not going to lose money; we're well secured. But I would suggest that if your customer goes bankrupt within one year of a deal, then the deal was not good business for you. Some practitioners in the organization wouldn't necessarily agree with that. They would argue that big fees against no losses is a business victory. A smart organization would have said we shouldn't do the deal—even while knowing that if we didn't, someone else would. That's a hard one to pull off, but it's essential as a judgment and it's essential to our success.

We don't have those values fully in place yet. Nor do we have a real vision of what we want the business to be. My sense is that if you put the top ten people in the business in ten different offices and talked to them separately, you'd get ten different views of what we're doing. That's not healthy. That's not how you build a smart organization.

How do you promote those values?

Inject them on a case-by-case basis. I am going to intervene in the corporate business for a short period of time to create a sense of purpose and direction. Lately, I've been spending time on the real estate area because it's under so much pressure. My role is to give people the psychological permission to do what's right, not what's expedient. I will bet you that right now, 90% of the banking institutions in the United States define success in real estate this way: don't let the comptroller of the currency come in and ask you for any reserves, don't increase your write-offs, don't increase your exposure.

That's not a good value judgment. A bank should not manage its real estate business simply to lower its profile. We should assess the business, stick with the customers that we're comfortable with on the projects we feel comfortable with, identify the ones that we don't, and get out of those as effectively as we can. If as a by-product of making such rational business-related decisions we have to take a few more write-offs or book a few more nonperforming loans, that is the price to pay. We should tough it out and accept it—even though the marketplace may punish us and our stock may suffer.

The main point is not whether I am right or wrong. The point is, we are using personal intervention to persuade the organization to respond to a strong message. Somewhere down the road, we'll go out and have a beer. Success will be if we can say, "You know, we played that pretty smart." Failure will be if we say, "How the hell could we have been so dumb to react that way?"

Personal intervention can start the process of changing values. How will you institutionalize the process?

In JENA, we just introduced a new organizational structure and management approach that addresses some of the issues we've been discussing. I think we've come up with a way to deal with Japan, Europe, and North America as a seamless market with no organizational separation that acknowledges geography, a truly global approach to the corporate business. We are going to eliminate the psychological notion that we are a geographically organized bank.

Can you describe the architecture of this new global organization?

It's built around 50 or so distinct units that we are calling activity centers. Three features distinguish an activity center: it has a clear manager, its business thrust is easy to describe, and it draws on dedicated financial and human resources. Activity centers come in four colors. There are trading units such as foreign exchange and government securities. There are customer-contact activity centers, units dedicated to serving the financial requirements of particular sets of customers. There are placing centers whose primary function is to market paper to insurance companies, pension funds, and other institutional investors. Finally, there are product centers, specialized finance operations such as leveraged capital or M&A.

There are two things to keep in mind about this structure. First, the activity centers are well-defined, stand-alone entities. We are describing the language for each of them, and we're keeping it simple—a loose-leaf notebook with 50 pages, one for each activity center. Each page has a description of what the unit is doing, a three-year outlook, and what has to change. We're keeping that notebook alive; it will constitute a living record of performance and development. And we're having monthly reviews for each activity center. We look each manager in the eye and say, "Here's how you have been performing relative to a yardstick of expectations."

Second, the activity centers are *not* independent lines of business. They have to collaborate extensively. The intersection between the customer people, the product people, and the placement people is very fluid. In the consumer bank, success transfer is a central mechanism for global success. In the corporate bank, we'll succeed only if we can collaborate successfully across borders and disciplines.

How do you think the new structure will affect behavior?

It's a revolutionary change, and we think it's going to be a liberating change. We have a highly talented group of people who are great at doing things but who don't necessarily know how to run things. Why have an elaborate management apparatus? We've gotten rid of two to three reporting layers above the activity centers. We don't want checks and checkers.

We've also cleaned up the financial language. In the past, we collected financial results for a whole bunch of profit centers within the corporate bank. From now on, we are going to produce profits at only the consolidated level; there will be no intermediate P&Ls. This should reduce the political pressures, all the struggles over which group should be allocated what costs. We will have lots of other performance indicators for units within the corporate bank.

Let me make another point. Mike Callen, our sector executive for JENA, is going to run this operation. We're looking at this as essentially two layers of management: Mike and the 50 people who run the activity centers. So he has a very complicated job. We've also named 8 coordinators—very senior, very talented people who play critical roles. They act as player-coaches for various activity centers. They have to be visible in the marketplace. They have to be knowledgeable about what's going on in relevant activity centers, about the level of professional training. But the coordinators are *not* an intermediate reporting layer. They work alone, they don't have staff, and we don't want P&Ls from any of them.

Go back to the hospital metaphor. Mike Callen runs the hospital. The coordinators are like senior doctors on the most serious cases. They bring in the surgeons, the anesthesiologist, the nurses, and the special equipment to make sure the procedure happens right. Their psychic reward is that they're publicly visible, and they have the clout to pull together Citicorp's global resources to make things happen.

What's the key to making this new structure work?

We're building a 50-person team that feels a common ownership of the business. I don't think it's impossible to get 50 people to believe the same thing. It turns out this is a fairly homogeneous group; most of these people have worked with each other before. We may have events, perhaps three times a year, that bring them together as a way to build trust and teamwork. And we're creating a vision for the business that all 50 understand and buy into—a vision statement that emphasizes the collective success of JENA, which is to serve a defined set of customers. Each month, people will see performance numbers reporting on business across the activity centers.

Does the reorganization mean you have to change how you evaluate group performance?

Yes. We've always been great at managing individual perform-ance reviews. We look at you and say, "You did a good job this year, but we think you're going to do better next year," or, "You're terrible, you've got a year to shape up." We've got that down pat—to the point where people salivate over it, they become hyper. But we haven't been good enough at the more subtle art of evaluating our collective professional competence and organizational effec-tiveness. How does the team do?

We're putting in a cross-evaluation system much like the ones universities have. Their peer reviews look at the nature of the research going on in a department, the quality of the students, and the size of the department vis-à-vis its intellectual space. It's pos-sible for a university to have too many great Shakespearean schol-ars, given everything else it has to cover. That is true for us too.

Once a year, then, or maybe every 18 months, we'll have a "visiting committee" that reports on the quality of the people we put up against approximately 40 marketplaces in Japan, Europe, and North America. This peer review assesses the competence and dynamic functioning of a department, not individual players within departments.

We're working on the mechanics; we have some differences on details. But it does help to be CEO when you want to make big changes. We're doing the reviews. We won't like how they're done every time, so we'll change them and get it right.

This new global organization might also require changes in indi-vidual rewards and compensation.

Many of our high-bonus professionals are coming off a model that paid out lots of money, and it's been corrupting. This process is going to change. The new system needs a lot of flex. I believe strongly in arbitrary compensation. If you trust someone to make a business judgment, you ought to trust that person to evaluate individual performance without some cookbook recipe. People pre-fer cookbooks to help them defend their decisions. But what you really want is to decide how big a pot to create based on overall performance, rank your people, pay them accordingly, and be pre-pared to defend the result in the same way that you defend a business decision.

I want our people to feel they're within a band of fairness on financial compensation and then to think about other things: their job, the quality of their colleagues, the customers they deal with, their sense of organizational pride. Those are the values I'd like the compensation system to reflect.

Let's talk about the transformation process itself. It sounds like you're playing a hands-on role.

We are implementing; we are writing code. It takes a lot to get me into this mode, but once you do, I stick with it.

What persuaded you to get so involved?

In addition to the obvious responsibilities that come with the job, the thing that motivates me more than anything else is personal and professional pride, running a business that just feels right. It's almost like neatness, like lining your socks up in your drawer. No one but you knows your socks are lined up, but it matters. I want to retire saying that I've put together a business of which I'm personally proud. We're pretty well along in many parts of the business, like consumer and international. We can't say that yet on the corporate side. Our revenue momentum isn't anything like what it should be. We are not as good as we can be. JENA should be able to earn $800 million a year for us again, it should be a big business and occupy a lot of key space.

What were the warning signs in the organization?

We started detecting attitudes, a tonality, that I didn't like. We were becoming deal junkies. I got a memo on the Campeau deal that told me we had big fees before it described the transaction. All of Wall Street had the same attitude, of course, and it was hard for me to tell if I was just getting too old for this, that the world was changing in ways I didn't like, or if something was out of kilter.

We've made it clear that we don't want to hear a lot about fees in our memos or our priorities. Doctors charge for their services, but I hope to hell their medical reports don't say, "Patient Smith spent two days in the hospital, and he owes us $5,000." We've also reclarified that every credit will have one set of initials—we call them the senior reporting initials—with clear responsibility for the loans. We have some credits now with so many initials that it is impossible to figure out who the hell did what. That never would have happened ten years ago. It shouldn't happen again.

Any change agent needs a team to carry the changes forward. How are you building your team?

I'm not sure we have a team in the sense you mean. I had only two jobs of any consequence in the bank before becoming chairman, one was running the operating group and the other was running the consumer bank. In both cases, the vision drove the people equation and created the team. I got into situations where I was either forced or asked to become an architect. We went through a learning process, came up with a notion of where we wanted to go, and signed up a set of people to make it happen. As the vision matured, the people changed. What stayed constant was the absolute commitment to building the business.

So given a vision, the team tends to be whatever people can move us down the road at that point in time. At GE, Jack Welch seems to have decided how he wants the company to be run, and he and his team are in the process of inculcating that style in large numbers of people. I have a different approach. I have a clear vision of what we want the place to be—and that's the constant. The team tends to be people we find who can help us move down the road. On the corporate side, I have a vision of what the business is and how it should be managed. We've got people signed up, and we're going to make it happen.

Critics argue that you waited too long to initiate the JENA reconfiguration. Why did it take so much time?

It had to be last. First, there was the need to jump on the foreign debt issue. When I became chairman, our total equity was $5.7 billion, and since then we've taken LDC reserves alone of $4 billion. So this was a top priority. In order to work the cross-border issue, I had to network the chairmen of all the banks, all the ministers of finance, the presidents of all the countries. Getting to know these people personally, so I could deal with them effectively, was very time-consuming. Even today, I will drop this other work to go down to Brazil. They owe us $3.4 billion plus $500 million in back interest. Brazil is the eighth largest economy in the world, a key leader in the group of newly industrialized nations. They should not be a bad debt or a drag on our capital.

There was also a cultural factor. The dominant culture of most banks, and almost all bankers, is corporate banking. I did not come out of that business. So there was a certain humility, a politeness quotient, that may have held me back, especially given the lack of perceived need. When I took over in 1984, the units that we now call JENA had operating earnings of $380 million. Last year, they had operating earnings of $719 million, which seemed like great progress. As I started sensing problems, I started getting involved, but I was slow off the mark.

In some ways, it's easier to go to another organization if you want to make change. You have none of the human ties, none of the politeness factor, and you have more permission to do things. The circumstances that cause you to go into a new place usually give you license to act.

How do you respond to the proposition that Citicorp's financial condition may hamper your organizational agenda?

We're being criticized mainly on our real estate assets and on the capital front. Both criticisms are valid, and I take them to heart. One thing I hate is for people to dismiss criticism. That's a passport to suicide. At the same time, we cannot overreact. We shouldn't play to the bleachers.

I've gone deeply into the credit portfolio and the credit process, and it's fair to say I've been hurt by it. I haven't told the world that, because who cares? But I'm a little embarrassed professionally—maybe more than a little embarrassed—that I didn't jump on it sooner. We were warned about real estate two years ago, we were warned again a year ago, and we pooh-poohed it. Now I'm damn embarrassed because the critics were right and we were wrong. Sure, the market's changed; we didn't know two years ago what we know today. Values have gone down. But the fact is, they're more right and we're more wrong.

The capital thing is also valid. Visibly, statistically, we look a little naked. Now the statistics may not be worth that much—except everybody looks at them, so you have to pay attention. We've made a calculated decision that this is not the time to raise new equity, which frankly is right for the stockholders. We don't lack the capacity to absorb any of the risks we're dealing with. We can, if necessary, liquidate assets and take other steps that would generate the necessary resources to cover any risks we have, even Brazil. The regulators would agree with me on that. However, until we rebuild our capital some more, we're going to take some heat in the stock market. Our credit ratings have been banged around a little bit, but we have to do what we think is right. We are on a trajectory to rebuild the capital, but it is an inch a day, and we have lost some flexibility.

When will it be fair to judge your progress at implementing the changes you are trying to make at Citicorp?

In terms of the institution as a whole, building the kind of global financial organization I would like to lead, we're dealing with a time horizon of six or seven years. Short-term progress will show much sooner. We have lots of work to do; we're building a global business.

PART
IV
Perspectives on Change

1

Consensus, Continuity, and Common Sense: An Interview with Compaq's Rod Canion

Alan M. Webber

In February 1982, Rod Canion, Bill Murto, and Jim Harris, three Texas Instruments alumni, founded Compaq Computer Corporation, launching what has become the fastest growing company in U.S. business history. In 1983, its first full year of operation, Compaq recorded revenues of more than $111 million—a record for the most successful first year of sales. In 1984, Compaq achieved sales of $329 million—a record for the most successful second year of sales. In 1985, Compaq's sales of more than $503 million made it the first company in U.S. business history to reach the *Fortune* 500 in less than four years. In 1987, Compaq passed the $1 billion mark in annual sales, hitting this mark faster than any other company. In 1988, sales passed the $2 billion level. And in 1989, Compaq's worldwide sales approached the $3 billion barrier.

Behind this remarkable financial performance is Compaq's unique management process. The company's corporate culture is based on teamwork and consensus management and a continuous effort to maintain the benefits of a small company, even as Compaq experiences phenomenal growth. But what is most intriguing about Compaq is a series of counterintuitive notions that combine to create the company's management process. For example, the CEO of the country's fastest growing company insists that he is not an entrepreneur. While the company's product-introduction strategy depends on speed to market, Compaq believes absolutely in a slow, methodical, decision-making process. In an industry that is driven by innovation, Compaq defines innovation as staying within the boundaries of accepted industry standards. Because the company's labor costs are so low, says the CEO, the company must hire its people very carefully. In a company that has achieved such remarkable financial results, cost ranks relatively low on the list of manufacturing priorities.

In this interview, conducted by HBR editorial director Alan M. Webber, Rod Canion, Compaq's founder, and former CEO and president, explores these surprising notions and the management approach that guides his company's rapid growth.

HBR: Compaq has spent a lot of time defining and developing its culture. How would you describe your corporate culture?

Rod Canion: Compaq stresses discipline, balance, continuity, and consensus. That's the way to survive in an industry that changes as fast as ours does. There are lots of values behind these characteristics, but perhaps the most important is teamwork. That means treating other people with respect and expecting to be treated with respect.

No management system can force people to do things they don't want to do. So when we started Compaq, our basic philosophy was to create an environment where people can stay enthused about the company and not be frustrated by red tape and unnecessary burdens. When you come to work day after day after day for a year, superficial things wear through quickly. You find out that either you enjoy work and get lifted by it or you get dragged down by it.

It's not how hard you work. People work as hard at Compaq as at any other company, maybe harder. But work here isn't drudgery. It doesn't use up their energy on negative things. It doesn't mean fighting off people who attack you in the company or filling out forms or doing unproductive work. People don't enjoy that, and they'll leave eventually. But if you spend 80% or 90% or, if you're really lucky, 98% or 99% of your time on productive things, you leave work feeling that you've accomplished something.

Why is the corporate culture so important to you?

Our culture is designed to keep the characteristics of a small company alive while the company grows. In 1983, we were growing by leaps and bounds. We saw bureaucracy creeping in and development cycles stretching out. At that point, I realized that the company was getting too big for me to be everywhere or for the management team to mandate and enforce short development cycles through strict planning and reporting. Trying to force short development cycles on people would have failed miserably.

I concluded that what we really needed to do was tell people what was good about what they had been doing. I wanted to make them aware of the fact that they'd worked together as a team, that they'd done things in parallel. I wanted to get them to look at what we'd been doing that had worked and consciously try to keep the small-company advantage. We started doing that in 1984, and we've kept doing it. That's what our quarterly company meetings are all about. We get everybody together at a companywide meeting to talk about Compaq. Typically, we hold four meetings over two days at a nearby church that holds about 2,000 people. We go over the past quarter's performance, show a couple of videos, address issues as varied as speeding on campus or smoking in the offices, and then answer questions. Everybody takes it as a personal job to keep the culture—to keep the good qualities of a small company as we get big.

What's the secret to continuity?

You can't have continuity unless you retain people. We're able to learn as a team and then build on stable layers of new people, year after year. Low turnover is fundamental and distinguishes Compaq from lots of our competitors, particularly those in Silicon Valley. Most companies would point to compensation plans, stock options, and bonuses as the way to keep people. But really, they're just there to prevent people from being stolen. It's not pay or stock or anything else that keeps people. It's whether they're drained or charged emotionally. People stay when they enjoy what they do. People stay when they fit the culture, when they are working in a supportive, helpful environment, and when they get fulfillment from working as part of a winning team. It's dissatisfaction, more than money, that leads people to leave.

I learned that lesson early in my career. Halfway through my tenure at Texas Instruments, I left to go to a small company here in Houston. I did it basically for money. I wasn't looking for a job. They came to me and showed me all this money, and I thought, "That's great." Six months later, I realized that there's a lot more to life than money. Money is important, but even more important is enjoying what you do and being really excited about it. So I went back to TI. Compaq wouldn't be here today if TI had continued to be a challenging place to work. I enjoyed most of my career there, and it was only in the last year that I really got frustrated. That was the critical factor in my deciding to leave.

But can't you live with a little bureaucracy as long as the company keeps growing? Growth has a way of curing all ills.

I would say that growth *hides* all ills—until the growth stops or slows down. At Compaq, we know that growth is a two-edged sword. It does a lot of good things for a company, and it's an environment that you want to maintain. But depending on growth as the antibiotic for whatever ails you will eventually get you into serious trouble. In fact, growth can be a disease, rather than a cure. We're trying to manage growth, and whether or not it's fatal, by managing the culture.

That doesn't sound like the ideas of a typical entrepreneur.

I never viewed myself as an entrepreneur, either when I quit TI or when I started Compaq. I always thought of an entrepreneur as someone who can't work for anybody else and has a burning desire to make his or her own idea known. That just didn't fit me or any of our team. And our not being classic entrepreneurs has been a real benefit for Compaq. The typical entrepreneur has the problem of dealing with all the things success brings, things he or she didn't really want in the first place. But because we were really more typical businessmen starting our own company from scratch, when we did grow successful, we had the skills and orientation necessary to manage that growth.

We've talked about continuity; what about discipline and balance?

Our entire orientation toward customers and technology—and the process that brings the two together—depends on discipline and balance. Our management process is designed to meet customers' needs, use the latest technology, and—most important—get to market quickly. The last part of that—getting to market quickly—allowed us to come from behind in the early days, to pass the competitors, and to continue to be out in front of our bigger competitors who don't have short development cycles. To accomplish that in a way that doesn't burn out our people requires discipline and balance.

Where does the sense of discipline come from?

I think it comes from our roots in engineering. Both Jim Harris, the vice president of engineering, and I were engineers, and Bill Murto, our former vice president of sales, had worked closely with us. That background created a sense of tough-minded pursuit of facts, of pushing until you get to what you think is really the right answer. That attitude was there initially. It was the way people operated with each other—and it grew. It wasn't viewed as threatening because it went hand in hand with the consensus process. But consensus doesn't work unless you have the discipline to keep digging for the facts that you need to make a good decision. Consensus isn't getting everybody to agree to vote for the same thing. Consensus is getting people to believe that you've got the right facts and the right reasons to make the right decision.

How important is the consensus process to Compaq's mode of operation?

It is fundamental. Our management process is based on the concept of consensus management. The real benefit of the process is not that you get the answer but all the things you go through to get the answer. You get a lot of facts, you get a lot of people thinking, and the result is that everybody owns the decision when you get through.

Originally, we used consensus management at the top to address the really tough, critical, long-term decisions. But as people participated in the process, they could see how to use it at all levels. Today it permeates the company all the way down to the manufacturing floor. When something isn't working right, the teams get together and try to figure it out.

Isn't that quite a lot to invest in a decision-making process?

It's what makes Compaq so successful. I remember when I was moving into the ranks of management at TI. I was worried about making the wrong decision. So I talked to one of my mentors, and he said, "As long as you're right 51% of the time, you're OK." I accepted that answer at the time.

Today I'd say that you need to be right 100% of the time. You may not achieve it, but that should be your goal—to be right all of the time. You need to keep striving for that goal, which means paying attention to every detail and putting everything in its proper order. Being right all of the time also means that you don't just do the best you can as an individual. You use all the resources that are available to you. You use the whole team. And the team keeps pushing and digging until everyone can agree on the decision.

If you do the best possible job, then the best the competition can do is tie you. Our basic philosophy is to push harder and more thoroughly, to push until we get more facts and the best answer. It also means recognizing that there are times when the right decision is no decision. I used to hear the saying, "Any decision is better than no decision." But that didn't seem right to me because when you make a decision, it ripples, it propagates. If that decision has to be changed, then other things have to be changed too.

What role does the boss play in this process?

That's one of the key differences in the consensus process. The normal way a company works is that a team comes to the boss at the end of the process and presents its results. So if the boss has something to contribute, he says, "No, we really want to do it this way." Since he's the boss, he usually gets his way. But a lot of bad things happen right there. The people feel that he's changing the decision just because he wants to or because he can. Also, the boss doesn't have all the information they do, so his critique may not even be correct.

At Compaq, the consensus process does not assume that because I'm the boss, I have the final answer. It's built around a team, and any time there's a team of people, you expect everybody to contribute in one way or another. If I'm going to contribute an idea, experience, or knowledge, the best time for me to do it is early in the process rather than at the very end. That way people don't think of it as getting my stamp of approval; they think of it as getting my contribution.

What's an example of the decision-making process making a difference at Compaq?

Take our approach to the laptop market. The first time we looked at that market was back in 1984. Following our usual methodical approach, we did some market research to find out what was out on the market and what the technology allowed people to do. We were researching companies that took the latest, smallest technology and did the best they could with it. Then we tried to figure out the number of potential customers there were for that type of product so we could make a go or no-go decision. In parallel, we were doing a number of other things, including preliminary design work and even prototyping for our own laptop.

Now in the laptop case, the go or no-go decision came down to one meeting. And what made it particularly interesting was that I was the driver behind the project. I liked having a laptop with me, and I wanted us to produce one that was better than anything else on the market. At this meeting, a fairly young researcher presented her facts and recommendations.

Her conclusion was that there was a market for a Compaq laptop, but it wasn't very big. We looked at how she had come up with her numbers, and we came up with a set of facts we could all agree on. In the end, we concluded that while we could sell some laptops, those sales didn't justify the effort we were going to put into it. There were better opportunities, like the desktop line. So in spite of a strong desire on my part to go into the laptop market, the process worked and we decided not to do it.

Yet here you are in the laptop market now.

Sure, because that meeting was not the end of the story. We decided to focus on other opportunities—on getting into the desktop market, which turned out to be the right decision. But we continued to look at laptops, which is also part of the process. We did several more prototypes and more market research, and the next time the issue came to a head was in early 1986. At that time, the laptop market was beginning to grow with Toshiba. We considered getting into it then.

But once again, the laptop was up against another opportunity, the 386 desktop product, which provided a tremendous differentiation opportunity, a chance to establish real leadership. So again, we decided to focus our resources on that product. And again, I'd say that our process produced the right decision.

What led to the decision to launch the laptop?

The way we finally developed our laptop reflects another important thing that distinguishes Compaq—our attitude not to accept the general preconceptions of the industry. Every time we spot an industry preconception, we see it as an opportunity and test it. Most of them may be right, but often enough they're wrong. We feel that if we follow our processes—and we're confident they're right—we can go against the industry's conventional wisdom.

In the case of the laptop, all of the products that came out in the last part of 1989 demonstrated a set mentality. Every one of our competitors came out with a small, notebook-size computer with a floppy disk and no hard disk. The reason was obvious: you couldn't get a hard disk into a computer that size. The conventional wisdom was that if it can't be done, nobody will do it. And if nobody else does it, you're safe if you don't do it.

We came at it another way. We said, we're not going to offer a computer that doesn't have a hard disk in it. So much of the market today demands it, we've got to deliver it. Let's figure out what it takes. Sure enough, we found out we could do it. So when we finally made the decision to go with our own laptop, we were able to use technology to meet our customers' needs and be the first to market. And again, we were fortunate to make the right decision.

The laptop was one success that went against conventional wisdom. How important is that approach to Compaq's success?

A lot of the things that helped Compaq move out in front went against generally accepted opinion. I think that gets back to discipline, thoroughness, and our decision-making system. A part of the consensus process is not just coming up with the best decision that the group can make today. It's being willing to recognize when you really don't have enough information to make the right decision. So you say, "Time out, let's go get more information." And you keep doing that until you have enough information to make what the group believes is the right decision.

Another part is keeping an open mind so that people feel that it's OK to ask questions and test assumptions. In many company cultures, if you question people, they think that you're trying to shoot them down. The result is that people won't speak up. They may speak up if it's important but not if it's just a little deal. But then a lot of those little deals add up, and they can end up getting you off the right track.

Is there something in particular that distinguishes the way you approach a problem?

We work hard to ask questions. If I had to characterize our way of thinking, it is "Why not do that?" It's practically an inside joke. If somebody says that we can't or shouldn't do something, the automatic response is, "Why can't we do that." If there's a good reason, then that's the end of it. But if the "reason" is just a blanket statement or a remark in the trade press that "this is what everyone is thinking," we know that's not a good reason.

We can see today that what separated Compaq from the pack were decisions that other companies didn't make. We're testing ideas, getting people to think in a different way, and asking questions. We're looking for the assumptions that aren't justified. As I listen to people, I listen for what fits together, for where the holes are, or for the one assumption they've made that may not be right on. It comes to the point where the more traditional a thing is, the more you question it. If it's traditional, maybe you're just accepting it without really testing it.

How did that attitude get started?

We've always been caught up in the idea of testing boundaries. You never know unless you try. At the beginning of 1983, we were just starting to ship our first product, and we needed to find a new vice president of sales. We sat down and asked ourselves, if we could have anybody in the world to do this job, who would we get? It seemed obvious that he or she should be somebody who had been through it, who knew all the dealers, and who had a lot of experience.

Only one person fit that description: the IBM PC sales manager. Of course, conventional wisdom says you can't hire away a guy with 20 years experience at IBM. It's a safe company, a good job, a key role. You can't get him to leave that and come to a startup.

But as luck would have it, when I ran into him at a PC conference, I approached him, and he didn't turn me down. A month later, we had gone through the process, negotiated with him, gotten him comfortable with a small company, and hired him.

How has this attitude affected the way you do business?

It's one of the things that has distinguished Compaq. For example, to some people, a slow, methodical process conflicts with speeding a product to the market. That may seem to be true because of history or other people's expectations. In fact, we've heard a lot of criticism from other companies that like to run and shoot. They announce a product early, but then something goes wrong, and they end up with six-month delays. There is a very strong, fundamental belief at Compaq that following a methodical approach as quickly as you can almost always leads to the best and fastest solution. When you seem to be moving slowly, if you're taking careful steps that turn out to be right, you get where you want to go faster than by speeding along and making mistakes that slow you down or permanently derail you.

Is it true in technology as well?

That's exactly what happened with our decision to go with the 386 processor. What was working in our favor was our mind-set and attitude. The industry tends to follow certain preconceptions about how things ought to work. One of those is that IBM is the company that always has to bless a new processor design. It's interesting how quickly that attitude evolved. After all, when IBM entered the PC market, there were already a lot of companies out there with "better" products. But IBM dominated and became the standard. Any company that jumped out in front of IBM risked being incompatible. In fact, we realized that IBM had done such a good job of setting the standard that it wasn't an IBM standard any more—the industry itself was now supporting the standard. So the key to any next product was to be compatible with existing standards and offer improvements.

In the processor area, there weren't a lot of choices. Intel was developing the next step beyond the 286, the 386. Because of our attention to compatibility all along, we understood where the risk areas and the safe areas were. We looked at the 386 and concluded that we could offer a compatible product that ran all of the software and delivered the advantages of speed and power that the 386 processor had. And we could do it first. We could use conventional wisdom about IBM's leadership to take a position ahead of IBM. And we could do it without sacrificing compatibility.

It sounds as though Compaq adopted a long-term orientation toward the business right from the beginning.

Our business changes so fast that the only way to survive is to think for the long term. When things change as rapidly as they do in our industry, the long term comes sooner rather than later. So thinking long term turns out to be just a commonsense thing to do. We have an aversion to making bad short-term trade-offs, seemingly for a short-term good.

When you think that way, and it becomes a part of your culture, it affects everything you do. For example, you don't try to squeeze the last dollar out of a supplier or try to trick a dealer to get a small advantage, because those things never last. They may last for six months, but problems will catch up with you the next time around. If you want to be around for the long term, you have to invest in developing a supplier, developing a dealer. You have to create a stable, fair, and win-win situation every time you can.

There's another element to the long-term focus. A company that wants to be a leader for a very long time has to apply its limited resources, energy, and people to the most important things. Dealing with short-term issues, such as constantly changing suppliers or dealers, wastes energy and resources. It keeps you from getting on to other opportunities.

If your focus is on the long term, how do you set company plans?

We set directions rather than goals. We pay more attention to managing the direction we are going in, how we are making progress, and how we are doing things than we do to setting a specific goal and then meeting it. In other words, someone who is meeting goals but doing it in the wrong way—not building a team that could keep it going year after year—might have to be replaced. But someone who isn't meeting goals but is really doing all the right things to get us there over the long term may actually be a hero because he or she is laying the pieces in place to get the job done right.

How far do you take this idea of setting directions rather than goals?

You shouldn't get the idea that we don't have plans. In order to be able to buy land and build buildings, we do have to plan. But the plan doesn't drive the company. The plan is a tool that we use to communicate with groups that need coordination. We have certain revenue targets for a year, for example. We have a goal, but we all know that it's a goal for planning purposes and that the numbers are wrong. We say that a lot: "These numbers are wrong. We just don't know if they're high or low." Saying it out loud reinforces the idea that those aren't magic numbers that we have to do whatever it takes to hit.

We learned that from the beginning when it became clear that we had no way to set and then meet company revenue goals. Our first year, we had revenues of $111 million. When we started, if we had set a revenue goal for everyone to hit, it certainly wouldn't have been $111 million. At the outside, it might have been $50 million.

If we had passed the $50 million goal in the third quarter, everybody probably would have coasted on to the end—at least, that would have been the temptation. On the other hand, what if we had set that goal and come in at $35 million? Now, $35 million would have been a phenomenal first year. But everybody would have said that we didn't meet our goals.

That's why today we accept that things change. What's really important is that we're doing the right things in manufacturing and marketing and throughout the company—the things that will give us maximum growth. We believe those things will work over the long term—even if they seem not to be working now. You don't just abandon them to hit the numbers. You have to have consistency and continuity; you can't switch back and forth. You can't tell people to think long term and next quarter tell them to make their numbers. You train people by all your actions over time. You communicate more strongly with your actions than your words.

How would you describe Compaq's approach to competitive manufacturing?

There's a whole science to our manufacturing approach, and it begins with carefully setting priorities. What do we want our manufacturing organization to gear itself to do? When we asked ourselves that question, quality turned out to be number one but keeping costs low was not number two. In fact, cost was way down the list, after flexibility in shifting the product mix and speed in bringing products to market. We geared our manufacturing to the change that is such an important part of the industry, rather than to trying to change the industry. Our approach was to stress flexibility and speed, rather than assume that the market wouldn't change.

Or take our view of our work force. Since we have relatively low labor costs, we feel we should hire our people very carefully. Some people might consider that counterintuitive, but we think it's common sense. After all, if you look at a typical computer that we build, the actual human labor that goes into it compared with the material that we buy outside is pretty small. So we feel that we can afford to increase that percentage with slightly higher labor costs if the result is reduced quality problems and more efficient teamwork. Rather than squeeze labor costs down by 10% and reduce the quality of people, we are willing to increase it by 15% and get the best people who are going to make everything work better.

How did you come up with these manufacturing priorities?

Our manufacturing priorities grew out of the consensus process, out of different teams bringing up issues for discussion. The marketing people would look at our costs and tell us that we needed to lower them. Our factory people would say that we could have lower costs, but that would mean that we'd have to give up some flexibility. We talked about it, gathered facts, and finally concluded that to get lower costs on a repeat product basis, we'd have to build in a pipeline, which automatically reduces flexibility. In the early days, IBM, the King Kong of the industry, had a manufacturing philosophy that believed in 90-day windows during which nothing changed. They tried to get dealers to give them a 90-day order that didn't change. But of course, in the computer industry, that isn't the real world.

The dealers never had the right amount of inventory; they had either too much or too little. They would cut way back on their orders, or they would double their orders. So it was clear that in the PC market, a pipeline wouldn't work; there just wasn't the stability. The environment forced us to decide that there was real value in being able to switch our production from one model to the next—say, from one desktop or portable to another—to get the sales that existed. We wanted to be able to deliver whatever the dealers ordered. The way we looked at it, it wasn't cost versus flexibility. It was how we were going to respond to the market.

If quality is the top priority, what is the Compaq idea of quality?

Quality isn't whether or not your products work. Quality is how people do their jobs. Quality is defining your job and then meeting the expectations. When you do that, you raise everyone's consciousness that everything is important. Every piece of the company is important.

How did you arrive at that definition?

I think that attitude goes back to the first two or three years of the company, when there were relatively few people. Back then, there was a lot of opportunity, certainly a lot more than we could possibly handle. Everyone in the company had to organize his or her own tasks, and we had to decide how many people we were going to hire and which areas would get the people. We realized that there shouldn't be any jobs in which it didn't matter whether you were there that day or not. We were counting on everyone, no matter the function or part of the process. It's important, or it's not there.

We try to communicate this feeling throughout the company. It's not one little piece that you could look at and say, "That's it." The feeling has to be everywhere. It's in the factory, in the way it looks. It's an open, pleasant factory with trees in it. The Cokes are free. And that's not by accident, that's by design. We have company picnics. We have company meetings. Those events mean different things to different people. It's a half day that you get to do something that's different and maybe a little fun.

How would you describe Compaq's approach to innovation?

In any situation where we're looking for creativity, we begin with the customers' needs. We always start by trying to figure out what we must not change in order not to violate the needs of customers. They define the boundaries, the framework of things that are fixed. Then, in the areas where we can innovate, we try to be as creative as we can.

This has really been our approach to the whole product area: innovating within a framework. We knew from the very beginning that we had to produce not only a good hardware product but also one with good software. And that meant the product would have to be compatible with the IBM PC. So we told our engineers—we drilled it into their heads—that they couldn't violate anything that would prevent the software from running. Be creative, but don't violate these fundamental rules.

That approach has made the difference. Early on, a lot of companies had products that the industry magazines reviewed as being more innovative than Compaq's products. It amazed industry experts that these products didn't sell. It took a long time before people understood why our products sold and other people's didn't.

Do you apply this notion of innovation in other parts of the company as well?

We had the same attitude when we opened our Scotland factory. Our approach reflected a clear and thorough understanding of our target. We wanted to create a model of success for any foreign factories we would build in the future. The thing we worried about the most was that something wouldn't work. Here, in Houston, we live in an ideal world, a controlled, self-contained factory environment. Since we were going across the ocean to a different culture, we wanted to be conservative about everything. We decided to take what worked and transplant it carefully to the new factory. The Scottish teams were eager to improve on the process. But we told them, don't improve it now, let's get it up and running with no problems. We can improve it later.

What is your approach to new-product development?

The whole new-product cycle from the concept definition, research phase, design, testing, and into manufacturing has been the heart of the company's success. It's the foundation of everything else. It has meant having the right product at the right time—consistently, over and over again. The reason for it, I believe, is our use of a process that doesn't rely on luck or the vision of just one or two people.

Our process involves a team that deals with new product ideas. There's a core—people who are involved all the time—and others who are part of the team, depending on their area or the type of product. But it's not just a matter of focusing on a specific product. The team also deals with long-range strategic issues, for instance, how RISC-processor technology is going to affect the market. Some people see that issue as black and white. We see it as a force that will affect things in many different ways. The team also looks at what our competitors are doing. We identify things we don't know or aren't sure about and ask a team to research carefully a specific question, gather more information, and then revisit the question a few weeks later. It's a building process. It's not one 15-hour meeting. It's five 3-hour meetings over a period of months, where we build our knowledge and understanding until finally everything we need is there to make a decision.

What is it that makes a company a leader in a certain industry?

To be a leader, you have to do more than just get out in front. A lot of small companies go for the headlines by announcing a product first. That works to get headlines, but it doesn't work well to get sales because you have to combine being first to the market with having credibility with customers so that they'll follow you. Leadership to me is about not being held back by your competition and also having credibility and clout with the customers so they'll go with you.

2
The Value-Adding CFO: An Interview with Disney's Gary Wilson

Geraldine E. Willigan

Gary Wilson, the executive vice president and CFO of the Walt Disney Company since 1985, has gained wide recognition for his creative asset management and shrewd financial techniques, not to mention his multimillion-dollar compensation. Clearly, Wilson is a first-rate CFO. But he is more than an expert financial technician. He is also a strategist, a long-term thinker, an innovator, a creator of value. His influence reaches beyond the usual confines of finance. Indeed, while he holds the top finance job at the world's most successful entertainment company, Wilson doesn't see himself as a financial executive. "I look at myself as a business strategist with a strong finance background," he explains.

This distinction is powerful. In the 1980s, CFOs expanded their responsibilities from arranging loans and issuing financial statements to protecting the company from unwanted suitors. Wilson represents the next step in the evolution of the CFO's role by demonstrating that a CFO can create value, not just account for and defend it.

According to Wilson, a CFO adds value "just like all the great marketing and operating executives—by being creative." That means rethinking assumptions about ownership and control, what an asset is, how to optimize capital costs while achieving strategic goals, and what really drives a company's value.

Wilson's biography is littered with examples of the kinds of imaginative deals that result—such as the off-balance-sheet financing he used during his 12 years as treasurer and then CFO of

Marriott Corporation. Marriott sold its hotels and contracted simply to manage them, allowing Marriott to expand quickly without having to tie up capital in low-return real estate assets. Wilson used a similar approach in creating the financial structure of Euro Disneyland.

Wilson is one of the few CFOs who started his career with entrepreneurs rather than in the finance department of a large corporation. As the CFO for a private Filipino-owned company, he developed many of the skills and philosophies he has applied since. He says, "Functioning at a senior level in a small company gives you a broader view of the business and provides opportunities to be creative." Wilson even learned about LBOs in those early days when the Filipino entrepreneurs assumed enormous debt to buy an agribusiness conglomerate.

In this interview, conducted by HBR associate editor Geraldine E. Willigan, Wilson talks about what comes naturally to him: combining financial sophistication with an imaginative, strategic approach to business—with exciting results.

[Ed.'s Note: Mr. Wilson is now director and principal adviser to Disney, and co-chairman of Northwest Airlines, Inc.]

HBR: Is the role of the CFO different today from what it was 25 years ago?

Gary Wilson: The CFO has become much more important. Twenty-five years ago, you didn't have to be a rocket scientist to be a top financial executive. Today a CFO needs more technical and strategic skills because the financial game has changed. Back in the 1950s, it was a big deal if the prime moved a quarter of one percent in a year, and leverage was low because of a depression mentality. Then in the 1970s and 1980s, we experienced high inflation and correspondingly high financing costs. The deregulation of the financial markets in the early 1970s required more complex and creative ways to finance companies. Optimizing capital costs became a key factor in making companies economically competitive.

As demand increased for competent finance people, more creative executives entered the financial profession, and some of these talented executives started doing more than just finance. When I joined Marriott, there wasn't a great finance guy in the company. Today most of Bill Marriott's executive team have finance backgrounds. While Marriott is the consummate operating company, the key operating executives now have strong financial talent.

What's your role at Disney?

I look at myself as a business strategist with a strong finance background. Michael Eisner, Frank Wells, and I manage Disney strategically. Michael is the world's finest creative executive, in my opinion. Frank is our chief operator, and I lead the strategic and finance effort. As a result of our collegial team approach, I'll get my nose into marketing and operating issues as well as finance matters.

My formal responsibilities are finance, strategic planning, and real estate. But I view my most important function as conceptualizing and implementing the company's overall strategy to maximize shareholder value. I try to spend as much of my time on strategy as possible.

There aren't many finance people who are responsible for the strategy of the business. I did that in my position at Marriott by accident. So now I do it at Disney by design because it was so successful at Marriott.

Why were you able to assume a different role from most CFOs?

I'm one of the few CFOs who started in small business. I worked for entrepreneurs for ten years before I was recruited by Marriott. Even Marriott was relatively small when I joined in 1974—only half-a-billion dollars in volume. Functioning at a senior level in a small company gives you a broader view of the business and provides opportunities to be more creative. I performed most financial functions myself because small companies can't afford large staffs. I was the only one there to do it. I know what it's like not to have enough cash to meet the payroll. I know what it's like to pay 20% for loans. I've actually traded in foreign currencies. I've been involved in a wide spectrum of situations that prepared me well for developing business strategy in larger companies.

People who start out in big companies frequently get notched in a specialized functional area. A finance person might become treasurer in the big company, then treasurer in a bigger company, but will maintain a very narrow view of the business and may have problems adjusting to different business situations. This speciali-zation tends to keep executives from developing a strategic view of the business as they mature professionally.

Was your small company background a disadvantage in some areas—such as understanding Wall Street's sophisticated deal making?

I believe it was an advantage. Take LBOs. We all marvel at them, but small businesses have been doing them for a long time. Now that LBOs have come to corporate America and are on a giant scale, they get lots of attention. But I have been involved in LBOs since I started my career in Manila in 1965. A group of smart local businessmen bought an agribusiness conglomerate on borrowed money—just like Sir James Goldsmith is proposing with BAT in England. Our goal was to improve operations, sell assets, and pay down the debt. We sold a cement plant, a jute bag factory, and a small sugar mill and used the cash flow from one large sugar mill to repay debt and buy the largest construction company in South-east Asia. Today the company is one of the best managed and most profitable in the Philippines. My dad did an LBO with a little printing plant—he bought it with borrowed money and turned it into the market leader before selling it to his employees 20 years later.

You say you get involved in marketing and operations as well as in finance. Do you see your role as keeping those functional areas in balance?

The CEO has to keep the functional organization in balance, although I can influence it. Maintaining balance among operations, marketing, and finance is crucial to a great company. Companies that are weak in a particular function generally aren't market or industry leaders. But I've never seen a company that's equally good in every area. Companies are like living organisms with unique histories and cultures. Their functional strengths and weaknesses tend to reflect their leadership and culture. Football teams are the same way. Super Bowl champions are generally well balanced, with no functional weaknesses.

Are Marriott and Disney balanced?

When I joined Marriott, it was a great operating company, but had very little financial or marketing sophistication. It was seriously unbalanced. The company has always had a strong operating culture because the Marriotts themselves were strong operators and personally focused management attention in that area. Today Marriott is one of the world's great operating companies. I was responsible for getting the financial side up to snuff. By the time I left Marriott in 1985, finance was at least as strong as operations. Marriott has improved as a marketer and is good, but not great, in this functional area.

Disney is culturally a very creative company. Michael Eisner reignited Disney's inherent creative energy and brought great marketing strength to the company in 1984. Disney also has become financially sophisticated. While operations are strong at Disney (particularly in our film groups), rapid expansion requires that we pay constant attention to this crucial functional area.

You've said your primary job is to help develop strategy that creates shareholder value. How does Disney create value for shareholders?

By growing cash flow and earnings at 20% annually and reinvesting cash flows productively to achieve in excess of 20% return on equity. It takes enormous energy to create and implement such a plan. The Disney franchise is really the linchpin in our value creation. It's the finest consumer franchise in the world. Most assets show up on the balance sheet—films, parks, hotels—all of which you can put a value on. But some of Disney's key assets are not on the balance sheet. You could say the Disney franchise is an intangible asset, but to the people who go to the parks, the Disney aura is very real. And it produces very tangible results.

In the past five years, we've unlocked and marveled at the wonderful things that can be done with that franchise. We're continually amazed at how Mickey Mouse is received, whether we're selling a bond issue, a new movie, or a consumer product or opening a new park. When we were launching our share issues for Euro Disneyland last October, for instance, we invited a hundred European institutional investors and analysts to Walt Disney World in Florida for three days. We let them enjoy the product. Subsequently, the response to the initial public offering of Euro Disneyland shares was incredible.

How do you unlock the value of the Disney franchise?

Through the efforts of dedicated, smart, creative people. It's the same whether you're coaching an athletic team or managing a business, winners have the best people. Disney is a good example of what I mean. In 1984 when I was at Marriott, we had the opportunity to purchase Disney for the present day equivalent of $16 a share. Our analysis showed that was a full value for the shares, and we didn't pursue it.

Disney now trades for $120 per share. The reason it's worth so much more is because a talented group of people, through their creativity, have taken the Disney franchise and made it hum. We've opened retail stores, marketed the parks better, built hotels, and made hit movies. It's amazing how much value can be created by giving creative people responsibility for a great but undermanaged franchise like Disney.

Investors value a company by projecting the future cash flows and discounting them to present value at an appropriate discount rate. Disney's cash flows can be projected with relative certainty for a much larger period than, say, those of a disco or a restaurant concept. The restaurant may be unique and popular, but how long can you project those cash flows before the fad dies? Five years, six years, ten years? Mickey Mouse has endured for 60 years. I am confident we can continue to make him go for a very long time. And the longer investors can project growing earnings, the greater the value of the Disney franchise.

Is that true for other assets—it takes creative people to realize the value?

Yes, people are everything. There are many examples of great names that have been languishing for years and have been brought back by good management. Take a great name in hotels, like the Ritz. It hasn't been managed well for years. A group bought the Ritz name and is developing well-managed, deluxe hotels to leverage the name. Polaroid was screwed up for a long time until my colleagues, Roy Disney and Stanley Gold, tried to take it over. Suddenly, management got "religion" and decided to leverage the balance sheet and manage the company better. We'll see if they can succeed. Pan Am has a great name in the airline business, but it's not doing well because it's been poorly managed for years. New management is trying to turn it around, but management neglect takes its toll over the years and many analysts question whether the Pan Am name will survive.

How does a CFO create value?

Just like all the great marketing and operating executives—by being creative. Creativity creates value. In finance that means structuring deals creatively. For example, we monetized about $750 million worth of royalties from Tokyo Disneyland. We have substantial yen inflows from the park, and we felt the yen was getting too strong in 1988. Our royalty stream from Japan was becoming very important to our earnings, and I didn't want our dollar earnings to be subject to volatility because of something beyond our control—namely, the yen/dollar exchange rate. So we decided to hedge our yen position.

We came up with an idea that in effect sold to Japanese investors a 20-year stream of yen royalties. To decide what that stream was worth, the investors discounted the earnings at their required return, about 6%. The present value of that earnings stream discounted at 6% came to about $750 million. In May of 1988, the exchange rate got to 124 yen to the dollar, which we felt was high, and we consummated the transaction. In effect, we got money at a 6% discount rate, reinvested it at a minimum of 10%, and hedged our royalty stream against yen fluctuations—all in one transaction. Since then, the yen has weakened, which was an added bonus to the transaction.

The Euro Disneyland financial structure was probably the most creative and generated the most value of any deal I've ever been associated with. I won't bore you with the details, but some security analysts have attributed $15 to $20 of Disney's share value to the Euro Disneyland structure.

Besides using the assets creatively, how else do you manage the balance sheet?

There are two key things on which a strategic CFO must focus: first, investing the company's assets productively to achieve its

strategic objectives, and second, financing the assets at the opti-
mum cost of capital. So on the left-hand side of the balance sheet,
we must invest in assets to provide growth at our targeted returns,
and on the right-hand side, we must finance the assets in a way to
optimize the cost of capital. Optimizing the cost of capital means a
generous sprinkling of relatively low-cost debt, because it's the
cheapest form of financing. The after-tax cost of debt is somewhere
around 6%, whereas the cost of equity is probably 15% to 20%.

*If you think proper capitalization includes lots of debt, why does
Disney have so little of it?*

It's the problem of plenty. We have excess cash flow relative to
our investment opportunities, which makes it difficult to optimally
capitalize our balance sheet. That's the challenge we've been facing
for the past couple of years.

What should we do with our excess capital? There are only two
choices. We can either increase assets or decrease equity. Our clear
choice is to invest the capital productively through acquisitions in
our existing lines of business. But in today's market, driven by
LBOs, we can't find acquisitions that meet our return requirements.
We've bought some little things, like the Muppets, that fit nicely
into our business. But we are content to hit a few singles and wait
patiently for the right pitch to hit a home run. In fact, I think one
of Disney management's biggest accomplishments over the past five
years is being patient—and refraining from overpaying on acquisitions. We might miss a few deals by being conservative, but our
investors can be confident that what we do buy has good value.

What criteria do you use when considering an acquisition?

First, we look at the strategic fit. Then we see if the project meets
our financial objectives. There are companies we would like to
acquire for strategic reasons, but it has been tough to make the
acquisition prices work for us economically. That's why the Muppets deal was good for us. There was a lot of opportunity for us to
add value through the films, parks, and retail products—that overused word, synergy.

Other companies have the same problem of not being able to
justify acquisitions financially because there are so many financial

buyers bidding up values. There's a lot of money available for LBOs right now, and a lot of people are doing deals.

Will you lower your financial objectives if prices stay high?

Our financial criteria are based on sound economics demanded by our shareholders. Therefore, we can't lower them unless financial markets dictate a change. We'll continue to be very conservative about our investments. We've been at the acquisition game for five years now and haven't done anything stupid yet. Besides, markets don't stay up forever. In a free-market system, excesses occur frequently, but rationality always returns to the marketplace. Remember oil prices that were never going to fall! Or take real estate. Real estate developers will build anything a financial institution will lend against. They'll build steel factories in Manhattan if they can get 100% financing! The REITs (real estate investment trusts) in the early 1970s leveraged, leveraged, leveraged—until the gasoline crisis and recession came in 1974. Then they had a huge problem that lasted for over a decade.

It's the same with LBOs in today's market. Financial institutions make so much money on lending fees that they'll finance anything that looks reasonable. And what looks reasonable becomes more liberal every day, until the point when somebody has a problem. Junk bond investors got their pound of flesh, but they are starting to pay the price now that a few firms have gone bankrupt and the market has turned against them.

You have lots of cash, but you still choose not to own Tokyo Disneyland, Euro Disneyland, and the Silver Screen movie-making partnerships. At Marriott, you didn't own the hotels. Why don't you want to own those assets?

Tokyo Disneyland was done before new management arrived on the scene. We would have loved to own Euro Disneyland, but we agreed to the French government's request to sell 51% of the company to the European public. The most we can own is 49%, the least is 17%.

But in general, we choose to own only those assets that give us the return we want and the growth we need to meet our business plan. At Marriott, for example, our strategic plan was to grow rapidly in hotels, a very capital-intensive business. Owning the hotel consumed a great deal of capital at relatively low returns. The returns were low because they were real estate assets. Pension funds and other investors consider them a relatively safe investment, so they didn't require a high return on them. But a public company like Marriott had to have high returns if we were going to sell at a high stock multiple. And the reason a lot of people weren't excited about the hotel business in the 1970s was because they had to own all this low-return real estate.

We said there are really two aspects to the hotel business—the management of the hotel and the real estate. As I said earlier, Marriott had a very strong operating culture. It was, and still is, the best hotel operator in the world. We knew how to manage the hotel bottom line very well. Most hotel companies really don't have the discipline to manage the food and beverage and banquet businesses, but Marriott did because of its roots in the restaurant business (remember the famous nine-seat root beer stand where Marriott started). Yet Marriott was the tenth-ranked hotel company. It was an also-ran. So to grow, we decided to sell off the real estate to investors desiring real estate returns. Then we'd take our great operating talent that was producing profit margins far superior to the competition and simply manage the real estate for lucrative fees.

How did that arrangement help you achieve your strategic and financial goals?

We could make our profits with very little capital investment. Our ROE went from 9% to over 20% very quickly. And we could build a lot of hotels because somebody else was financing them. Therefore, we could grow very fast. Marriott grows in excess of 20% annually—in a capital-intensive business. The only limit to our growth was the management we could train—not capital, which was constraining our competition. It's a rather simple concept, but it worked. That's why Marriott doesn't own many hotels. It's managing billions of dollars of hotels that are owned by others. It has 75-year management contracts on literally thousands of hotel rooms, which it couldn't have had if it had had to own them all. The owners of the real estate are getting the returns they want, whereas Marriott is generating very big returns from its intangible asset, which is over 30 years of experience in running hotels at superior profits.

Why didn't you apply this off-balance-sheet financing to Disney's U.S. theme parks and hotels?

When I first came to Disney, everybody expected us to sell the parks to financial buyers and manage them under contract. But after analyzing Disney, it became apparent to us that the parks themselves were very high return assets with a relatively low tax basis. Park earnings were growing greater than inflation, and we thought cash flow could be improved through better marketing and pricing. We didn't foresee major capital needs because of Disney's strong cash flow position. Therefore, selling parks was a high-cost source of financing that wasn't prudent to pursue.

We also own our own hotels for much the same reason. They're relatively more valuable than normal hotels because they are running at extremely high occupancy and room rates. If we decide to make a major acquisition and need capital to finance it, selling parks or hotels under management contract is an alternative. It carries a relatively high capital cost, however, because of taxes due when the assets are sold.

Since 1985, you've used partnerships to finance Disney's films. What did the Silver Screen partnerships accomplish?

Investors have looked at the film business as being inherently volatile. Disney's objective was to mitigate that perceived risk. Silver Screen accomplishes that by shifting the primary financial risk to outside investors in return for a share of the profits. Since Disney has produced a string of hit films, and the ancillary markets—particularly home video and foreign television—have exploded, Silver Screen investors have received good returns.

We're considering financing future films in-house rather than through Silver Screen, however, because our film group management is so professional and successful and because the film business is becoming much less risky. When theatrical revenue was the primary source of film income, the risks were enormous: a film was either a hit or a bomb depending solely on box office results. As we move into the 1990s, domestic box office sales amount to only 20% of a film's total revenues. The home video and television markets dominate film profits and produce income that is much more stable, which reduces the risk in the film business overall.

Do your financing methods mean you lose control of the assets?

Anytime we do a financing, we make sure we maintain effective management control. A Marriott management contract gives Marriott control for many years. Silver Screen and Euro Disneyland give us virtual management control.

How do you achieve total control when you're a minority owner, as in Euro Disneyland?

Our French park is set up as an SCA [*Societé Commanditée par Actions*]. That's a unique French corporate form that is very similar to a U.S. limited partnership. We're the *gerant,* or general partner. The SCA structure allows us to control management, even with a minority shareholding. Of course, we can get terminated for gross misconduct, but otherwise, our control is pretty firm.

The structure also benefits the investors because it ensures that Disney's license agreements will remain in force. If somebody were able to take over the company and terminate our management and then manage the company improperly, it's conceivable that we would have grounds to terminate the Disney franchise. That would be an unacceptable risk for our European shareholders.

We've been able to negotiate such terms because both Disney and Marriott have a unique franchise. Both are leaders in their respective industries, so they can control the terms of the contract. A weaker hotel company or a weaker entertainment company wouldn't be in that position. That's why it's always best to be the market leader. Leadership helps in any commercial relationship—whether it is with distributors, suppliers, customers, or "guests," as we call them at Disney.

Your financing arrangements leave you with a lot of excess cash, which is attractive to raiders. Does that concern you?

My view has always been that in a free market, people can raid you. The best defense is to manage the business in such a way that you have a high market multiple. If the market places a high value on the company, it's very difficult to be taken over. Look at Disney's multiple. Nobody's going to buy us. They can't afford to. Management strength is another good defense. We're very management intensive. If somebody buys Disney, we'll probably all leave, and no one will take that risk, particularly the bankers who finance these transactions. Obviously, if we screw up and Disney's future prospects don't look so good, then we might be threatened. But I don't think that's going to happen, so takeover is not something I lose a lot of sleep over.

Do you think hostile takeovers happen only when managements flounder?

In my opinion, the vast majority of takeovers were companies that were not properly managed in some important function. Frequently, it was improper financial structure that the raider corrected through leverage. But remember, Disney was a hostile takeover, and look what happened. The company was flat on its back, and now it's the darling of corporate America—all in five years.

Does there come a time when a company matures and begins to generate more money than it can invest in continued growth? Is that what's happening with Disney?

I look at General Motors and AT&T as mature companies because they are huge and have limited growth prospects. I don't think Disney is in that mold because the entertainment market is growing rapidly worldwide, and we can capture an increasing share of that market through our creative energy.

What is the critical difference between Disney and AT&T?

There's still a lot of growth we can accomplish. Our financial goals are "20–20"—a 20% ROE and 20% growth in cash flow. If we had a less aggressive management who didn't care about growing, you might say that Disney is mature. But I haven't been involved with a company that couldn't grow aggressively, and I've been in business for 25 years.

Since I joined Marriott in 1984, there has not been a year in any company I've been with that it didn't grow at 20% a year. At

Marriott, it took a lot of creativity because we were in a low-growth business. We had to grow by taking market share. When traditional hotel growth became difficult, we invented the Courtyard concept to capture the lower end market segment with a fresh, new product. Our strategic planning group actually created that product in the early 1980s, and it provides much of Marriott's hotel growth today. The same creative effort produced Marriott's product for the elderly care market.

Do you think the time will come when Disney doesn't have a lot of growth left in it?

You can't grow something at 20% forever. Through the magic of compounding, it becomes the world! There will probably be a time when Disney's growth rate will fall, but that won't be in my lifetime. We can grow through the 1990s just by growing our existing products and managing our existing businesses better. And we would like to buy a major related business, which could provide even more earnings growth since we'd finance it with our debt capacity.

And when our existing growth prospects wane, we will create something new—we are working on some of these projects now. Growth becomes tougher as a company gets larger, but that's what good management is all about. That means at Disney we'll probably have to invent a new kind of entertainment center that goes in big cities or a new hotel resort concept to entertain guests in a nonpark setting. There's lots we can do with the Disney franchise.

Are the incentives there for managers who are not also majority owners?

It doesn't take a private company to motivate managers. Disney emphasizes pay for performance, so the incentives for management are huge. I don't see any difference at all. In fact, a lot of companies that have gone private will probably go public again once management gets the debt paid down and the stock is hot again. That's the only way you can create value and liquidity.

Does your emphasis on meeting financial objectives inhibit Disney's creativity?

The financial function provides the economic discipline in a well-managed company. The planning and control system imposes discipline on the operators who are committed to meeting operating and capital budgets. For example, we had a budget to build our Studio Tour in Florida. There's no change in that budget—unless Michael Eisner himself goes in and says we need to do this or that to improve the show. We're very disciplined about budgets—if we deviate from them, we know exactly why we're doing it. Movies are the same way. Under our Silver Screen deal, we get paid a bonus for producing under certain negative costs. So that's the target. And we hit it. It's a great discipline.

The operating and creative people don't always like this discipline—or "financial box," as Michael Eisner calls it. We swear at each other a lot in the process. But if the company had financial guys that were pushovers, we'd lose financial discipline. Look at how many of the small, independent producers in Hollywood don't have any financial controls. Many have gone bankrupt because the creative executive runs it with no discipline—he hires his girlfriend as the star and shoots in Rome. It just doesn't work. Our film group runs it like a business, and our guys are the best in the world at producing not only hits but also a great bottom line.

Some people say Detroit's downfall was people who understood finance but not cars or manufacturing. Do people ever accuse you of running the company by the numbers?

Sometimes. It's part of the turf. But we give our creative people and operators a big box within which they can exercise their prerogative. In films, we recognize that the script is the most important creative decision, so our creative people make those decisions. But when it comes to producing and marketing the films, it's got to be economic. Our creative people are pretty disciplined anyway because most have come from large entertainment companies, like Warner or Paramount, which are well managed.

It's true that the typical finance executive likes doing things the traditional way, whereas a marketing executive will tend to be a little more off-the-wall and willing to try different things. But is running things more conservatively good or bad? It's a question of how good the finance person is or how good the marketing executive is. Unfortunately, the automobile companies have had poor leaders whether financial or otherwise. It's the classic example of an ingrown business that didn't focus strategically on the customer or on its worldwide competitive position. Again, it all comes back to people.

In my view, a CFO should be first and foremost a strategic business executive. Creating value for shareholders is what any business executive's primary economic objective should be. That means CFOs should help create the strategic plan that's going to achieve the corporate goals of growth and return on capital—and then help make it happen. How do you do that? With good people. A great team of people can make almost anything work.

3

The Business of Innovation: An Interview with Paul Cook

William Taylor

Paul M. Cook, founder and CEO of Raychem Corporation, is in the business of supplying technology-intensive products to industrial customers in sectors such as aerospace, automobiles, construction, telecommunications, and utilities. Raychem builds products that connect, seal, and protect signal-carrying cables for telephone networks and cable television systems. It manufactures much of the high-performance wire and cable that runs through military and commercial aircraft. Self-regulating heaters based on conductive polymers ensure the smooth flow of oil through pipelines in harsh environments and deice rails for mass transit systems.

On a more basic level, though, Paul Cook is in the business of innovation. Since its founding in 1957, Raychem has pursued a consistent and ambitious strategy: to master a set of core technologies and create thousands of proprietary products based on those technologies. Today Raychem generates annual revenues of more than $1 billion through the sale of some 50,000 products. For most of those products, it is the world's leading supplier; for many, it is the only supplier. Its products have found receptive customers around the world. Raychem generates more than 60% of its revenues outside the United States and has extensive manufacturing and research facilities in Western Europe and Asia. The company has more than 900 U.S. patents with some 300 pending, as well as some 3,000 foreign patents with another 9,000 pending.

Raychem's powerful market position has contributed to outstanding financial performance. It consistently earns gross margins of more than 50%, unrivaled in the industries in which it operates.

The company has no net bank borrowings. Its price-earnings multiple of 30 is well above market averages.

Innovation at Raychem goes beyond products. Indeed, the company is in the process of reinventing itself. For its first 25 years, Raychem recorded explosive growth (averaging 25% per year) as it tapped the global potential of its products. Since the early 1980s, as growth slowed, Raychem has worked to develop new core technologies and to position itself in new markets. Its recently developed expertise in thin-film and liquid-crystal displays has created a role for the company in burgeoning markets for computer touch-screens and "switchable windows." A ten-year initiative in fiber optics has made Raychem, through its Raynet subsidiary, a leading contender to bring fiber optics to the home—a vast global market worth billions of dollars.

Mr. Cook, 65, is a graduate of the Massachusetts Institute of Technology and a former head of the Radiation Laboratory at the Stanford Research Institute. He has stepped down as Raychem's CEO but is still chairman. The interview was conducted by HBR associate editor William Taylor.

HBR: What's the secret to being an innovative company?

Paul Cook: There is no secret. To be an innovative company, you have to ask for innovation. You assemble a group of talented people who are eager to do new things and put them in an environment where innovation is expected. It's that simple—and that hard. There are, after all, a limited number of things management can ask for. We get innovation at Raychem because our corporate strategy is premised on it. Without innovation we die.

And I don't mean just from the engineers. Innovation is as much about sales or service or information systems as it is about products. We spend twice as much on selling as we do on research and development, so creativity from our sales force is just as important as creativity from the labs. How do you sell a product no one has seen before? How do you persuade a customer to accept us as a sole source for an important component? There's no one in any organization who can't be clever and imaginative about doing his or her job more effectively. We expect innovation from our secretaries and the people on the loading docks as well as from the scientists.

Still, few American companies are as innovative as they could be—or must be—to survive intense global competition. What's missing?

You won't get innovation without pressure. Most companies put pressure on their sales force to go out and get orders. They put pressure on manufacturing to cut costs, increase yields, improve quality. But they forget the importance of pressure when it comes to new products and processes. We want to grow this company from $1 billion a year to $5 billion, and we don't do big acquisitions. The only way to get that kind of growth is to get more and better products out the door faster.

I'm convinced that's a big reason Raychem grew so explosively in the early days. When we started the company, we didn't know what products we were going to make. We knew the first electron-beam machines were coming to market from General Electric, and we knew there were potential industrial applications for the technology. So we bought a machine. And pretty soon we started running out of money. We were under enormous pressure to find successful products—and we did. We came up with lots of good ideas because we had to. People need a fair amount of pressure to have creative ideas.

How do you maintain pressure in a successful global company?

Everyone has heard the cliche, "management by walking around." Well, you can't walk around 30 plants in 12 countries, which is what Raychem has right now, without dropping from exhaustion. But you can practice what I refer to as "management by calling about." Almost every day I use the telephone to contact Raychem people somewhere in the world. "How did your experiment go last night? What results do you have this morning? What are your ideas for a new approach? Why don't you fax me your product plan?" If you keep the pressure on in a constructive way, if you demonstrate genuine curiosity about what's happening in the labs, it stimulates people to keep the creative process going.

Why do organizations need such pressure and prodding? Isn't innovation the most exhilarating part of being in business?

What separates the winners and losers in innovation is who masters the drudgery. The creative process usually starts with a brilliant idea. Next you determine whether, if the brilliant idea worked, it would be worth doing from a business standpoint. That's the exhilarating part. It may be the most stimulating intellectually, but it's also the easiest.

Then comes the real work—reducing the idea to practice. That's the drudgery part of innovation, and that's where people need the most pressure and encouragement. You can draw a chart of how the original excitement of a new idea creates all kinds of energy, but then people go into the pits for a long time as they try to turn that idea into products that are reproducibly manufacturable. That's when you use the phone and the fax machine. That's when you have review meetings between the technical people and senior management. That's when, as CEO, you show the entire organization that you are just as interested in new product and process development as you are in manufacturing costs, sales, or quality.

We don't often hear the words "innovation" and "drudgery" together.

Too many people still think innovation is about one brilliant technologist coming up with one breakthrough idea. It's not. When we started Raychem, we began to learn what radiation chemistry could do. Within three or four years, we had generated virtually every idea behind the products we're selling today, and we're still working on that original inventory of ideas. Ten years ago, after we began work on conductive polymers, we identified a market for all the manifestations of the technology that totaled $747 million a year. We made our "747 list" and began working through it. At the time, it was a $5 or $10 million business. Today we're up to $150 million a year. So we still have a long way to go.

Or think about semiconductors. I can make a case that the semiconductor world hasn't had a really new idea for 15 or 20 years. Those companies have essentially been practicing the same technology. They've learned more about it, they've penetrated it throughout the economy, but the core technologies haven't changed that much. The pioneers of the semiconductor industry could recite within the first few years all that could be done with the technology. The winners have been the companies that reduced the technology to practice most quickly.

Does that explain some of our competitive slide against the Japanese?

This is where the Japanese are eating us alive. They're making us look like amateurs in product development. American technologists are still without peer in terms of the imagination they bring to problems. No one can question our technical brilliance. The Japanese don't pioneer the brilliant solutions, but they find the brilliant solutions. Then they bring them over to Japan and master the drudgery to reduce them to practice. Japan may not have the Nobel laureates yet, but I'm not sure it needs them to flourish. And if it wants them, all it has to do is create the right environment and that will happen too.

What's frightening to me is the thoroughness with which the Japanese scan the world for important technologies, learn them, know the patent literature, know the technical literature, and turn over every stone. We've been working on shape-memory alloys for almost 25 years. The Japanese keep knocking on our doors; they want a license from us. They are the only companies in the world besides Raychem that see the potential for this technology. In fact, whenever we find technologies that we consider powerful, for which we have great expectations, it isn't long before the Japanese show up and say, "How about a license?" or "How about a joint venture?" We seldom get chased by American or European companies.

Can a company teach its people to be innovative?

No. Innovation is an emotional experience. You can train people technically, but you can't teach them curiosity. The desire to innovate comes partly from the genes; you're born with it. It also comes from your early life, your education, the kind of encouragement you got to be creative and original. Innovative people come in all shapes and sizes and in all personality types. Some people are happiest when they're wrestling with a problem; I'm one of those. Others go into a green funk. They're miserable and depressed until they have the answer. But you can't have a good technologist who's not emotionally involved in the work. You can't have a good technologist who doesn't wake up in the middle of the night searching for answers. You can't have a good technologist who doesn't come into the lab eager to see the results of last night's experiment.

So before you hire people, you ask about their childhood?

You bet. One of my most important jobs is finding the right people to add to the Raychem environment—people who genuinely want to serve the customer, who want to build new products that are superior to anything that's come before, who are willing to stick their necks out to do new things. That means learning how their minds work, what they think about, what excites them, how they approach problems.

The top management of this company spends a huge amount of time—I probably spend 20 percent of my time—recruiting, interviewing, and training. It's not unusual for a technologist candidate to go through ten in-depth interviews. Now some people do better in interviews than others. But by keeping the evaluation process broad, we usually get broad agreement on candidates. I can't think of anyone who's been a great success at Raychem who wasn't a big success in the interviews.

How do you motivate people over the long haul to keep them focused on innovation?

The most important factor is individual recognition—more important than salaries, bonuses, or promotions. Most people, whether they're engineers, business managers, or machine operators, want to be creative. They want to identify with the success of their profession and their organization. They want to contribute to giving society more comfort, better health, more excitement. And their greatest reward is receiving acknowledgment that they did contribute to making something meaningful happen. So the most important thing we do is build an organization—a culture, if you'll pardon the word—that encourages teamwork, that encourages fun and excitement, that encourages everyone to do things differently and better—and that acknowledges and rewards people who excel.

Of course, people do use financial yardsticks to measure how they're doing. So you have to pay well. We pay our people above average, but only slightly above average—sixtieth percentile or so. Bonuses give them an opportunity to move up a fair amount based on overall corporate results and individual performance. Every person in the company earns a cash bonus each quarter based on after-tax profits as a percentage of sales. Ten percent of our people are in a second bonus pool. The size of a pool reflects the performance of the group or division; the distribution of the pool reflects individual performance.

Some companies spread bonuses quite evenly among group members. We have a different approach. Typically within a division there are significant differentials based on performance. Having a big spread causes some unhappiness. But it also creates drive, because I think people respect how we evaluate their contribution. We don't just reward success; we reward intelligent effort. We've paid sizable bonuses to people who have worked day and night, with remarkable proficiency, on a year-long project—only to find the market had disappeared.

We must be doing something right, by the way. Our attrition rate is very low, and the number of people who have left to start businesses to compete with us is virtually nil. That's pretty unusual when you consider what happens in the rest of Silicon Valley.

Let's talk about technology. Increasingly, companies are trying to close the innovation gap by working with other companies—often their competitors—in strategic alliances, joint ventures, and research partnerships. Does this worry you?

Yes. No company can do everything, and we use partnerships on a selective basis. We're working with Nippon Sheet Glass on switchable windows and with Furukawa Electric in shape-memory alloys. But those and a few other alliances are the exceptions. I've always believed that truly innovative companies must build an intellectual and technical infrastructure around core technologies. At Raychem, those core technologies are radiation chemistry, conductive polymers, shape-memory alloys, cross-linked gels, liquid-crystal displays, and a few others. Companies need a single-minded commitment to their core technologies, a commitment to knowing more about them than anyone else in the world. No partnership or joint venture can substitute for technology leadership.

You also have to make sure your company has the very brightest people in your core technologies. Some who know the analytical part of the technology, some who know the molecular part, some who know the physics, some who know the chemistry. You make sure those people talk to each other, that there is regular and intensive interchange between all those disciplines. They have to work together, communicate, sweat, swear, and do whatever it takes to extract from the core technology every product possibility. The fax machine has been absolutely magnificent in that regard. Our technologists are using it to share sketches and plans, annotate them, and feed them back. The fax machine is much more important than videoconferencing as a tool for technical interaction.

Still, effective communication doesn't come easy. One of the problems with people at the cutting edge of their field is that they don't think anyone can teach them anything. That's why we recently started a "Not Invented Here" award at Raychem. We celebrate people who steal ideas from other parts of the company and apply them to their work. We give the person who adopts a new idea a trophy and a certificate that says, "I stole somebody else's idea, and I'm using it." The person on the other side, the person who had the idea, also gets an award. His certificate says, "I had a great idea, and so and so is using it." We hope to give out hundreds of these awards.

How does being committed to core technologies differ from how most companies manage technology?

Too many American companies are only immersed in their markets. They bring along whatever technology they think is necessary to satisfy a market need. Then they fall flat on their faces because the technology they deliver isn't sophisticated enough or because they don't know what alternatives the competition can deliver.

We think about our business differently. Raychem's mission is to creatively interpret our core technologies to serve the marketplace. That means we don't want to be innovators in all technologies. We restrict our charter to the world of material science, and within material science, to niches that can sponsor huge growth over a long period of time and in which we can be pioneers, the first and best in the world. And I mean the first. That means we can't just go to universities and find trained people; we have to train them ourselves. We usually can't use technologies from university and government labs, although we stay abreast of what's happening. After all, if we're a pioneer in a technology, how can we go to a university and learn about it?

Then we draw on those core technologies to proliferate thousands of products in which we have a powerful competitive advantage and for which our customers are willing to pay lots of money relative to what it costs us to make them. Think about that. If you can pioneer a technology, use it to make thousands of products, sell those products at high price-to-cost relationships to tens of thousands of customers around the world, none of which individually is that important to you, you wind up with an incredibly strong market position. That philosophy hasn't changed for 33 years. Our challenge has been to apply it to a bigger and bigger organization.

Why don't more companies follow this model?

Because it's a harder way to do business. Most companies say, "Let's pick markets in which we can be big players and move as fast as we can to do the simple things." More companies today want to be dominant players in big markets—you know, number one or number two in the world—or they get out. Jack Welch, General Electric's chairman, has followed that strategy very successfully for years. That's not our strategy at all.

A different, and I think more powerful, way to compete is to avoid competition altogether. The best way to avoid competition is to sell products that rivals can't touch. When we started Raychem, the last thing we wanted to do was make products that giants like GE or Du Pont would also be interested in making. We made sure to select products that would not be of interest to large companies. We selected products that could be customized, that we could make in many varieties—different sizes, different thicknesses, different colors. We wanted products that were more, not less, complicated to design and build. We wanted products with small potential annual revenues compared with the total size of the company, and we wanted lots of them.

After 33 successful years, I still have trouble pushing that vision inside Raychem; people struggle against it all the time. It takes a lot of confidence to believe that you can go out and master a technology, stay ahead of everybody else in the world, capture markets based on that technology, obtain broad patent coverage, and then end up with a strong gross profit margin in a protected business. People argue that it would be much easier, that we would grow more quickly, if we put less inventive content in our products and went for bigger markets. That's not my idea of a smart way to grow a business.

So innovation is primarily about pushing technology out the door?

Not quite. What we're really talking about is economically disciplined innovation. Sure, you have to know your core technologies better than anyone else. But you also have to know your marketplace better than anyone else. You have to understand your customers' needs. You have to understand whether your product is reproducibly manufacturable, which isn't easy when you're pioneering new technologies. You have to understand the competition's ability to respond to your innovation. You have to understand whether the product can generate a gross profit margin big enough to fund the new investments you need to keep pioneering and to allow for some mistakes along the way. For us, that means a gross profit margin of at least 50%. Unless you can figure ways to save your customers lots of money, to be economically important to them, and to beat the hell out of the competition with products for which they have no alternatives, and to do all that cost-effectively enough to earn big margins, you won't have economically successful innovation.

Don't all companies try to understand their markets and their customers?

But how do they do it? They go out and ask customers what they want. That's not nearly enough. I'm not talking about lip service. There are a whole series of questions that we have to answer before launching a new product. Will it save customers a little money or a lot of money? Will it make marginal improvements in the performance or efficiency of the customers' products or will it make major advances? What does it cost customers to use this new product beyond what we charge them? What are their overhead rates? What are the hourly rates for the people doing the installation? I could go on. That's why Raychem probably has more MBAs per capita than any other technology company in the United States. We have to know our customers' business problems and economics as well as we know our technology.

We also have to ask one last question: Will the customer accept a sole-source relationship with us? After all, we're in the business of delivering pioneering, proprietary products. An oil company can't decide to use one of our couplings for a pipeline in the desert and then bring in two other suppliers for the same product. We're the only supplier in the world. So we have to understand the customer deeply enough—and the customer has to know we understand him—that he has the confidence to establish a sole-source relationship with us for a new and novel product.

So companies aren't just selling innovation, they're selling confidence that they will stand behind the innovation?

Absolutely. Many customers have stuck their necks out to buy products from us that they have never seen before. That means we get into trouble from time to time. But I can't remember one case where this organization didn't rally day and night, as long as it took, to solve the problem. In fact, when you have those experiences, customers always wind up more friendly, more favorably disposed toward the next innovation. That's not the way we intend to do business, but it's part of the territory.

Customer responsiveness and trust can also lead to tremendous business opportunities. Cross-linked gels are now one of our core technologies. That business grew out of a very specific problem we had to solve for a customer. A hurricane hit Corpus Christi, Texas and knocked out a bunch of telephones. We sent down a task force at the request of Southwestern Bell and discovered that most of the shorting out occurred in certain terminal boxes. At the time we had a tiny research effort in the area of cross-linked gels, and we thought we could use the technology to solve the problem. It worked, even though we didn't understand all the principles behind it. So we plugged gels into research to explore what fundamental technologies were involved. We discovered all kinds of fascinating things and expanded the research effort. Today we probably have 100 people throughout the company working on gels. It's a profitable, fast-growing business.

How do you develop an in-depth understanding of markets?

You can't understand the market unless you get your technologists to the customer in a deep and sustained way. Your sales force, the traditional link to the customer, only gets you part of the way. It can open doors and find opportunities, but it can't really solve the customer's problems. And you can't pass the details of what the customer needs through the filter of the salesperson. You can't expect salespeople to have the imagination and expertise to know what can be accomplished through manipulating the technology.

We have technologists at Raychem who are superb in the labs. We have salespeople and marketers, most with technical training, who are superb at understanding customer needs. The person who can combine deep knowledge of the technology with deep knowledge of the customer is the rarest person of all—and the most important person in the process of innovation. We don't have very many of those people at Raychem, but those we do have are all technologists. We have never come up with an important product that hasn't been primarily the work of a technologist. That's because doing something truly important in our field requires knowing all the things that have gone before. You have to have the technology in your bones.

It's easier to teach a technologist economics than it is to teach an economist technology. And our technologists enjoy learning about the business. Whenever they go out to visit customers, they absolutely love it. It stimulates them. It excites them. It teaches them all kinds of things they wouldn't know if they stayed in the labs. It's a very important part of the innovation process here. That doesn't mean we do enough of it; nobody does.

What are the biggest obstacles to innovation?

For an organization to remain innovative, it has to be willing— even eager—to obsolete itself as fast as it can. So one of the biggest obstacles to successful innovation is success itself. All too often a company will develop an important new product and spend years asking itself the same questions—how can we make it a little better, a little cheaper, a little more sophisticated? Those are all important questions; there's always room for incremental improvement. But you can't let the entire innovative thrust revolve around making products faster, better, cheaper. A truly innovative company never stops asking more fundamental questions about its most successful products. Are there whole new ways to solve the problem—ways that might cut costs in half or double or triple performance?

So Raychem is working to obsolete its own products?

Every day. Right now we are in the process of obsoleting one of our best products, a system for sealing splices in telephone cables.

That product generates $125 million of revenue per year, more than 10% of our total sales. We introduced the original splice closure, which was based on our heat-shrinkable technology, about 20 years ago. It absolutely took over the market. Our customers, the operating telephone companies of the world, have been thrilled with it. We also do pretty well on it financially—gross profits are well above average.

Now we could have kept on improving that product for years to come. Instead, we've developed a radically new splice-closure technology that improves performance tremendously, and we're working very hard to cannibalize the earlier generation. We introduced this new technology, which we call SuperSleeve, in the last few years. Today we're about halfway through the conversion process; 50% of our splice-closure revenues this year will be from the new technology, 50% from the old. By the end of next year, we want virtually 100% of these revenues to be from the SuperSleeve technology. In fact, we recently closed our only U.S. manufacturing line for the old technology.

How's that different from what any good company does—once an old product runs out of steam, you introduce a new product?

That's precisely my point—our old product wasn't running out of steam. Our customers had virtually no complaints about it. But because we knew the product and its applications even better than our customers did, we were able to upgrade its performance significantly by using a new technology. Our margins on the new technology, at least until we get manufacturing costs down, are lower than our margins on the old product. We had to do an aggressive selling job—and take a short-term financial hit—to persuade customers to adopt the new product.

Why are we doing it? Because we understand that if we don't obsolete ourselves, the world will become more competitive. We'd spend most of our time and energy reducing costs and outmaneuvering the competition that springs up. And for all that, we'd wind up with products that are only incrementally better, not fundamentally better.

Remember, we want products for which there is no competition. Even if we could have maintained our margins on the old product— and we probably could have by reducing manufacturing costs to keep pace with declining prices—we don't want to play that game.

So today we're capable of delivering a demonstrably better product at the same price. And we're trying to persuade our telecommunications customers to write new specifications that require performance as good as what SuperSleeve can deliver. That's the game we want to play. And it's one of the hardest games any organization can play.

Are there other obstacles?

Size is the enemy of innovation. You can't get effective innovation in environments of more than a few hundred people. That's why as we continue to grow, we want Raychem to feel and function less like a giant corporation than a collection of small groups, each of which has its own technical people, marketing people, engineering people, manufacturing people. Sure we want to get big. But we must stay innovative.

Innovation happens in pockets, and the location of those pockets changes over time. So we play musical chairs with people and make extensive use of skunk works and project teams. Using small groups also allows us to make sure that a technologist is at the head of the group making the decisions. I prefer to put development decisions on the backs of technologists rather than on business-people. I don't want our new product teams automatically going after the biggest markets. I want them going after the best way to develop the technology along proprietary lines so long as growing and profitable markets exist. Once the product succeeds and your problems become cost, quality, and efficiency, then you can think about putting different managers in charge.

I'm surprised you haven't mentioned money as an obstacle.

Innovation takes patient capital. American companies just aren't spending enough on R&D. If companies increased their R&D spending by 2% of sales, and therefore lowered profits by 2% of sales, they'd be much better off in the long run—and so would the United States. Normally, we spend 6% or 7% of sales on R&D. This year we'll spend more than 11% of sales on R&D, even though revenues are flat and margins down a bit, because we're working on several technologies that are going to materialize into really good businesses. That's an extraordinary commitment for us to make during a disappointing period, but it's the kind of commitment more companies are going to have to start making.

Let me give you a specific example. About 25 years ago, we learned that the Naval Ordnance Laboratories were experimenting with metals that shrunk with incredibly high force when heated. We were in heat-shrinkable plastics, so we thought this was something we should know about. We started some research. We developed a metal coupling to join hydraulic lines for the F-14 fighter, and the Navy bought it in the second year we had the technology. So we continued the research and made major investments. We kept pushing to get manufacturing costs down. We searched for markets in which these shape-memory alloys could have explosive growth.

Last year, for the first time, we made money on that technology. We stayed with it for more than two decades. We are without question the world's pioneer. We have patents coming out of our ears. After 25 years, shape-memory alloys are on the verge of becoming a big and profitable business. And believe me, we are going to stick with that technology.

But you know the corporate lament: Wall Street won't let us make the investments we know we have to make to stay competitive.

Wall Street does apply pressure; Raychem's market value dropped by 10% in one day last year when we reported disappointing quarterly results. But the analysts aren't totally unreasonable. Our fiber-optics subsidiary, which is one of the most exciting new ventures in the company, is a good example. We started exploring the fiber-optics area more than ten years ago. After we worked with the technology for a few years and made some technical discoveries, we began to see what was possible. We concluded it would take several hundred million dollars to bring the technology to market and make it profitable. So far it's taken $150 million to get Raynet on its feet, and we haven't made the first sale yet.

Wall Street was shocked when we told the analysts about Raynet. We had been secretly working on the technology for years so the competition couldn't find out. Wall Street is still nervous. But the more it learns about our system and the potential markets, the more comfortable it gets. We've also tried to be smart about the financing. We brought in BellSouth as a partner to share some of the costs. And we break out Raynet's financials so the analysts can evaluate our existing businesses on a stand-alone basis.

Sure, it takes some courage to tell Wall Street, "Dammit, I'm going to spend a couple more percentage points of revenues on R&D and let my profits go down. But I'm going to show you how over a period of time that investment is going to pay off." That's not an easy story to sell. But it is sellable—especially if you have a track record of effective technology innovation.

Based on our conversation, we might identify the following principles of innovation: necessity is the mother of invention. Invention is 1% inspiration and 99% perspiration. Possession is nine-tenths of the law. Is the secret to innovation rediscovering old truths we somehow forgot?

Not quite. There are at least three new forces today. First, intellectual property is absolutely key. We are always driving for an ironclad proprietary position in all our products around the world. The ability of companies from other countries to copy important developments has increased so much that there's no way for this society, with our high standard of living, to compete against societies with lower standards of living unless we have protected, proprietary positions. So we make aggressive use of intellectual property laws and work as hard as we can to get the rest of the world to adopt effective protections.

Second, technology is becoming more complex and interdependent. To practice pioneering innovation, you must develop a critical mass of many different skills. If you're a small company, you better restrict yourself to one core technology in which you can do this. If you're a big company, you better take advantage of your technology scale and scope. You can't make that assumption anymore. You have to use your leadership position to push the frontiers of the technology, or you won't be a leader for long.

What's the third difference?

Innovation is a global game—both on the supply side and on the demand side. Raychem's most innovative lab is our telecommunications lab in Belgium. It's a relatively small facility, but it's a melting pot of scientists and engineers from Belgium, America, England, France, and Germany. I can predict with a good deal of accuracy how a technologist brought up in the Flemish region of Belgium will approach a particular problem. I can tell you how a French engineer might approach that same problem. You have to create an organization that can mix and match all of its skills around the globe.

On the demand side, you can't leave a technology window open in another geographical marketplace. You have to fight foreign competition before it starts. Twenty years ago, MITI [Japan's Ministry of International Trade and Industry] targeted radiation chemistry as one of its industries of the future. MITI supported a lab in Osaka and tried to get the technology off the ground. Today there are 30 Japanese companies with radiation-processing technology, but together they probably have only 20% of our business. Why? Because we took the threat seriously; we refused to license our technology. We also built a business in Japan so that Japanese companies couldn't get a safe haven in which to charge high prices, grow their businesses, and then give us trouble around the world. If you want to lead with a new technology, you have to lead everywhere.

Can any company be innovative?

Every company is innovative or else it isn't successful. It's just a question of degree. The essence of innovation is discovering what your organization is uniquely good at—what special capabilities you possess—and taking advantage of those capabilities to build products or deliver services that are better than anyone else's. Every company has unique strengths. Success comes from leveraging those strengths in the market.

4
Championing Change:
An Interview With Bell Atlantic's CEO
Raymond Smith

Rosabeth Moss Kanter

Competing in the telecommunications industry is increasingly a world game. Rapid scientific advances are increasing communications speed and blurring the distinction between information technologies and communication technologies—computer companies are in the communications business, and telephone companies are selling systems integration. The old-fashioned Phone Company—once a monopoly in the United States and a government ministry elsewhere—is now subject to forces of competition, through changing regulation or privatization.

Few industries as old have been transformed so dramatically in such a short time, and further transformations are on the horizon. The U.S. edge in the telecommunications sector may well depend on the skill with which change—human, organizational, and technological—is managed.

Bell Atlantic Corporation was formed in 1983, in preparation for the breakup of the Bell System telephone monopoly on January 1, 1984. It is one of seven U.S. regional telecommunications holding companies (sometimes called "baby Bells") created when AT&T was required by judicial decree to divest its local telephone operations, ushering in the era of greater competition.

Bell Atlantic began with a charter to provide local telephone service in six mid-Atlantic states and the District of Columbia. By 1990, Bell Atlantic was introducing new products and services at a rapid clip, starting ventures and forming alliances throughout the

world, and pursuing leadership in the information technology industry of the future. The corporation reported 1989 earnings of
over $1 billion on revenues of $11.4 billion, with 76% of its revenues
from its regulated local telephone business.

Bell Atlantic's vision centers around the creation of the "Intelligent Network," a computer-driven network capable of transmitting
audio, video, and data signals through speedy fiber-optic lines.
Calling itself the world's most efficient telephone company, Bell
Atlantic today has the lowest costs among the regional firms. It
provides telephone service over 17 million access lines—more lines
than any other baby Bell.

Raymond Smith, 53, became Bell Atlantic's CEO in January 1989,
adding the responsibilities of chairman of the board in July 1989.
Earlier in his career, he managed operations, regulatory affairs,
engineering, and finance for AT&T, rising to the presidencies of
the Pennsylvania and Delaware companies, positions he held when
Bell Atlantic was formed. A year after Bell Atlantic's inception, he
moved to the corporate team as vice chairman and chief financial
officer (1985 to 1987) and then president and chief operating officer
(1988). He worked closely with his predecessor Thomas Bolger to
shape the business concept and to eliminate vestiges of the traditionally complacent, monopolistic mind-set known as having "Bell-
shaped heads."

Mr. Smith spoke with HBR Editor and Class of 1960 Harvard
Business School Professor Rosabeth Moss Kanter about the CEO's
role in transforming a monopolistic, bureaucratic corporation into
one that is both efficient and entrepreneurial.

*HBR: How did you view the state of your business when you became
Bell Atlantic's chief executive?*

Raymond Smith: I saw that the way we had been managing all of
these years was going to have to change. The problem was clear.
The intrinsic growth of the core business would not sustain the
company in the competitive global economy of the twenty-first
century.

The difficulty of addressing our basic business problem was
complicated by competition on one side and regulation on the other.
Even our 3% projected growth rate was subject to considerable,
well-financed competition in the most profitable lines. As a regulated company, we owed a subsidy to the local telephone rate-

payers, so we were limited in what we could earn in the core business. And the legislation and judicial decree that broke up the Bell System restricted the kinds of businesses we could enter. For example, the Cable Act of 1984 kept Bell Atlantic from competing in the cable television business in our region.

How did you think the company could increase its rate of growth in revenues and earnings?

We identified five initial strategies. Four of them would sound familiar to many businesses: improved efficiency; substantially improved marketing to protect market share; new products and services; and entirely new businesses operating outside of our territory and outside of the United States.

The fifth strategy was one we had to work on right away. It involved regulatory reform that we called "incentive regulation" to allow us to benefit from our own initiatives while protecting the telephone rate-payers. We worked intensively with regulators and crafted social contracts with consumer groups and those most affected by telephone rates, such as senior citizens and people with disabilities.

With incentive regulation accomplished, we could concentrate on the business growth strategies. But none of our strategies could be achieved with the company culture in place after the breakup. So I had to focus on the culture first.

What was wrong with the culture?

The company had grown out of a long-standing monopoly, with the centralized organizational structure and culture of a monopoly. In the old Bell System culture, no operating company could introduce a product of its own. The way a small work center in a small town in Pennsylvania would operate was mandated by the central staff. There was no strategic planning, no product development, no long-range planning in the operating companies. It was all centralized at AT&T.

What was the consequence of that?

The operating companies had an implementation mentality. They did not understand the initiative, innovation, risks, and accountability necessary to meet our business goals. Managers were held accountable for implementation of a process or practice exactly as it was written, not for the end result. Managers simply could not imagine rewriting a process even if they knew a better one. They were maintenance managers, not business managers.

When I told those same managers that we wanted improved marketing, new products, and new business, it was a mental shock. We had no experience to draw on. And the ways we were accustomed to operating impeded our ability to achieve our goals.

How so?

Cross-departmental competition raised costs and prevented new initiatives. This problem was a consequence of our heritage.

The old Bell System was like a great football team with the best athletes and the best equipment. Every Saturday morning, we'd run up and down the football field and win 100 to 0 because there was no one on the other side of the line of scrimmage; we were a monopoly. Being human, the football players found their competition inside the team. This sometimes resulted in lowest common denominator solutions and substantial inefficiency. Despite dedication and hard work, it often took more resources to get things done than were ever really needed.

The conventions of behavior grew out of cross-departmental competition and were very parochial. There was no true unifying concept to rally around. I represented my department, you represented your department, and we behaved as if we were opposing lawyers or political opponents.

When did you begin to see that this kind of behavior had to change?

In the early 1980s, when we began to see real competition. Tom Bolger, my predecessor as CEO, and I agreed that we needed a new culture to support our business strategies.

Where did you start?

We started by articulating the values of the corporation. I was personally involved, with another officer, in the design of seminars

We have the obligation to:

Participate in the development of the values, purpose, goals, strategies, and corporate positions of Bell Atlantic and communicate our endorsement to all of our employees.

Provide vigorous input into corporate decisions while maintaining a clear focus on Bell Atlantic's interests.

Work diligently to see that decisions important to Bell Atlantic are made in a timely fashion.

Dissent or escalate problems or decisions when we believe Bell Atlantic's interests are not being served but enthusiastically support the final decision once it has been made.

Obtain the necessary information to communicate Bell Atlantic's values, mission, goals, strategies, and corporate positions to all of our constituents.

Define our roles and manage our organizations in a manner that will support the goals of Bell Atlantic while meeting our local obligations to employees, customers, and communities.

Support and encourage local proprietorship, pride, and accountability within the framework of Bell Atlantic's goals and objectives.

Look beyond our groups or companies to encourage teamwork, and integration among the Bell Atlantic family of companies.

Encourage innovation within our organizations and share the benefits of that innovation with other Bell Atlantic units.

Find creative solutions to the inevitable disputes that arise from sharing resources among the various Bell Atlantic groups.

Avoid short-term expediencies that will be detrimental to Bell Atlantic's long-term strategies and objectives.

Create an environment for individual initiative, growth, and development.

In brief, Bell Atlantic executives are the role models of the corporation, obliged to demonstrate constructive teamwork and be exemplary representatives. We lead the planners, strategists and implementers of the Bell Atlantic plan. With our employees, we show the Bell Atlantic Way.

We made quality a corporate imperative in our 1989 strategic plan, designing a Quality Improvement Process using the Baldrige

in which 1,400 managers spent half a week to think through
values and state them clearly. At the seminars, a draft was han
out for discussion. These managers were actively engaged in edi
the document word by word. New categories were suggested; ev
tually, "teamwork" became "respect and trust." I attended virtu;
every seminar and met with the participants for five or six ho
a week.

Ultimately, we agreed on five values: integrity, respect and tru;
excellence, individual fulfillment, and profitable growth, with
paragraph of description explaining each.

*What happened when the sessions were completed and the state-
ment of values was published?*

Not enough! It became very apparent to me and to the managers
involved that we needed to move from general statements of values
to concrete behaviors and work practices, or what we called the
"conventions" of day-to-day business life. So when I became CEO,
I announced a ten-year transition to a new way of working together.

*Every corporation today is full of rhetoric like "it's time to change"
or "we need a new way" or "we want to get rid of bureaucracy."
What did you do to show people that you meant it?*

One of the first steps I took was to engage the senior officers in
a serious examination of our obligations to the corporation. I personally prepared a list of 12 specific guidelines (see Exhibit I). In
a series of day-long meetings, I suggested to each of the top 50
people in Bell Atlantic that they had broad corporate obligations
that went beyond their departmental responsibilities. There were
arguments and debates about the obligations, but in the end they
stood. It took a year to get the required understanding and commitment.

Exhibit I.   The Obligations of Leadership

As Bell Atlantic executives, we have the special obligation to provide
an ethical leadership that goes beyond our departmental or subsidiary
goals.

Award criteria and starting our own Quality Institute. We developed an organized program of internal communications for all employees outlining our obligations to each other, the opportunities ahead, and the need and reasons for change. We called this the Bell Atlantic Way.

What is the Bell Atlantic Way, and why did you think you needed it?

Simply stated, the Bell Atlantic Way is an organized, participative method of working together that allows us to get the most out of our own efforts and maximize our contribution to team goals. The Bell Atlantic Way includes the conventions of daily behavior subscribed to by all of us.

In a large business, the most important determinant of success is the effectiveness of millions of day-to-day interactions between human beings. If those contacts are contentious, turf-oriented, and parochial, the company will flounder, bureaucracies will grow, and internal competition will be rampant. But when employees behave in accountable, team-oriented, and collegial ways, it dramatically improves group effectiveness.

The Bell Atlantic Way isn't limited to a list of dos and don'ts, but it does seem to boil down to a few specific behaviors. For example, the plaque on my desk says, "Be Here Now." That just means that it's important that I listen and be totally involved in any discussion we may have. I'm not looking over my shoulder. I'm not taking phone calls. I'm not doodling or having side conversations while you are making a presentation.

In such a large corporation, how do you get people to operate by these codes of behavior?

With the help of consultants, we designed forums to introduce the Bell Atlantic Way to 20,000 managers. The officer group, roughly 50 people, attended first. Then the officers acted as executives-in-residence at forums for the rest of the managers and supervisors. Most of us have been through the sessions two or three times.

We teach the conventions, we don't just talk about them. Each one is impressed on forum participants in experiential exercises that help us examine ourselves and remind us of our obligations to each other. And our responsibilities don't stop at the end of the forum. I'm spending a great deal of my own time in the field meeting with employees and talking about the Bell Atlantic Way. Each of the officers has developed departmental programs of reinforcement and support back on the job.

Why is it important for you and the other officers to spend scarce executive time on this, involving yourselves in a personal way?

We must ourselves model what we are asking others to do. We call this "the shadow of the leader." We are asking people to change their behavior, to accept a new set of conventions for working together. And I try to provide reinforcement in every way I can. For example, I always wear my Quality button to impress colleagues with my rabid dedication. It serves to remind us that we have a very special obligation to support those who are supporting the corporation.

It took about a year for top management to internalize the concepts of this change, to recognize it, and to begin to support it fully. Now changes have started to accelerate. We're seeing as much change every three months as we used to see in three years.

What are some tangible signs of change?

The language is changing. The decision process is changing. People are becoming more accountable, more team-oriented, and more effective. For example, our budget process is no longer bitter and contentious. It's still painful and always difficult, but it's much less of a hassle and never personal.

There has been remarkable improvement among the top 400 people of the company who decide on budgets, projects, priorities, and resource allocation. As corny as it may seem, managers will now open sessions saying, "We've got to break the squares today," referring to one of the Bell Atlantic Way games—meaning we've got to compromise here, break out of thinking about only our own territories. We may know that the corporation has to reduce budgets; so we all must give something up for the good of the whole company.

In the old culture, if I contributed resources for the good of the corporation, I'd lose the support of my own group. Now it is no longer acceptable for someone to say, "I've done my bit. I've met my goal. I'll sit back until you meet yours." It's not acceptable to complain to third parties about the boss or the company or some other department. Someone who does that is likely to be asked, "What did they say when you told them?" One manager said that bitch sessions used to be the social event of the week, but now they're no fun. We expect people to accept accountability for results.

How do you get accountability?

We had to make sure that our reward system encouraged people to focus on results consistent with larger business goals. The first step was to base compensation on corporate and team results as well as individual results. Today the corporate performance award is a much higher percentage of compensation than it was in the past. It used to be zero—or such a tiny percentage that it never meant anything. Now the award has a long-term as well as a short-term component for a growing percentage of managers, and it is worth more than a few bucks. It's also flexible; the definition of team can include local groups as well as the whole corporation.

A significant factor in an individual's performance evaluation is whether they have also contributed to the overall team goals. Our team goals include customer service. We look at the customers' attitudes through telephone surveys—whether or not they feel we are conforming to their requirements 100% of the time. We must reach a minimum level of performance on customer service measures before there are any corporate incentive awards.

Our reward and appraisal system is not perfect, but at least it is getting better. However, even the best evaluation system will not produce the desired behavior unless people understand our business problem and our strategies.

Do your employees get this basic business information?

Now they do, but that was not always the case. As I traveled throughout our company before becoming CEO, I found that very few people really knew what we were trying to do as a company. Sometimes they understood the departmental objectives, and certainly they knew their own objectives, but most people had no idea how to put their day-to-day work life into a corporate context. Actions of the corporation such as the purchase of a new business or the consolidation of an operations center were often a mystery.

How did you clear up the mystery?

My senior officers and I wrote out what we thought was the basic business problem we were trying to solve. We added the specific strategies to solve it, the departmental goals, and finally the individual objectives that were the employees' contributions to the goals. Then we shared it with everyone.

This was somewhat new. The notion of intellectually engaging all of our employees in the solution of the basic business problem was so different from the past that we had to communicate clearly and personally. So we asked the 400 top people in the company, the key managers and communicators, to understand the overall strategy totally and fully, internalize it, and go forth and share it with others. There was a brief hiccup in the company while this idea was absorbed, but then it took off.

You were also giving top managers a big kick in the pants. You were arousing them to action. Shouldn't they have known the strategy and been communicating it all along?

I don't think of it that way. From my first day on the job, I should have made sure that we were all on the same wavelength. I didn't realize that everyone wasn't behaving like a CEO and thinking about the basic corporate problem all day long. When 99% of someone's efforts are engaged in getting a departmental job done, the broad goals of the corporation begin to fade if they are not constantly reinforced. As the head coach and teacher, I hadn't really taught the game plan or the course well enough. So I went on the stump, enlisted the aid of a number of others and spread the word.

Now the top 400 certainly know our business problem. They know our purpose, vision, and strategies, and how they fit together. Because the top 400 talk about this, thousands of other Bell Atlantic employees know it too. They can translate their personal and departmental objectives to those of the company. This makes it easier to deal with the tough realities we face.

What are the tough realities?

We had to eliminate jobs to get our costs in line and reduce wasteful bureaucracy. This is one of the biggest culture shocks we faced. People used to join a Bell System company with the expectation that they'd be taken care of from cradle to grave.

We've tried to do two things to cushion the blow. The first is to level with people. We tell them about the problems in the United States—the troubled companies and the layoffs, plant closings, and ruined careers that come from complacency. We explain that this is the way life is in a competitive world. Wishful thinking won't bring back the old world of no change and total security.

In U.S. business today, the understanding of the real world is vital to survival. In our industry, for example, we have a choice of having a larger number of low-paid employees who will be subject to layoffs, or we can have a smaller group of well-paid, efficient employees with security obtained through hard work and providing customers with more value than they can get elsewhere.

The second thing we do is to try to make stressful changes like downsizing in a participative manner. We eliminated one whole level of management, and we did it by involving the employees in the decision. We had no overall template for the organization, the way the Bell System did in the past. We allowed each organization to eliminate the level it wanted the way it felt was appropriate. After all, almost any organization will succeed if the people feel empowered, are recognized for what they do, and understand the purpose of their jobs.

The idea for this initiative came from New Jersey Bell. The officers thought they could run the business more efficiently if they eliminated a management level, but they wanted to leave the choice of which level to the departments. The departments examined the situation and made the right decision. It worked so well, we made this a Bell Atlantic-wide effort. People in jobs that were about to be eliminated participated in the discussions. Naturally, they were not enthusiastic about cutting their own jobs, so in practice the decision was left to the boss. Still, the "soft" aspects of the organizational change—appreciation, recognition, sharing—were given as much importance as the hard side of reducing the head count.

Was work eliminated along with the level? The criticism of down-sizing in many companies is that the people are gone, but the work remains.

Unfortunately, that's true. We saw no way to eliminate all the work first. We reluctantly concluded that we had to reduce the force and then empower the people to eliminate the rest of the work.

On the first day of the new organization, some groups had only eight people to do the work load of ten. But the individual departments were empowered to create the organization they thought would be most efficient. They worked hard to eliminate those activities that were least important. That sort of prioritizing can't be done by some superstaff.

What made you believe that people who had been accustomed to following central mandates would be effective at setting priorities?

People were able to do this because of what they learned from the Bell Atlantic Way. An important part of change is moving from a culture in which people are handed procedures to follow mindlessly to one that helps them make tough choices. This is a difficult process and we're still involved in it. It requires guts and a lot of honest communication.

In the seminars, we play a game with poker chips. The blue chips are valuable; the white chips are practically worthless. Participants learn that it is vital to understand priorities and know what those priorities are based on, such as the goals of the corporation and not just the goals of the subgroup. The blue chips mean First Things First—priorities. I carry one in my wallet as a reminder.

How do people feel about being involved in a tough restructuring process?

In our regular employee survey, workers cited our downsizing as one reason for improved morale. They told us that although resources are very tight, Bell Atlantic is now a much better place to work. They said since some of the disaffected, cynical people have left, there is much less time for bureaucracy.

What else are you doing to reduce bureaucracy?

We are determined to revolutionize staff support, to convert a bureaucratic roadblock into an entrepreneurial force.

Large staffs that are not subject to bottom-line pressure tend to grow and produce services that may be neither wanted nor required, and their allegiances generally lean toward their professional positions rather than toward their clients. We had to do something to change this.

Three years ago, when I was vice chairman and the staffs reported to me, I decided to place the control of discretionary staff and support expenditures in the hands of those people who were paying for them, that is, the profit centers, the bottom-line groups. We also had to eliminate duplicate staff groups at corporate headquarters and in the operating companies.

Our approach was to create small profit centers within the staff groups, called client service groups or CSGs. For example, the training department became the Training and Educational Services CSG. The accounting department formed the Accounting Operations CSG.

How do the client service groups work?

They sell their services both to the corporate headquarters and to the operating companies. Each year, CSGs develop a budget and an array of products or services based on what Bell Atlantic clients have committed to fund, plus approved amounts for ad hoc or unanticipated business. They have to meet market tests, providing the same value as any outside organization. The CSGs' total annual expenses must equal anticipated revenues (billing credits) from customers. The goal is to break even.

CSGs market their services continuously through items in internal publications, CSG newsletters and brochures, 800-number hotlines, and exhibits at trade shows. The Training and Educational Services CSG publishes a 370-page catalog of offerings. The Information Systems Professional Services CSG heralds new software, programming possibilities, and applications in a regular newsletter.

CSG account managers stay in touch with customers to learn about their needs, answer their questions, facilitate provision of services, and forecast demand. Monthly bills from the CSGs to customers itemize specific services and costs in detail, helping clients to understand and control these costs.

The profit-center customers have to follow a few simple rules. They must give the client service group an opportunity to bid on a project, formally or informally. If the internal organization wins the bid, they use the internal organization. If an outside company wins, they can use the outside firm. But they cannot create their own media group or their own business research group. We want no internal competition.

What happened when you introduced this major structural change?

First of all, it was believed that the client service groups wouldn't work. In some quarters it was considered a dingbat idea that would go away. Still, the first year got off to a pretty good start.

The second year brought a budget crunch and nearly destroyed the process. The budgets of the client service groups were cut by the central financial staffs without the clients' agreement. This is absolutely counter to the rules we devised. It wasn't done surreptitiously, just out of misunderstanding, but it happened. The new groups called foul, and we did some damage control to restore their budgets. There were also cases in which individual departments tried to form their own support groups under different labels, under different names.

In the third year, there is no question that the client service groups are working.

What results are you getting?

Market pressures are keeping the client service groups at a reasonable level. Expenditures for discretionary staff services are generally flat, while other corporate expenses have gone up. Because of pent-up demand, some CSGs have seen their budgets increase; for example, internal clients wanted more operations support programming. But the Business Research CSG encountered a substantial decline.

The most important fact is that spending for discretionary staff support activities is now controlled by the clients. That's changed the whole nature of staff groups. Not everyone is totally comfortable with this yet; it is much more fun to set a budget based on your professional opinion and let other people pay for it than to compete for resources. The idea is so different that it is very tender and will require careful cultivation.

I see great progress in attitudes and behavior. We put on one of the largest technical expositions in the United States to let our vendors like AT&T, IBM, and Siemens show us their stuff. Last year as I was walking through it, I was astonished to see the Medical CSG selling its services. I turned the corner, and there was another client service group hawking its wares. Both were selling back to their own company as vigorously as any vendor.

Because they have to do the work of selling their services to their clients and all the additional accounting, the groups are learning to be business managers. They are slowly becoming more entre-preneurial.

Are other people at Bell Atlantic acquiring entrepreneurial skills?

We are committed to identifying potential corporate entrepre-neurs, training them, and developing their ideas into new busi-nesses. We do this primarily through our Champion program (see Exhibit II).

The Champion program arose from one of our companies, Ches-apeake & Potomac Telephone, and we spread it across the whole corporation in 1989. The program provides seed money, guidance, and training to potential entrepreneurs who propose new products and services. People at any level can make proposals. If projects are accepted, their proposers can run them. And they can invest a portion of their wages in the project, in exchange for the prospect of a piece of the action when their product has been marketed.

Are you getting results?

In the first year, 36 Champions were accepted into the program. In 1989, 39 were added. By late 1990, there were about 33 products and services in the pipeline, several of them near the commercial-ization stage. Projects include *Creative Connections,* a line of de-signer phone jacks; *Emerg-Alert,* prerecorded emergency messages targeted to latchkey children and the elderly; *CommGuard,* a pack-age of backup phone services in case of a system breakdown; local usage information services for all lines in a Centrex system; and a do-not-disturb service.

Exhibit II.   Championing New Business Ideas

Bell Atlantic's internal entrepreneurship program, Champion, develops profitable new products and services based on employee ideas and efforts. The program encourages employees to develop skills they might not use in their regular jobs, especially entrepreneurial, risk-taking, market-driven behavior.

Employees submit revenue-producing ideas to the Champion program staff of the Bell Atlantic Intrapreneurship Division in Maryland. They complete a self-selection process to determine their skills, motivation, and enthusiasm. Supervisors, professionals, and middle managers are eligible.

If the ideas are accepted, the newly minted Champions may devote five hours per week of company time to the project (and any amount of their own time). They are trained in market analysis and entrepreneurial techniques and given budgets of up to $1,000 each to test the marketability of their ideas.

After three months, Champions submit "business opportunity assessments" of their ideas to a committee of selected senior managers. Champions receive awards of up to $1,000 if they have done thorough marketing studies.

If the ideas pass the screening stage, Champions are loaned to the New Business Development Group for six months, where they are trained in how to develop a business case for their proposed products. Then they conduct trials to determine if the proposed products have market potential.

If the products are introduced on the market, a business team is formed. Champions may become project managers for up to three years, leaving their previous jobs.

Champions may invest 10% of their base salaries in the product for three years, receiving 5% of the product's net revenue for those years instead of individual performance awards. At the end of this period, Champions move on to other assignments.

Champion's most noteworthy success is *Thinx,* new software so innovative that its creator, Jack Coppley, was one of five finalists for *Discover* magazine's award honoring engineers and scientists making technological breakthroughs. *Thinx* is an intelligent graphics program integrating data with images to help users explore relationships visually and apply data or calculations automatically.

Jack learned about Champion when he attended a meeting introducing it in 1988. At that time, he was a budget manager for the network services staff, but he was intrigued by the opportunity Champion represented. Some of Jack's initial ideas were rejected, but his software idea was warmly received.

After going through the steps to test the idea and develop the business plan, Jack became head of a 20-member team that worked out software glitches, chose the *Thinx* name, and designed packaging. The product was unveiled at Comdex, a large trade show, in November 1989. Jack came home with triple the number of customer leads he had anticipated. In September 1990, *Thinx* hit the market and received rave reviews.

Champion has now become an actual revenue source in our strategic planning process. That's the ultimate testimony of importance in a corporation—a business plan with dollars of investment and targeted returns. In five years, we expect annual revenues of over $100 million from Champion projects. My question when I first saw the 1995 projection was, "Is this hope or smoke?" I was told that the figure was conservatively stated!

There are potentially thousands of great, innovative ideas in a company our size. The Champion program encourages people to take responsibility for acting on them.

How do the internal cultural and operational changes you've described translate into advantage in the marketplace?

We were always an efficient company, but our new approaches are breaking new ground. Our management process provides another major differentiation factor in world markets. When you match our track record of efficiency and quality service with a state-of-the-art understanding of how to manage large, technologically complex organizations, you've got a terrific package.

The most efficient communications networks in the world don't come from just modern switching machines but from computer operating systems and skilled technicians that operate them—all working in an empowered, accountable organization.

This forms an excellent launching pad for new businesses. Our systems-integration business, for example, is a natural evolution of that theme. It began as a computer-maintenance business with

relatively low margins. But it has evolved into the largest independent field-service business in the country, adding products and
services and moving up the value chain to application software,
disaster recovery, system operation, consulting, and so on.

*You have a very strong vision for what the information system
linking the world will be in the future.*

It's probably the most important vision in our corporation. I think
it is the major contribution that Bell Atlantic will make to the
United States. We see the Intelligent Network changing not just
our company but changing civilization.

The Intelligent Network means virtually unlimited memory and
logic, instantaneous transport to anywhere in the world, providing
intellectual linkages between human beings. These links are equivalent, in my mind, to the revolution of the printing press or perhaps
even writing or speech. In the near future, a telephone conversation
could start in English at one end and be heard in French or Japanese at the other. Information will eventually go to wherever a
person is—at home, at work, in a car, or strolling in the park.

What steps are you taking to realize this vision?

We are building the Intelligent Network for the service area in
the Bell Atlantic regulated territory. We have introduced 30 new
technology-based services, more than any other regional company.
We are leading in deploying the nervous system of the Intelligent
Network, Signaling System 7. We've added massive computer capacity and will have a million miles of fiber-optics transport
throughout the territory in the next few years. The computers hold
extensive database information about customer needs and wants.
Fiber optics allow a signal to travel 10,000 times faster than copper
wire.

By being focused in the transport and use of information, we
realized the capabilities of the Intelligent Network. Our densely
populated territory allowed us to visualize and build these kinds
of links easily. We concluded, perhaps before others, that this
network architecture was a revolutionary way to provide intelligence. We coined the term "Intelligent Network" and began to sell
it to our counterparts. The Intelligent Network is a new notion that

came out of our search for distinction, our search for a future. The whole world has now accepted it.

How is Bell Atlantic gaining the resources and capability to realize the Intelligent Network vision worldwide?

We recognized very early on that we needed strategic alliances. We've formed partnerships with Siemens, IBM, NTI, and others, including big companies, small companies, and government ministries (see Exhibit III).

Partnering is a very serious business in Bell Atlantic. Some companies seek strategic alliances because it seems like a good idea in theory or it looks good to be associated with prestigious partners. But often the overall goal of the alliance is lost in the process. Substantial investments are made by large corporations, but little top management attention is given thereafter. Predictably, the local bureaucracy sets up prickly barriers and mousetraps to prove that the new joint venture partner doesn't really understand the business and is an enemy, not a friend.

Exhibit III.   Bell Atlantic Reaches Out: Emerging World Alliances

---

North America[1]
California
    Sun Microsystems (1990)
        workstation support, Eastern regions
Illinois
    RR Donnelley (1988)
        directory graphics joint venture
Massachusetts
    Digital Equipment Corporation (1990)
        expert system sales
Connecticut
    Deloitte & Touche (1990)
        expert systems development
Virginia
    American Management Systems (1989)
        systems integration joint venture

Exhibit III.   (continued)
Europe
Belgium
  Bell Atlantic-Europe headquarters (1989)
France
  CGI Informatique (1990)
    U.S. Local Area Network support with CGI-USA
Spain
  Telefonica (1988)
    cooperative marketing, installation of operating support
    system
Germany
  Siemans and IBM (1987)
    Intelligent Network product/market study
Czechoslovakia
  Czech & Slovak Posts & Telecommunications Ministry and US
  West (1990)
    cellular mobile networks and packet data networks
Norway
  Norvans (1990)
    bid for secondary cellular licenses
Italy
  Olivetti (1990)
    third-party computer maintenance; installation of operating
    support system
Netherlands
  PTT Telecom (1988)
    installation of operating support system; bid for cellular
    license

Asia
Korea
  Korean Telecommunications Authority (1990)
    cooperative development activities
Taiwan
  Directorate General of Telecommunications (1990)
    Agreement to join in a broad range of activities

South Pacific
New Zealand
  Freightways, Fay Richwhite, Ameritech (1990)
    New Zealand Telecom purchase

[1] Bell Atlantic's traditional U.S. telephone district included New Jersey, Pennsylvania, Delaware, Maryland, Washington, D.C., Virginia, West Virginia.

We can't afford to make that mistake because alliances are too vital for our growth plans, especially outside of the United States. The international field almost always calls for the formation of consortia because of the scale of investment or the preference of governments for local participation. We had to have partners in every one of our investments.

To make sure we are working with our partners effectively and building on their capabilities, we have had to develop a culture of tolerance, listening, and intellectual curiosity, not intellectual arrogance.

How did you develop that culture?

Once again, we turned to the Bell Atlantic Way. A year or so ago, we gathered together 75 people involved in our international business, from lawyers to salespeople to the head of the international business unit. We included all the officers and me.

We went through experiential training, exploring attitudes, and making behavioral commitments. We identified the real purpose of international expansion, which was not to get things "on the board" or "to score" but to produce solutions to the business problem. We wanted long-term investments in our field that would have acceptable risk profiles and higher growth rates than we had in our core business. We worked on how individuals could commit themselves to assist the new effort, to produce real results, not binders, reports, or smoky projections.

In the past, those kinds of understandings were attempted through a memo or at best a brief meeting. No real interaction, no joint understanding, no commitment, no internalization. New activities were launched without any serious preparation.

In your quest for a more entrepreneurial culture, have you had any personal setbacks?

My biggest personal setback was self-inflicted. In my first year as CEO, I was intensely frustrated because people didn't immediately understand my notions of empowerment, accountability, and teamwork. I finally learned to be less impatient.

How did you come to change your own behavior?

A lot of the impatience was coached out of me. One of the aspects of the Bell Atlantic Way is that everyone has an internal coach; mine is Anton Campanella, our president. Somebody said the reason Campy and I got each other as coaches is that no one else wanted us. There is a certain amount of truth to that.

Coaching is not seen as the least bit corny or unusual in our company. Once a week one of us will ask, "Can I coach you on something?" In the past, I've never been able to do that comfortably. I was never able to do it without it being unnecessarily evasive on the one hand or unnecessarily unpleasant on the other. Now the process is acceptable. It is group sanctioned. It is the way we've decided we're going to work together.

I really know we're doing well when I walk into a room of people and they are discussing a project with tremendous excitement, a project that is going to move our corporation ahead significantly, and I've never heard of it. That is a wonderful feeling.

PART
V

The Politics of Leadership

1
Yasuhiro Nakasone:
The Statesman as CEO

Alan M. Webber

In 1982, Yasuhiro Nakasone became prime minister of Japan, capping a political career that had begun in 1947 with his election to the House of Representatives. In the intervening years, Mr. Nakasone held an impressive array of offices within the Japanese government, including minister of state, director general of science and technology; minister of transport; minister of state, director general of the Defense Agency; minister of international trade and industry; and minister of state, director general of the Administrative Management Agency. During this period, Mr. Nakasone also held a succession of increasingly powerful and important positions within Japan's ruling Liberal Democratic party.

His term as prime minister was marked by Japan's significant emergence on the international scene and redirection internally—shifts that were not only attributable to Mr. Nakasone's personal leadership but also embodied in his own political style. Mr. Nakasone was the first Japanese prime minister to participate aggressively and forcefully at the annual economic summit meetings of the seven leading Western nations, emphatically announcing Japan's arrival as the world's emerging economic power.

He also confronted the challenges of rising trade friction between Japan and the United States during his administration and relied on his personal relationship with President Ronald Reagan—the "Ron-Yasu" relationship—to resolve these tensions. Overall, Mr. Nakasone expressed the view that Japan should "internationalize" in accordance with its increasing economic power. Domestically, Mr. Nakasone spearheaded administrative reform of the government—privatizing some government-held operations and reducing the size and scope of the bureaucracy. He also launched efforts within Japan to shift the economy from export-led growth to growth through domestic demand.

Since leaving office, Mr. Nakasone has remained a powerful and active figure in Japanese politics; he recently established the International Institute for Global Peace, a research foundation focusing on international security issues in politics and economics.

This interview was conducted by HBR Managing Editor Alan M. Webber.

HBR: Do you think the United States has reached the peak of its power and is headed for decline?

Yasuhiro Nakasone: No! I am sure that most Americans would disagree with what Professor Kennedy says in his book, *The Rise and Fall of the Great Powers*. From what I hear at various seminars, most researchers also disagree with him. I do, too.

One must appreciate the United States's military strength and its accumulation of scientific technology. People from all over the world go to the United States to live, and they have become an important element in building the United States. The frontier spirit of your country is still very prominent. As a result, intellectual stimulus is prominent, too. Unless these elements disappear, the United States will remain at the top. Japan does not have these elements.

What is Japan's role in the future? Will Japan's economic strength lead to the emergence of a "Pax Nipponica"?

I cannot even think of a "Pax Nipponica." Japan is still immature in many ways.

For example, it has been only 40 years since Japan rebuilt itself from the ruins of World War II. We have had a trade surplus for a short period of only 20 years. The United States is 200 years old. It has been emerging for the past century and has become a gigantic force over the past 50 years. England has been powerful for 200 years. Japan has had only 20 years.

Japan has a historical background of being isolated for a long time. Because of global changes, because of geopolitical and geo-economic reasons, Japan has prospered. However, we are still trying to mature into a fully global or internationalized country. The outlook of Japan's politicians and people is still lagging somewhat behind the United States and England. Politics must take the lead, and that was the commitment I made as prime minister.

How, then, would you describe the U.S.-Japan relationship?

Before the 1983 Williamsburg summit, I told President Reagan, "You be the pitcher, I'll be the catcher." I also told him, "But once in a while, the pitcher must listen to the catcher's good advice." This is the kind of relationship I have in mind. This is the relationship I believe will continue for the foreseeable future.

Nevertheless, we see continuing stress in the relationship between the United States and Japan. The two countries are becoming not only closer allies but also tougher competitors. When you were prime minister, how did you manage the conflicts in this relationship?

One of the features of American democracy is that you tend to be emotional. After some time you become cool, and introspection follows. It's this kind of flexibility that is your country's best feature. But when you become emotional, we sometimes get upset and ask, "Why don't you understand us?"

Therefore, what is most important for Japan-U.S. relations is that there must be mutual trust between the top leaders, between the Prime Minister's office and the White House. That will influence everything below them.

As an example, there was the FSX issue, involving the production of a new fighter plane. The FSX issue was a very complex matter for Japan. But the issue was settled through compromise. I was able to believe and trust President Reagan. That conviction was conveyed to Casper Weinberger and Yuko Kurihara, and then it was transmitted down to the lower operating bureaucracies in both our capitals. If this issue had been handled from down to up, then it definitely would not have worked.

As Japan has grown, the area of contact has become greater. And frictions have also increased. That is inevitable. What is important is the commitment to resolve these frictions through negotiations and meetings and to agree on the means of settlement for such negotiations.

Take the Persian Gulf issue. As you may recall, there was the issue of whether Japan would send mine sweepers. This issue was settled by Japan providing aid and electronic equipment for the Gulf Coast countries.

In regard to trade friction, we had MOSS (Market-Oriented Sector Selective) negotiations. They helped a great deal to alleviate the tension. We talked to each other concerning the automobile-parts industry, for example. In this way, we can agree on the procedure for settlement. Then eventually these frictions are resolved.

Today Japan is financing roughly 30% of the U.S. federal deficit. Should the United States be concerned about its growing dependence on Japan's capital?

The fact that Japan's capital is invested in the United States means that we are committing our future to the United States. It means that we do not have any uncertainty concerning America's future. Europeans must feel the same. The United States has been safer than other places, and this conviction still continues.

If we may, we are concerned that you have not put enough effort into erasing your twin deficits. You are making some efforts, but you are still not very successful. I want you to continue your efforts. This is important advice in view of our commitment to work together.

What about the concern in the United States caused by Japan's growing direct Japanese investment? Do you think this issue poses a threat to the U.S.-Japan relationship?

First, looking at recent statistics, the United Kingdom actually has the largest amount of investment in the United States. Then comes Holland. Japan is third, followed by West Germany. Japan probably stands out because of some unfortunate purchase behavior that hurt general public sentiment. Consequently, when we proceed with such investments, we must be aware of the attitudes and feelings of people. It is not good to buy a historically symbolic building in New York or an established golf club that Americans are proud of or a residential building just to resell it for a profit. We have instructed business leaders to be very careful and aware of this.

Second, the current wave of investment is a result of the high appreciation of the yen, and it is questionable how long this will last.

Third, liberalization of investment is absolutely necessary for the development of the world economy. Such liberalization will smooth out obstacles in international economic relations. For example, Japan's direct investment will help employment in the United States. That is why American governors come to Japan saying, "Bring your company, bring your company!" Quite a few states have set up offices in Japan. I think we should cooperate in this way.

However, I would also like to see investments from the United States coming into Japan. There are good opportunities in Japan, but there is a lack of research and effort on the United States's part. Whether it's Coca-Cola, Kentucky Fried Chicken, or IBM, the ones that have tried have succeeded. The American market is tremendous and self-sufficient; as a result, there is not enough enthusiasm toward outside countries. Investment should be reciprocal.

Given the fact that Japan's investment in the United States actually trails that of England and Holland, do you think the American reaction reflects any racist sentiment?

I don't think there is any racism involved. After all, Americans are cosmopolitan. However, when a newcomer arrives with such force in such a short period, it naturally creates surprise or shock. The British and Dutch have been in the United States for over a century. Their presence has become part of the customs and practices in America. Japan is the newcomer.

You would like to see reciprocal investment, but many American business leaders contend that they cannot invest in Japan as easily as Japanese companies can in the United States. When will it be easy for a U.S. company to buy a Japanese company, for example?

Generally speaking, Japan is just as open as other countries. We conduct our free-market economy and free enterprise impartially. Our markets are as open as those of Europe. Our markets are more open than France's, and we are at the same level as England and

Germany. Unless we keep it this way, Japan will not be able to continue its economic growth.

But Japan also has a history of over 2,000 years; the tradition of old Japan and the new modern society of science and technology coexist. This is one of the distinct features of Japan, a feature we must maintain.

So in Japan, as opposed to in the United States, the capital and management of a company are separated. Shareholders have very little interest in the way a company is run. They entrust the managers on a long-term basis of five to ten years. The managers are well aware of their responsibility. That is the established practice.

The trade union's opinion also weighs strongly. Management is only possible through the joint efforts between the union and the managers. Japanese capitalists don't have as much freedom as those in the United States. There aren't as many products sold in Japan. There are many joint ventures, however. And also many technical tie-ups. This is the difference in socioeconomic climates.

A current issue between the United States and Japan involves the difficulty of managing the distribution system in Japan. Do you agree with many Americans who say that this is a problem?

Criticism of the Japanese distribution system is correct—not 100%, but most of it. Japan has historically been an isolated island with a large population to support, and it has had to distribute domestically. In order to support this population, many steps were created; from wholesalers to retailers there are many layers in between. Now we have too many of these steps. We ourselves are having trouble with this system.

When large-scale supermarkets and department stores try to open in the regional areas, they always meet resistance. The local people and the large-scale store owners discuss this expansion, and the owners must obtain permission before opening their large-scale stores. This is not free competition. This must be changed—it is not in the interest of the consumer. However, we would have to provide an alternative for people to transfer their jobs, which we cannot do all of a sudden. So we are trying to find a way of opening the markets through a "soft landing." For example, we are exploring ideas such as changing these small stores into specialty stores, like boutiques, or joining small stores together to develop large-scale stores by themselves. These kinds of reforms have progressed a great deal.

Most observers in the United States and Japan agree that American companies have had a competitiveness problem. Why? Who is to blame?

United States competitiveness has improved recently; exports are increasing rapidly. During my time in office, however, competition from the United States was falling for many reasons. One is the corporate structure and environment of the United States. The United States has a huge market that can be self-sufficient. So it can buy and sell on its own and be well-off. It is happy enough with its domestic markets.

Forty years ago, the United States held the lead in technology and products. So it didn't have to put much effort into exports. But now Japan and the Newly Industrializing Economies (NIEs) have caught up. Some American corporations, contented with the lead, weren't making much effort. It's not surprising that they should start losing.

As an example, there are very few American businessmen who can speak Japanese. Also, very few of them know about Japanese society. And there is not much market research either. If they cannot sell their products abroad, they tend to blame the overseas market.

But Japan and European countries have small domestic markets—plus they have to worry about earning enough foreign currency. Corporations make an incredible effort to export. They work hard at market research; they work through agents; they make efforts to sell directly; and they have the determination to build competitive products.

There is also the important issue of producing only high-quality products. In the past, we used to hear about the "Monday lemons" that American automobile companies produced—automobiles that would tend to break down early. We learned from such lessons. We were much more elaborate with regard to quality control. We tried very hard to establish a reputation for making products that were free of defects. With all these factors combined, the Japanese worked incredibly hard to produce high-quality, competitive exports.

How much of the competitiveness problem is a result of the macro-economic policies followed in the United States over the past eight years? Did supply-side economics hurt U.S. competitiveness?

There are two sides to supply-side economics. On the one hand, the United States experienced a rapid increase of exports from Japan, the NIEs, and the European Community. The strong dollar acted like a black hole absorbing stars. This resulted in the sudden increase in the U.S. deficit. So supply-side economics clearly hurt the U.S. efforts in competition.

On the other hand, the United States acted like a tractor that pulled along the lagging economies all over the world. And supply-side economics also increased employment in the United States.

Today, however, the budget and trade deficits remain for the United States to deal with. So looking back, that is one detriment that we can observe.

What lessons about management and competitiveness can Japanese and American managers learn from each other?

Our strength is that Japanese managers have a long-term approach to investing and organizational reforms. They always foster their successors over a period of 20 to 30 years. They will find talented, young employees; they will train these young employees; and out of three or four candidates, the future president of the company will emerge. This is a different approach from American businesses.

Loyalty toward one's company is very strong in Japan. Sometimes the company is as important as one's family. Japanese companies also take very good care of their subsidiaries. They encourage these smaller companies to make sure that they will achieve the same standards as larger companies, in both funding and technology. The bond between the large companies and their subcontractors is different in the United States.

In Japan, we do not admire mergers and acquisitions—we try to keep that at arm's length. Today Japan's capitalism has become too heavily concentrated on *zaiteku*—financial management. It's becoming a casino economy. Observing this recent phenomenon of *zaiteku* financial management, I'd have to say that capitalism in Japan has degenerated.

The strength of the United States is in the great amount of research and development done there. You have strength in the basic sciences. Compared with this, we are stronger in applied sciences. To give you an analogy, we have the *kiribana,* or cut flowers. We tend to *arrange* things. In American society there is much intense intellectual stimulus. These creative activities naturally affect industries and always provide new frontiers—in high tech or any other area. Whether it's IBM or AT&T, there is a very deep reservoir of technological and scientific research. Also, there are very good insights into sales, marketing, and merchandise.

One source of economic advantage for Japan seems to be the close working relationship between business and government. In the past, some people have even spoken about Japan Inc. to describe this relationship. How important is that?

Japan Inc. does not exist. Far from acting as Japan Inc. to increase exports, the government is now making an effort to reduce our trade surplus and to increase our imports. For example, the government asks for reports from automobile companies and television companies on how much they import. That was an important job for me when I was prime minister. So Japan Inc. does not exist.

Years ago, from 1946 to 1969, when Japan was rebuilding itself, with the plan of reducing its trade deficit to zero, we put much effort into exports. We implemented policies to encourage this. But after this period, Japan moved into a period of rapid growth. Since then, we have not done things such as providing favors for industries. But the government did have industrial policies—for example, which industries should be encouraged, and, due to this encouragement, what kind of infrastructure should be arranged.

The fact that the government employs a priority policy stimulates industries. These companies then increase their research in the appropriate direction, using their own research institutes or forming research cooperatives among themselves. With regard to high-tech industries, some research is done in government-established institutes, such as the Nuclear Power Research Institute or the High-Technology Research Institute. But we don't give any subsidies directly to private industry. This is how the government and industries cooperate. It is nothing more than that.

So the notion that the Japanese government plays a powerful role in shaping Japan's competitive performance is a myth?

The government doesn't do much at all, because the private sector is taking care of itself. This is an ideal state. Before my tenure, there was the Five-Year Plan for Economic Policy. But when I was in office, I changed the name to "Five Years of Perspective and Direction." We never had any Five-Year Plan. And in it were greater efforts to introduce a more free economic orientation.

For example, take superconductors or biotechnology. Right now, with regard to superconductors, companies are worried about other companies in Japan and also in the United States. Toshiba is always on the lookout for Mitsubishi. Mitsubishi is watching Fujitsu. And Fujitsu is cautious of Matsushita. The competition is incredible.

Japanese company executives dread looking at the morning paper, fearing that they'll see an advertisement for a new product from one of their competitors. That's how intense the competition is. That competition is what increases spending in research. So go ahead and try to find Japan Inc.

Still, compared with the United States, there is much more cooperation in Japan between business and government.

In the United States, the government is certainly more detached from business. That is why you have so many lobbyists in the Congress. But in the United States, you have high military expenditures. If you look at research expenditures worldwide, the United States has a high amount in government research, higher than in the private sector, because the United States has military research. When you compare that form of subsidy, I think that there is more government intervention in the United States.

Since the issue of competitiveness surfaced in the United States, some have argued that, to be more competitive, we need our own version of Japan's Ministry of International Trade and Industry (MITI). Do you agree?

Each country has a government that meets its own political and economic needs. Whether America needs a MITI or not is something that the American people would determine.

From your position as a world leader, what advice would you offer to political and business leaders in the United States?

I would ask politicians of the United States always to look at horizons all over the world, not to look just in their own districts. The U.S. Congress is a Congress of the world. It is not just the Congress of the United States. Its effects are global.

To the business leaders, I would advise you to maintain the frontier spirit. Innovations and discoveries in science and technology always come from the United States. Do not let this strength wane.

What about your own assessment of the Japanese business community? When you were in office, what kind of relationship did you have with business leaders?

I am very grateful to the Japanese business world. When it comes to national and international matters, Japan's business leaders are capable of thinking outside their companies' affairs. This is a sign that Japan's businesses have gained a global perspective.

They also cooperated with my programs of administrative and fiscal reform. With their techniques in corporate management, they proposed reform plans for inefficient government practices.

Reduction of government spending and of manpower, privatization, these agenda items met vehement resistance from the opposition parties. But business leaders cooperated as if they were one with us. Things that were thought impossible to accomplish were made possible because of business leaders' insight and cooperation.

Also, they are very conscious of the role they play internationally: for example, the increase of Official Development Aid and the acceptance of trainees from developing countries. We have 5,000 trainees from China and several thousand from Southeast Asia. They are accepted into these businesses. This is one of the reasons the NIEs are succeeding in development.

Also, Japanese companies are donating substantial amounts of money to American and European universities and museums. This is part of our effort to get rid of the stigma "the economic animal." This is a sign that Japanese business leaders have become internationalized.

You served as Japan's leader from 1982 to 1987. From your experience, what makes a person a leader?

It's the same whether it's business or government. You must be able to set goals, persuade everyone, and have everyone participate. And you have to help create enthusiasm. That is all.

What goal did you set for Japan?

For Japan to embark on playing a global role—economically and culturally. As far as the military is concerned, Japan will not be any threat to other countries. We will continue to operate along the guidelines of the U.S.-Japan Security Pact. The goal for Japan now should be to use our growing financial stature in global cooperation in economic and cultural matters.

Before you became prime minister, did you consciously prepare yourself and develop an agenda or program for your administration?

I prepared myself for almost four decades. For a period of close to 40 years, I wrote down thoughts or plans that occurred to me when I was riding in a car, on the train, or in an airplane. These thoughts amount to approximately 20 volumes. In 1978, four years before I became prime minister, I took the significant points from these volumes and wrote a book, *Theory of New Conservatism*. This is my "bible" on politics. When I became prime minister, I utilized the important points in this book. While I was prime minister, I always made notes and still do today; I always make notes. When I am in the car coming home from Zazen and I hit upon an idea or I have an introspection, I write it down.

What considerations shaped the way you, as the leader of Japan, thought about guiding your nation?

I always think of Japan in terms of the coordinates of history—the vertical axis of time and the horizontal axis of space. I always think in terms of where we are located, where we stand on these coordinates, and in which direction we should go. And I think of this future direction in terms of 10 to 20 years.

To do so requires a knowledge of the past. Therefore, the most important education for me is the study of history: world history, Japanese history, the history of diplomacy. The most important books to me are all history books—for me, political science books are history books.

During your tenure as prime minister, you undertook a major program of administrative reform of the government. What was your thinking behind these reforms?

I saw the need for administrative reform looking at the juncture of two spans—one of 120 years, the other of 40 years, following World War II. Looking over 120 years of Japan's history, that is, since the Meiji Restoration, Japan has been trying to catch up to Europe and the United States. The Japanese government became centralized and, like a locomotive, led the country. As a result, the political and social climate became bureaucratic.

But since 1970, Japan's capitalistic system has matured a great deal. Regulations, centralization, and bureaucracy became unnecessary and needed to be reformed by policies that we call "cheap government" or "new discipline of the bureaucrats." This is one span.

The other span began after the war. Following the 1960 Tokyo Olympics, Japan grew astronomically. The government became big and bloated and created many government institutions and public operations. I was faced with the problem of how to reduce the size of these operations and make them more efficient. I cut government subsidies, reduced manpower, regulated the number of government corporations, and transferred government-owned agencies to the private sector. For example, we transferred the National Railroad, NTT [Nippon Telegram and Telephone Corporation], and the National Tobacco Monopoly Corporation to the private sector. Otherwise, Japan's capitalistic system could not develop anymore. Therefore, we moved toward small government, deregulation, and privatization.

You also spoke about the need to "internationalize" Japan. What does that really mean?

Before I became prime minister, Japan was involved in international economic affairs. After I became prime minister, Japan became committed to world political affairs. Security must be con-

ceived on a global basis. The security of the free world is insepa-
rable from global politics. Working with these principles, I attended
the Williamsburg summit to commit Japan to world political and
security affairs.

Today Japan's economy and technology have grown to the point
where, rather than receiving economic and peace benefits, Japan
should provide these things. Otherwise, they will not exist.

*You also advocated increased defense spending by Japan. Is that
part of internationalization?*

We have no intention whatsoever of expanding militarily. What
we fear most is that other countries fear us, fear that we will expand
militarily. Of course, this is a result of the acute experiences of
World War II. Because it lessens the threat to these countries, the
security pact between Japan and the United States is extremely
important. As long as this treaty is maintained, the neighboring
countries should feel at ease. The relationship between Japan and
the United States will continue to develop a mutually complementary security relationship. As Japan grows so enormous economically and technologically, it becomes necessary to review the role
of each country in this security pact. We have to find appropriate
ways to expand our role to keep it complementary.

One more thing, Japan's military has orders not to expand.
Because of the recent high appreciation of the yen, Japan's defense
budget has become equal to that of England or France—about $30
billion. But we should not exceed England or France.

Then the issue becomes, where should we put this extra energy?
I believe we should put it to use by cooperating in the economic
and cultural fields, particularly in the Pacific and then around the
world.

At present, Taiwan, Hong Kong, Singapore, Thailand, and Malaysia are coming up, too. Their growth is due in part to their good
national policies and their social stability. But also because funds,
technology, and information have flowed into these countries from
Japan and the United States. The basis for all of this is the presence
of the U.S. military in Asia. With such a reality, the robust economic
energy felt in parts of Asia should be spread to other countries all
around the world.

This is one of the reasons we are rapidly expanding Japan's
Official Development Aid. We plan on spending more than $50
billion in the span of five years. Next year, we will surpass America

in absolute figures and become the world's biggest spender on international development. As long as Japan's economy continues to grow, this phenomenon will continue.

Your participation in economic summits represented a new international presence for Japan. How important are direct conversations between world leaders?

I cannot help but stress the importance of economic summits for Japan. It is far more important than the European and North American nations realize. The leaders of Europe and North America meet all year round, through NATO, the EC, and other organizations. Only once a year, however, does Japan join these meetings, and that is at the economic summit. That is why it is particularly important for Japan. The world is structured under the triangle viewpoint: North America, Europe, and Japan.

If you believe that these top-level meetings are so important, how would you assess the relationship between the United States and the Soviet Union, where no meetings were held for nearly six years?

What is most important in politics is how to find the right timing. This is true with U.S.-Soviet relations. It takes quite a long time for negotiations to succeed with U.S.-Soviet relations. The INF treaty was formed at the right time. Both President Reagan and General Secretary Gorbachev should be praised for this. If it had been sooner, it would not have succeeded. The INF was created because it had the potential agreement in Reykjavik as a foundation. Before the Reykjavik agreement, there was the deployment of the Pershing IIs. Through these processes, gradually things matured. The top leaders found the right timing and were very competent in what they did.

As prime minister, you not only changed Japan's policies but also changed Japan's politics. You were a much more visible figure and assumed much more direct power than your predecessors. What were the political changes that you made, and what were you trying to accomplish?

I was trying to inform my people of Japan's historical position. Japan has become a highly informationalized society. Japan is on a par with the United States in terms of television and mass media.

Political techniques must be changed from old ways or else they will be out of sync with present times. The tempo and rhythm are very important. Japan is a rapidly changing, highly compact society—like a crowded train running at 100 kilometers per hour.

It is necessary to have politics that can keep up with this rapid pace of change and high level of intensity. When the train arrives at the station and the doors don't open right away, the passengers will be upset. With politics, it's the same. You have to change the technique in accordance with the times. So you must directly address the people, obtain support from them, and then move the Diet. In other words, the Nakasone government is a "glider"—without the wind of the people, the glider will fall.

How were your political views received?

At first, my cabinet lost popularity. In fact, the polls went down to 30%. But then they went up, and we were able to maintain a 60% level of support. The reason I held office for so long was the support of the people. I changed the performance of the government.

There is that expression, "television democracy." I kept up with this phenomenon by utilizing my staff and "the brains." For example, I would take ideas for new policies out of my notebooks, speak to my staff or my ministers unofficially, and have them research these plans. It would take about six months for these plans to ripen. Then I would form an official committee with economists, academics, and journalists. The committee would deliberate over the new policies and submit their recommendations. The results of the research conducted by these committees would appear in newspapers and on television. This way, the public would learn; the members of the committees who were journalists, editorial writers, lecturers, or academics would publicize the research. So the committees were very effective as a medium for public relations.

That was one of the reasons I was able to obtain support of the public. At the Diet I was always criticized. "You are ignoring the Diet," they would say. "You are acting as if you're the president in the American sense."

But then I would tell them to look at the new constitution. Our new prime minister is based on the British parliamentary system. But at the same time, we adopted the presidential system of electoral states. In fact, in Japan this presidential system is more evident than in the Great Britain system. The emperor is a mere symbol with no political power. I am only working under the constitution, I would tell the Diet. The ways of the previous prime ministers were old fashioned.

Of course, I always presented my plans and views to the Diet. And many of them were successful. The reason for this was that I always kept the cabinet and party as one unit. The cabinet members—the minister of finance, minister of foreign affairs, chief cabinet secretary, party secretary, minister of justice, chairman of general affairs, the policy research bureau, and the chairman of the house of counselors—met regularly. I saw them as one unit so that we could face the formidable bureaucracy that we have in Japan. The Japanese opposition parties are very weak, so we don't have to worry very much about them. But the bureaucracy is very strong, and, when it came to deregulation or privatization, it was very resistant. This strong unification of the cabinet and the party was the key to successfully pulling down the bureaucracy.

What other techniques did you use in managing Japan's powerful bureaucracy?

One technique I used was to employ a merit system, after examining how high-ranking bureaucrats worked. For example, during the reform of the National Railroad, the head of the National Railroad indicated his reluctance to cooperate. So I accepted his letter of resignation forthwith, assessing that the circumstances no longer justified his holding the office. This reform succeeded at precisely that moment, that moment! After all, merit and punishment are very important. Of course, at the time, the opposition parties and the bureaucrats said, "Nakasone is a dictator."

These don't sound like traditional Japanese approaches to politics.

I came up with these political techniques after reading a book that came out when John Kennedy became president, *The Making of the President, 1960*. I learned a great deal from that book.

I thought perhaps you'd learned it from your time at Harvard.

It's true that I attended Henry Kissinger's seminars at Harvard. That may also account for it.

Sometimes leaders learn more from their mistakes than from their successes. Does this apply to you and your tenure as prime minister?

I will speak from my own experience. With regard to tax reform, I was in too much of a hurry. After the plan was first formed, I should have spent at least another year in having people discuss and deliberate over it. But because of our new budget, part of the tax-reform bill had to be incorporated in the following year's budget. So I had to hurry and I failed. In business or government, impatience can be a source of failure, even when the idea is sound.

In business, the grade that a manager gets is often judged by the company's profits or losses. How should a political leader's performance be judged? And how would you judge your own performance?

In the case of the political leader, he must endure the critical eye of history. So you might create very unpopular results when you implement your program, but ten years later you may be praised for the same policy. My teacher, professor, and evaluator is history.

2
Jimmy Carter:
The Statesman as CEO

Alan M. Webber

In 1976, Jimmy Carter—farmer, businessman, former naval officer, Georgia state senator and governor, author, and church leader—was elected president of the United States. With the memory of Watergate still fresh in the public's mind, President Carter appealed to voters by calling for honesty and integrity in government—the need for basic values guiding the country's leaders.

While in office, President Carter successfully championed a long and comprehensive legislative agenda, including passage of a national energy policy, deregulation of transportation industries and banking, and civil service reform. President Carter also negotiated a historic peace agreement between Israel and Egypt, established diplomatic relations with China, concluded the SALT II treaty, and gained ratification of the Panama Canal treaty. During his administration, the country was tested by an inflation-fanning oil embargo and the taking of American hostages in Iran. Both events gave rise to a feeling of American vulnerability to outside forces.

Former President Jimmy Carter is the founder of the Atlanta-based Carter Center, a nonprofit organization that works to resolve conflict, promote democracy, preserve human rights, improve health, and fight hunger around the world.

HBR: What makes a person a leader?

Jimmy Carter: The ability to accommodate the pressures of a competitive world is one of the prerequisites to success. During the difficult years of working one's way to the top, leadership qualities are tested. There may be tens of thousands of people who have the ambition to be president of the United States, or president of IBM, or of General Motors. But you don't inherit the presidency of a democratic nation or any of these other positions of leadership. Only a few individuals have the capacity to meet the competitive test.

What qualities determine success?

The ability to work with other people, the capacity to expand one's mind and one's heart as years go by, and to see the broader dimensions of the future. Most important, it's necessary not to fear the prospect of failure but to be determined not to fail. If a leader is not willing to attempt things that might not succeed, then he has little faith in himself or the goal he seeks to achieve.

How do values shape leadership?

High moral and ethical standards are essential, and they don't change from one job to another, or from one level of authority to another. Honesty, truthfulness, integrity, unselfishness—these are always there. And whenever a leader violates these basic principles, through arrogance or through ignorance, there's a derogation of duty.

Leaders also have a duty to understand the needs of people who depend on them. I've never been a victim of racial discrimination. I've never been deprived of basic human rights. I've never suffered from hunger or lack of shelter. As a businessman, a church leader, and a political leader, I became intensely aware of the needs of others in the deep South during segregation, although I wasn't always as courageous as I should have been in trying to alleviate these problems. But understanding the needs and suffering of others is a vital element for successful leadership.

Finally, there's a legal framework within which a leader must operate. The president of the country or of a company should display an exemplary commitment to the law. Any leader who deviates from compliance with the law, or compliance with the principles of a corporation, sends devastating waves of damage throughout the organization itself. Such conduct lowers the standards of performance of everyone who is aware of the violation.

Is there anyone who you feel embodies these qualities of leadership?

Harry Truman. He's kind of a hero for me in this century. I tried to measure up to his standards. I don't think Harry Truman ever told the American people a lie. I don't think Harry Truman ever violated the law. He had a respect for history and a respect for the office of president. As a consequence, I am certain that Harry Truman would never have done anything to bring discredit to his office.

As president, what were your experiences in dealing with business leaders? Both disappointments and successes.

We had some disappointments at first. For instance, even before I became president I could see that the U.S. automobile industry was making two very serious mistakes. One was the lack of fuel efficiency, and the other was environmental pollution.

So I called in to my cabinet room the chief executive officers—the chairmen of the board and the presidents of every automobile manufacturer in the nation—along with the autoworkers' union representatives. I told them we were going to pass some very strict air pollution and energy conservation laws. My hope was that they would take the initiative right then and commit themselves to producing energy-efficient automobiles that would comply with these strict standards. Their unanimous response was that it simply was not possible. I told them that automakers in Sweden and in Japan were doing it, so it *was* possible. But they insisted that they just couldn't make a profit on it because their profit came from the larger automobiles. So they refused to modify their designs.

Eventually we passed a law that required them, incrementally and annually, to improve their automobiles' efficiency and to comply with environmental standards. In the meantime, American manufacturers lost a lot of the domestic market. That was a case of the automobile industry being unwilling to look to the future. They could not see the long-run advantage, even though it might prove to be costly in the close-in years.

In general, however, I think the business community was quite helpful and enlightened when I was in office. There was a tremendous improvement in the efficient use of energy while I was there. The laws that we finally passed after four full years of tedious negotiation are still on the books. And now we can sustain any given gross national product using about 30% less energy than we did, say, ten years ago.

Another commitment my administration made, with which most business leaders helped me, was deregulating the private enterprise system. We deregulated oil and gas, airlines, railroads, trucks, the financial institutions, and communications, including radio and television. And we couldn't have done that without the support and leadership of enlightened members of the business community. They agreed to put their faith in a more competitive free enterprise system. In general, even including the airlines, U.S. industry and consumers have gained substantial benefits from deregulation.

How does becoming president change the way you think and what you think about in making decisions?

Becoming president generates and demands a much greater awareness of what one's predecessors have done. A leader must understand history, either within the corporation or within the nation. Quite often an awareness of what has gone before gives good guidance about how to handle current challenges or opportunities and helps avoid repeating mistakes. Leadership also requires a broad concept of your responsibility to others and your future effect on them. As you rise in corporate or political positions, you have an increasingly broad impact on other people's lives.

How would you describe your management style?

I have always tried to limit the number of specific duties that I had to manage. Where I could, I would delegate authority to others whom I trusted. I've done everything I could to master those duties that I considered uniquely mine, that no one else could perform. To do that, I would commit the time and concentrated effort necessary to go into considerable detail. Management, in my view, requires mastery of relevant details about one's own unique duties.

As president, you were constantly engaged in negotiation and me-diation—with business leaders, with the Congress, in the Middle East. You've even written a book on mediation, Negotiation: The Alternative to Hostility. *Why is negotiation so important?*

Every leader has to understand at least the rudiments of nego-tiation—because a chief executive officer in the White House, in the boardroom, or in the corporate executive offices is faced every day with potential conflict, with immediate subordinates, with the workers in the plant, with the sales force, or perhaps with com-petitors.

All negotiations, whether in government or business, require certain things. One is a proper respect for the people across from you whose opinions differ from yours. You can't be arrogant. You've got to give the people with whom you're contending your under-standing—not your agreement but your understanding. It requires some humility to recognize that you're not inherently better than they are.

A successful negotiation has to be voluntary and unanimous. Then you have an agreement. You also need to understand when an intermediary, an arbitrator or mediator, would help and when a direct approach is best. This has an important application in business. Altercations between two big corporations can often be resolved most easily through direct talks between the chief exec-utive officers. They need to be secluded but backed up and advised by their attorneys. Instead of going to court in an extremely expen-sive eight- or ten-year lawsuit, where no one wins, a direct en-counter like this is often the best approach.

During your administration, the United States confronted a series of economic, environmental, and military limits. How do you think a leader should contend with limits and the recognition of limits?

The recognition of limits shouldn't lead to a feeling of weakness. A shortage of raw materials, of arable land, or of pure air, are all real conditions that must be accepted and then corrected or accom-modated. The acknowledgment that we can't do anything we want to the environment is not an acknowledgment of weakness. Dealing with limitations wisely and successfully is a sign of greatness.

Business should readily understand this concept. Limits are

taken for granted in the competitive arena. Alternative products are on the market. Competitors are striving to be better, more desirable, or more efficient than you are. You also are limited by your customers' desires and tastes. You can't charge any price you want for most products. In business, limits are acknowledged and expected. So there's no feeling of inferiority. The same principle should apply to political leadership.

Yet that message of limits and restraints is tough to convey, particularly in politics.

That's exactly right. And I was not always successful in getting it across. It's always much more popular for someone to say, it's okay to do whatever you want, we're never going to run out of oil, forests, or other raw materials; to tell the American people the United States is so powerful, we can always live a happy life, regardless of what happens to the rest of the world; to say it doesn't matter how large our federal deficits are—our country is so strong, we can survive it. It doesn't matter what happens to the nation's agricultural community—we have enough land to survive. It doesn't matter about human rights violations around the world, because our people are secure in their basic rights.

This way of thinking is very attractive to the American people. These are messages they like to hear. We don't have to worry about others, we've got it made, and because of our great blessings, which are obvious, we must be God's chosen people. And if someone is poor, or destitute, or deprived, it must be because God looks on them with disfavor. To me, that is an incorrect approach to the world's problems. But it is a politically attractive approach.

Part of leadership is telling people news they may not want to hear. Is another part willingness to hear bad news from advisers?

It's a serious mistake for any leader to be surrounded by sycophants. It's just as erroneous to listen only to advisers who have a homogeneous approach to the important issues of the day. The stronger and more self-assured a leader is the more likely he or she is to seek diversity of advice. If you are insecure or don't have confidence in yourself, then you're apt to listen to a narrow range of advice.

I deliberately chose advisers with disparate points of view. The media criticized this as indicating disharmony in my administration. But especially in matters of foreign policy, I wanted the very conservative, stable, and cautionary reaction of the State Department on the one hand and the more dynamic, innovative advice from the National Security Council staff on the other hand. Sometimes the two points of view conflicted. But in foreign policy and defense, the final decisions were always mine. I wanted a broad assortment of opinions before I made a judgment. That's also why I brought in to the Oval Office members of the Congress from both houses and both parties, and listened to them: to make sure again that I had diversity.

Do we expect too much or the wrong things from our leaders?

In general, the American people credit the president with excessive power and authority in the field of economics. The president doesn't have much to do with the inflation rate, for instance. A little, but not much. He can affect the budget deficit. In economics and finance, the president must share authority with a tremendous free enterprise system and with the Congress and the Federal Reserve Board.

But in matters of foreign policy and defense, the president does have tremendous power and unique authority. Occasionally, he can even act unilaterally.

Because there is a misapprehension among the American people about this delineation of power, one responsibility of the executive officer is to define his or her authority and influence properly. I was not against using my legal authority to a maximum degree, but I was very careful to make sure that it was legal and proper when I did exercise authority. As stated earlier, I also consulted with others as much as possible.

How much consultation went into your decision and policy making?

Whenever I made a decision concerning foreign policy or defense, I worked it out in advance, initially with the secretary of state, secretary of defense, the joint chiefs of staff, the National Security Council, and the key members of Congress, both Democrats and Republicans. We would have a consensus before we made a major move on the Panama Canal treaty, for example, or with the negotiations on SALT II. As a result, Congress never reversed or refused a single proposal I made and changed my defense budget proposals minimally. It is extremely important to build into initial discussions the people who will eventually be responsible for the final definition or implementation of a proposal.

A large amount of consultation, however, increases the danger of leaks. What was your view of keeping information secret?

If you're a political leader, you have to decide about the level of secretiveness. In general, I think that some secrets contribute toward leaders' misusing and violating their positions. When secrecy is emphasized, it tends to be used sooner or later to cover up mistakes. And if those mistakes later become public, they will be more embarrassing than if they were acknowledged openly in the first place.

My inclination was to have as few secrets as possible. In general, we sought to reveal the facts to the American people. So I had frequent press conferences, and all my cabinet officers had orders to share their knowledge with the press whenever it would not adversely affect our national security.

How much of a leader's time should be spent on pursuing accomplishments and how much on selling accomplishments to constituents?

You have a choice at any time to concentrate your efforts on additional accomplishments or to publicize previous achievements. I don't want to appear too idealistic by saying this, but we deliberately kept a full agenda on the things we wanted to accomplish. Our agenda was always so ambitious that even after I was defeated in November 1980, we still had a highly productive legislative session. We finished energy legislation, we passed the Alaska Lands Bill after 20 years of fruitless effort, we passed legislation creating the Super Fund, and more.

I had envisioned publicizing my successes for political purposes in the 1980 election year. But, unfortunately, two things happened: the Iranian revolution precipitated a more than doubling of oil prices in less than 12 months, and the hostages were taken. The political and economic climate precluded my letting the public know what I had accomplished. But there has to be a combination of initiatives and publicity. Only by educating people on what you have already done can you retain adequate political support to pursue present and future goals.

What do you consider is the right way for leaders in this country to use their power?

Our country is certainly the most powerful nation on earth. Economically, militarily, politically, sometimes even morally and ethically. But that doesn't mean we can use this tremendous power to subjugate other people or to impose our will on others against their wishes. Or to intrude into the internal affairs of another country, unless our own security is directly threatened.

We should use our influence, not to create or sustain conflict and animosity and suffering throughout the world but to alleviate it. And although we have the most powerful military force on earth, we should use that force with great reticence. Whenever possible, we should use diplomacy and negotiation to alleviate friction, to bring disputing parties together, to resolve matters through peaceful means.

In the case of the Middle East, my predecessors and I were always eager to support any peace process that was initiated. Anyone in the Middle East who took one small step toward peace knew there was an eager partner in Washington. To me that was a proper use of U.S. power. We didn't inject troops into the Middle East. We didn't bomb villages or bomb Beirut. We sought opportunities to bring people together to work out a peaceful agreement, with our government acting as mediator.

That to me is a stamp of greatness, not weakness. We don't have to be a bully in the world just because we are the strongest.

3
Gerald R. Ford:
The Statesman as CEO

Alan M. Webber

In 1974, Gerald R. Ford became president of the United States under some of the most trying conditions in the nation's history, after the previous vice president, then the president, resigned amid public furor. When President Ford took office, he assumed the leadership of a government whose capacity to govern was open to question.

Over the next 3 years, by the force of his character and the power of his unquestionable integrity, President Ford helped restore the public's confidence and trust in government. His 25 years in Congress served him well as he assembled his own team and set about the difficult job of combatting the inflation and unemployment problems he had inherited. When he left office in 1978, the country had overcome its crisis.

The interview was conducted by Alan M. Webber, managing editor of HBR.

HBR: It's no exaggeration to say that when you became president in 1974, the government was in desperate circumstances. Watergate and the resignations of both Vice President Agnew and President Nixon had created a national crisis of confidence.

Gerald R. Ford: Many young people today don't recall the unhappy condition of the country on August 9, 1974. We were literally torn apart. My main concern was to overcome that crisis, to restore trust in government, to restore confidence that our country had weathered the storm. That was why I stated in my acceptance speech that our long national nightmare was over. I was seeking to restore our nation's faith and confidence.

If I'm remembered, it will probably be for healing the land. That doesn't mean that everybody agreed with everything I did. But we did return to a common level of understanding to guide the country's direction.

When the whole organization is in trouble, what special qualities does a leader need to assume command?

Particularly in a time of crisis, it all boils down to the character of the individual. As a new leader, you must be perceived as totally honest, dedicated to the proper goals, and possessed of the strength necessary to achieve results. Everyone must see you as a person of integrity—people on the inside with whom you work as well as people outside your organization. Everyone must understand that you take action only to pull things together, that you will act in the best interests of all concerned. You must make it clear that you are not seeking personal aggrandizement.

As a new president, I had to instill a feeling within the government that I was working to get things back on an even keel. And I had to deal with Congress to rebuild a constructive relationship with both the House and the Senate. My overall goal was to restore the public's confidence. Without that confidence, nothing productive can happen.

Parallels exist, of course, between the circumstances I inherited and those in corporations where previous management has been challenged for mismanagement or corruption. In those situations, a business leader faces the same kinds of problems I faced.

Are there any universal keys to managing in a crisis?

The short reply is people. You must assemble people you trust and who can carry out their duties. You cannot rely on those who have made mistakes. Whether they acted willfully or by happenstance, the people responsible have to go. Your new team members must be able to carry out their jobs as you direct. And the public must perceive them as capable.

In your case, how did you handle the tough personnel decisions?

I made some drastic changes in personnel. Some who left did so by choice, and I agreed to it. Some left because I felt they had to go. In government as in business, you must decide who's got to go. You cannot retain people with whom you're not comfortable. You cannot retain anyone who is perceived as incompetent. And you certainly can't keep anyone who can't or won't work with your team.

After you assemble the right people for your team, how do you go about using them properly?

You delegate to people the responsibility for running their own operations. You give them a firm outline of their duties, then hold them responsible.

After I found the people I wanted in my cabinet, I made sure they understood their charters and I held each one responsible for his or her area. If a question arose over who should handle something—and that does happen in government when one department's jurisdiction overlaps another's—I remained the final arbiter. On a number of important issues, I listened to two cabinet officers with opposing views. Each got to present his case. But as president, I reserved the right to decide.

Of course, I wouldn't always decide then and there. Sometimes I would listen to the arguments and give my answer later, although no later than the next day. Those things shouldn't linger. Indecision is often worse than wrong action.

How would you describe your management style?

I have spent my whole life trying to pull people together. I've always tried to create a team environment, whether it was in athletics, on board ship in the navy, or in politics. I think that's the only way to get the job done.

By stressing the team, though, you may not get the credit you deserve. Isn't that a risky approach to politics?

I am sufficiently optimistic—or sufficiently naive—to believe that if you do the job, sooner or later you'll get the credit. That doesn't always happen, but at least you have the satisfaction of doing things the right way. Some people manage by trampling on others. Some even succeed that way. But to me, that's anathema. In the long run you're better off working for results, and recognition will inevitably come.

Do you think it's important for a leader to project a vision that inspires and directs the organization?

Too often "vision" is just a fancy word people use to justify spending a lot of money. You can spend an awful lot of money on some pretty unattainable goals. That's why I'm a firm believer in a pragmatic approach. I'm more concerned with the nuts and bolts of getting from here to there.

My idea of vision is ensuring that we're making progress on a day-to-day basis. I want to know the accounting figures for how we did today and how we're going to do tomorrow—and how we're going to get there, in practical terms. Once you do that, you achieve some vision about what will happen down the road.

From time to time we see problems come up in the way the White House is managed—the Reagan administration's recent difficulties with the operation of the National Security Council, for instance. What do you think of the way that was managed?

The current situation is very sad. What surprises me is how far the National Security Council overstepped its legislated boundaries under its 1947 charter. It supposedly just evaluates recommendations to the president from the State Department, the Defense Department, and the Central Intelligence Agency. These recommendations deal with everything from weapons systems to foreign policy. To my knowledge, the National Security Council was only intended to evaluate, never to act operationally in the field on such matters. And it appears that the council operated against the wishes of the secretary of defense, the secretary of state, and maybe others. To use such a group—one that's neither planned nor competent to be operational—in this way is a tragedy.

Frankly, I don't understand why it wasn't managed better. Of course, you're bound to encounter some such problems. But that was comparable to a corporate chief executive assigning some youth to do something for which he doesn't have the competence, experience, authority, or background.

Another recurring issue is the role of certain government officials. What, for example, should be the role of the president's chief of staff?

The president needs a chief of staff who's a superb manager but who is willing to remain under the president's direction. The chief of staff shouldn't try to be president. And he should not try to project himself as the number two person in government. The number two person is the vice president. In my view, business should follow a similar organization. A conglomerate can't have some secondary official publicly telling heads of various subsidiaries what they should do. Those directives must come from the president or the CEO.

Does it really make sense to talk about managing something as large as the federal government?

There are 2,100,000 civilian employees and roughly the same number of people in military uniform. That's a big organization. And, of course, top government officials are handicapped by legislation restricting how you pay people, how you hire them, and how you fire them. It's particularly tough to manage that huge an organization with all those restrictions.

Is managing the government different from managing a business?

A lot of top businesspeople become totally frustrated when they move into a cabinet position as head of a department. They're used to much more power in business. And it's a totally different environment. In government, they must suddenly follow strict procedures and regulations. It's a difficult adjustment.

I've seen many first-class businesspeople throw up their hands and threaten to walk out of government after just a few months. Nevertheless, successful business executives can thrive as government officials. If they get past those first two or three months and learn to live with the frustrations that are part of the environment, they can do a top-notch job. But first comes that difficult period of adjustment.

Looking back on your term as president, did you have any frustrations or disappointments?

There were lots of frustrations and disappointments. I inherited an economic recession in late 1974 and early 1975. A large number of people were out of work. When you're president, it's frustrating that you can't just flip a switch and suddenly improve the economy. But of course it doesn't happen that way.

If you look at the statistics, we did turn things around. But there were some very frustrating, disappointing moments, periods when things didn't move as fast as we'd have liked. When times are tough you have to keep faith in what you've done and in your plans. You must remain confident that your policies reflect what's right, and hope things will work out. It takes patience. You have to believe that in six months or a year, what you've done and the decisions you've made will benefit the country. But in our society, you can't always remain so patient.

Do we have unrealistic expectations regarding the power of the presidency?

The American public holds an exaggerated opinion of the impact a president has on the economy. Certainly the president can affect things through monetary and fiscal policy. If a president neglects one or both, we're in trouble. But the public seems to think you can do even more—more, in fact, than is possible.

Throughout your career, you never aspired to the presidency. Your real goal was to become Speaker of the House. In retrospect, was that an advantage for you when you did become president?

Yes, it was. I had made no prior commitments. I was obligated to no one. I had made no campaign promises. That's a huge advantage for a president. And that's one fault of our current system. Presidential candidates travel the country for a year and a half or two years, gathering support from this group or that element of society. The commitments they make sound good on the campaign trail. But when you have to make a decision in the Oval Office, reality sets in. As practical concerns, those campaign promises cannot be met. That's why it saddens me to see our campaigns drag on for so long, with candidates swearing to fulfill so many commitments.

In my case, having made no such promises, I was in a good position. I never had to worry about what I'd said a year ago or two years ago, trying to win votes. I could make decisions based on what I thought was right.

Integrity was the watchword of your political career. How does business measure up to your standards?

All the businesspeople with whom I've worked reflect high standards of integrity, which I think is important. We all read about individuals who have violated a code of ethics, but I've had no personal experience with that in business. And I'll add this. In my 28 1/2 years in government—and that includes more than 25 years in Congress, where I met frequently with business representatives—nobody ever offered me a bribe or anything comparable to it. Maybe they suspected that I'd throw them out of my office. But I've never had that experience.

Yet today, again, scandals threaten business's reputation. Is there something besides regulation that might curb unethical activities?

I would prefer that we handle the matter of business ethics without excessive government regulation—because regulation by itself won't suffice. But somebody must look over all those shoulders to ferret out crime. There's a delicate balance between what industry can do to keep itself clean and what government must do to protect the broader interests of the public.

You sit on a number of corporate boards now. How do business leaders compare with government leaders?

I've been greatly impressed by the people with whom I've been associated in business. They have excelled to reach the top. And they have leadership talents, or they wouldn't have succeeded.

The best business leaders are very broad based. Naturally they have a command of the technicalities of their particular industry. But they also have a broader view of our economy and our political system.

What should be the role of business leaders in addressing national issues?

Too often in the past, businesspeople have been preoccupied with just running their organizations. And of course that's their principal duty. But for the benefit of the business community as a whole, our business leaders must also project themselves beyond their customers. They must reach out to communicate and participate in public affairs. That's particularly true of the people who run major conglomerates, both nationally and internationally. Today's business leaders are far better at that than those of 25 or 30 years ago. If they properly and honestly set forth their views, the public will respond. But too many of them either don't think it's important or hesitate because they don't feel qualified.

I think it's important for major industrial leaders to grant interviews with the news media. They ought to participate in both community and national activities. That's good for American business. More business leaders should do things that will convince the public that their interests go beyond just making a buck.

INDEX

The Harvard Business Review Book Series